2wkly
346

LawExpress
TORT LAW

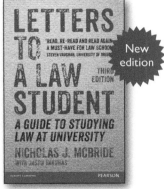

Law Express

TORT LAW

5th edition

Emily Finch
University of Surrey

Stefan Fafinski
University of Leeds

PEARSON

Harlow, England • London • New York • Boston • San Francisco • Toronto • Sydney • Auckland • Singapore • Hong Kong
Tokyo • Seoul • Taipei • New Delhi • Cape Town • São Paulo • Mexico City • Madrid • Amsterdam • Munich • Paris • Milan

Pearson Education Limited
Edinburgh Gate
Harlow CM20 2JE
United Kingdom
Tel: +44 (0)1279 623623
Web: www.pearson.com/uk

First published in 2007 (print)
Second edition published 2009 (print)
Third edition published 2011 (print)
Fourth edition published 2013 (print and electronic)
Fifth edition published 2015 (print and electronic)

ISBN: 978-1-292-01286-5 (print)
       978-1-292-01344-2 (PDF)
       978-1-292-01808-9 (ePub)
       978-1-292-01304-6 (eText)

British Library Cataloguing-in-Publication Data
A catalogue record for the print edition is available from the British Library

Library of Congress Cataloging-in-Publication Data
Finch, Emily, author.
   Tort law / Emily Finch, Senior Lecturer in Law, University of Surrey,
Stefan Fafinski Research Associate of Oxford Internet Institute. -- Fifth edition.
       p. cm. -- (Law express)
   Includes index.
   ISBN 978-1-292-01286-5
   1. Torts--England--Outlines, syllabi, etc.   I. Fafinski, Stefan, author.   II. Title.
   KD1949.6.F56 2014
   346.4203--dc23
                                    2014006358

10 9 8 7 6 5 4 3
18 17 16

Print edition typeset in 10/12pt Helvetica Neue LT Std by 35
Print edition printed and bound in Great Britain

NOTE THAT ANY PAGE CROSS REFERENCES REFER TO THE PRINT EDITION

Contents

Supporting resources

Visit the *Law Express* series companion website at **www.pearsoned.co.uk/ lawexpress** to find valuable student learning material including:

- A **study plan** test to help you assess how well you know the subject before you begin your revision
- Interactive **quizzes** to test your knowledge of the main points from each chapter
- Sample **examination questions** and guidelines for answering them
- Interactive **flashcards** to help you revise key terms, cases and statutes
- Printable versions of the **topic maps** and **checklists** from the book
- **'You be the marker'** allows you to see exam questions and answers from the perspective of the examiner and includes notes on how an answer might be marked
- **Podcasts** provide point-by-point instruction on how to answer a typical exam question

Also: The companion website provides the following features:

- Search tool to help locate specific items of content
- E-mail results and profile tools to send results of quizzes to instructors
- Online help and support to assist with website usage and troubleshooting

For more information please contact your local Pearson Education sales representative or visit **www.pearsoned.co.uk/lawexpress**

Acknowledgements

This book is dedicated to STG.

We are, as ever, grateful to all who have offered feedback on the last edition of *Law Express: Tort Law*, particularly the anonymous academic reviewers who provided some suggestions for improvement. We have been pleased to incorporate these as best we could.

We'd really like to hear what you think of the book, which you can do by visiting **www.finchandfafinski.com**, Twitter **@FinchFafinski** or email to **hello@finchandfafinski.com**.

Emily Finch and Stefan Fafinski

Publisher's acknowledgements

Our thanks go to all reviewers who contributed to the development of this text, including students who participated in research and focus groups which helped to shape the series format.

Introduction

Tort is one of the core subjects required for a qualifying law degree so it is a compulsory component of most undergraduate law programmes. It is usually taught as a first- or second-year subject as many of its concepts are relatively straightforward and it bears a certain resemblance to criminal law since it involves a similar two-stage process: the imposition of liability and the availability (or not) of a defence. Aspects of tort will appear in other subjects studied on the law degree: there are elements of negligence in employment law and environmental law whilst harassment is a prominent topic within family law. As such, it is important to have a strong grasp of tort both as a subject in its own right and because of the role it plays in many other law subjects.

Tort covers a wide range of issues that are pertinent to various aspects of everyday life such as the working environment, neighbour disputes and injuries sustained on another's premises. Negligence is a vast topic within tort that covers the many ways in which people inadvertently cause harm to each other. Due to the familiarity of many of the factual situations that arise in tort, students frequently feel quite comfortable with the subject. This can be a problem, however, if the situation gives rise to an outcome that seems unreasonable or unfair. It is important to remember to put aside instinctive evaluations of the situation and focus on the methodical application of the principles of law derived from case law and statute.

This revision guide will help you to identify the relevant law and apply it to factual situations which should help to overcome preconceived notions of the 'right' outcome in favour of legally accurate assessments of the liability of the parties. The book also provides guidance on the policy underlying the law and it identifies problem areas, both of which will help you to prepare for essay questions. The book is intended to supplement your course materials, lectures and textbooks; it is a guide to revision rather than a substitute for the amount of reading (and thinking) that you need to do in order to succeed. Tort is a vast subject – you should realise this from looking at the size of your recommended textbook – so it follows that a revision guide cannot cover all the depth and detail that you need to know and it does not set out to do so. Instead, it aims to provide a concise overall picture of the key areas for revision – reminding you of the headline points to enable you to focus your revision, and identify the key principles of law and the way to use these effectively in essays and problem questions.

📖 **REVISION NOTE**

Things to bear in mind when revising tort law:

- Do use this book to guide you through the revision process.
- Do not use this book to tell you everything that you need to know about tort but make frequent reference to your recommended textbook and notes that you have made yourself from lectures and private study.
- Make sure that you consult your syllabus frequently to check which topics are covered and in how much detail.
- Read around the subject as much as possible to ensure that you have sufficient depth of knowledge. Use the suggested reading in this book and on your lecture handouts to help you to select relevant material.
- Take every possible opportunity to practise your essay-writing and problem-solving technique; get as much feedback as you can.
- You should aim to revise as much of the syllabus as possible. Be aware that many questions in tort that you encounter in coursework and examination papers will combine different topics, e.g. nuisance and trespass to land or employers' liability and trespass to the person. Equally, defences and/or remedies could combine with any of the torts. Therefore, selective revision could leave you unable to answer questions that include reference to material that you have excluded from your revision; it is never a good idea to tackle a question if you are only able to deal with part of the law that is raised.

Before you begin, you can use the study plan available on the companion website to assess how well you know the material in this book and identify the areas where you may want to focus your revision.

Guided tour

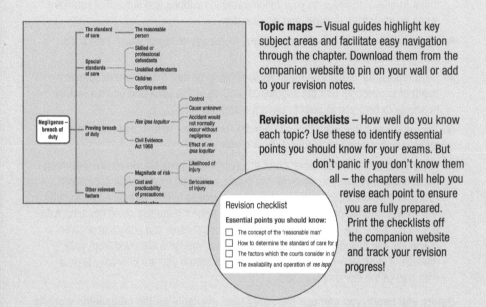

Topic maps – Visual guides highlight key subject areas and facilitate easy navigation through the chapter. Download them from the companion website to pin on your wall or add to your revision notes.

Revision checklists – How well do you know each topic? Use these to identify essential points you should know for your exams. But don't panic if you don't know them all – the chapters will help you revise each point to ensure you are fully prepared. Print the checklists off the companion website and track your revision progress!

Revision checklist

Essential points you should know:

☐ The concept of the 'reasonable man'
☐ How to determine the standard of care for p
☐ The factors which the courts consider in d
☐ The availability and operation of *res ispa*

Assessment advice – Not sure how best to tackle a problem or essay question? Wondering what you may be asked? Use the assessment advice to identify the ways in which a subject may be examined and how to apply your knowledge effectively.

> **ASSESSMENT ADVICE**
>
> Causation and remoteness are topics which are often overlooked by students.
>
> **Essay questions**
>
> Essay questions on causation and remoteness are not popular topics, so students tend to avoid questions involving these issues. It is often the case that when essays on these topics appear in examinations as the only essays on negligence, students who have revised duty and breach tackle the questions on the basis of this revision and skirt over, or ignore altogether, issues of causation and remoteness. This is an extremely poor strategy; you *must* answer the question that appears on the exam paper, not the question that you hoped would appear. To adapt the question to the material that you have revised does not attract any credit; you would be better placed

Sample questions with answer guidelines – Practice makes perfect! Read the question at the start of each chapter and consider how you would answer it. Guidance on structuring strong answers is provided at the end of the chapter. Try out additional sample questions online.

> ■ **Sample question**
>
> Could you answer this question? Below is a typical essay question that could arise on this topic. Guidelines on answering the question are included at the end of the chapter, whilst a sample problem question and guidance on tackling it can be found on the companion website.

Key definitions – Make sure you understand essential legal terms. Use the flashcards online to test your recall!

> **KEY DEFINITION:** Economic loss
>
> Financial losses which are not attributable to physical harm caused to the claimant or his property. It includes loss of profits, loss of trade and loss of investment revenue.

Key cases and key statutes – Identify and review the important elements of the essential cases and statutes you will need to know for your exams.

> **KEY STATUTE**
> **Civil Evidence Act 196**
> 11 Convictions as eviden
> ...
> (2) In any civil proceedin
> been convicted of a
> court-martial ther
> (a) he shall b

> **KEY CASE**
> *Bonnington Castings Ltd v Wardlaw* [1956] AC 613 (HL)
> *Concerning: causation; multiple causes of damage*
> Facts
> The claimant contracted pneumoconiosis after working for years in dusty conditions. There were two main causes of dust in the foundry, one of which was required by law to be extracted. It was impossible to prove which dust the claimant had inhaled.

Make your answer stand out – This feature illustrates sources of further thinking and debate where you can maximise your marks. Use them to really impress your examiners!

> ✓ Make your answer stand out
> An occupier may try to avoid liability by using an exclusion notice rather than a warning sign. A detailed consideration of exclusion clauses is beyond the scope of this book, being an issue covered in the law of contract. Mesher (1979) summarised the position in relation to exclusion clauses and occupiers' liability.

Don't be tempted to . . . – This feature underlines areas where students most often trip up in exams. Use them to spot common pitfalls and avoid losing marks.

> ! Don't be tempted to . . .
> Be careful not to assume that the 'but for' test of factual causation is so straightforward or obvious in a problem scenario that it is not worth mentioning. Factual causation is a key part of negligence and you will lose marks if your analysis is not complete and thorough.

Revision notes – Get guidance for effective revision. These boxes highlight related points and areas of overlap in the subject, or areas where your course might adopt a particular approach that you should check with your course tutor.

> **REVISION NOTE**
> The main remedies for trespass to land, as with so many other torts, are damages and injunction, covered in Chapter 14. It would be useful to take a moment to refresh your memory and consider the way that these remedies operate in relation to trespass to land.

Exam tips – Feeling the pressure? These boxes indicate how you can improve your exam performance when it really counts.

> **EXAM TIP**
> Why would we include a section on ineffective defences that can never succeed? The answer is that they are frequently argued as defences to nuisance so it is important to be aware of them in order to reject them as ineffective.

Read to impress – Focus on these carefully selected sources to extend your knowledge, deepen your understanding, and earn better marks in coursework as well as in exams.

> **READ TO IMPRESS**
> Cartwright, J. (1996) Remoteness of damage in contract and tort: a reconsideration. 55, *Cambridge Law Journal*, p. 488.
> Weir, T. (2002) Making it more likely v. making it happen. 61, *Cambridge Law Journal*, p. 519.
> Wright, R. (1985) Causation in tort law. 73, *California Law Review*, p. 1735.

Glossary of terms

Glossary – Forgotten the meaning of a word? This quick reference covers key definitions and other useful terms.

> The glossary is divided into two parts: key definitions and other useful terms. The key definitions can be found within the chapter in which they occur, as well as in the glossary below. These definitions are the essential terms that you must know and understand in order to prepare for an exam. The additional list of terms provides further definitions of

Guided tour of the companion website

Book resources are available to download. Print your own **topic maps** and **revision checklists**!

Use the **study plan** prior to your revision to help you assess how well you know the subject and determine which areas need most attention. Choose to take the full assessment or focus on targeted study units.

'Test your knowledge' of individual areas with quizzes tailored specifically to each chapter. **Sample problem and essay questions** are also available with guidance on writing a good answer.

Flashcards test and improve recall of important legal terms, key cases and statutes. Available in both electronic and printable formats.

'You be the marker' gives you the chance to evaluate sample exam answers for different question types and understand how and why an examiner awards marks.

Download the **podcast** and listen as your own personal Law Express tutor guides you through answering a typical but challenging question. A step-by-step explanation on how to approach the question is provided, including what essential elements your answer will need for a pass, how to structure a good response, and what to do to make your answer stand out so that you can earn extra marks.

All of this and more can be found when you visit **www.pearsoned.co.uk/lawexpress**

Table of cases and statutes

Cases

▌Statutes

▉ Statutory instruments

▉ European legislation

Negligence:
the duty of care

1

Revision checklist

Essential points you should know:

☐ The composite elements required to establish the tort of negligence

☐ The general definition of the legal duty of care

☐ Liability for omissions and the acts of third parties

☐ The principles of negligent misstatement

☐ The definition of economic loss and the limited circumstances under which it may be recoverable

☐ The changes to the extent of economic loss introduced by *Anns*, *Junior Books* and *Murphy*

☐ The definition of psychiatric injury and how it applies to primary and secondary victims

☐ The duty of care in relation to special claimants and defendants

■ Topic map

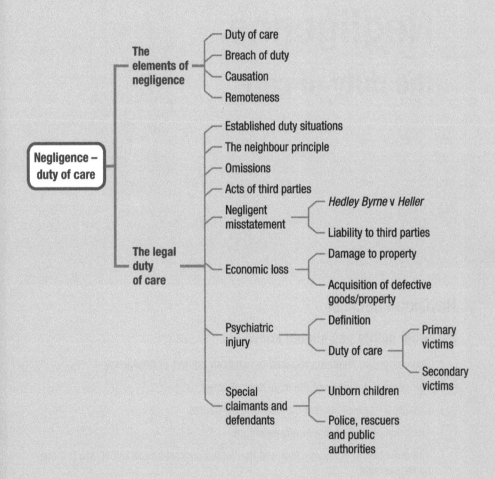

■ Introduction

Negligence has grown to become the largest area of tort law.

In everyday terms, negligence means failure to pay attention to what ought to be done or to take the required level of care. Its everyday usage implies a state of mind (carelessness), whereas the tort of negligence is concerned with the link between the defendant's behaviour and the risk that ought to have been foreseen. When revising negligence, be careful not to let the everyday meaning of the word distract you from the legal meaning of negligence.

As negligence is such an immense topic, it has been broken down into three chapters in this book. It may help to think of this chapter as dealing with the question of whether or not the defendant has a legally recognised duty to take care, while the following two chapters deal with whether the defendant has been careless (breach of that duty) and whether that carelessness caused the harm suffered by the claimant and that the harm gives rise to a legal claim (causation and remoteness).

ASSESSMENT ADVICE

Essay questions

Essay questions on the duty of care in negligence could concentrate on one particular duty situation in particular or cover several of them in a much broader evaluation of the role of the duty of care in negligence. Broad questions tend to be unpopular with students as many of the situations which limit the duty can be overlooked in selective revision. This means that, equipped with a good understanding of all the duty of care situations covered in this chapter, you would be well placed for your answer to stand out among those of your more ill-prepared colleagues. Remember that unpopular questions tend to be done either very well, or very badly.

Problem questions

Problem questions on negligence are very common. They can often include non-standard duty of care situations. For example, in a negligence scenario involving three parties, one might suffer physical loss or damage, one might suffer economic loss and another psychiatric harm. If you had just focused your revision on the 'standard' duty of care in negligence, you could lose out on many of the marks available for such a question. In all duty of care problems, remember to be methodical when applying the case law relating to the special duty situations to the facts given and work through each of the elements of the duty in turn.

■ Sample question

Could you answer this question? Below is a typical essay question that could arise on this topic. Guidelines on addressing the question are included at the end of the chapter, whilst a sample problem question and guidance on tackling it can be found on the companion website.

ESSAY QUESTION

The scope of the duty of care in negligence depends ultimately on the courts' assessment of the need to protect society from the carelessness of others.

Discuss.

■ The elements of negligence

KEY DEFINITION: Negligence

A breach of legal duty to take care which results in damage to the claimant. (Rogers, W.V.H. (2002) *Winfield and Jolowicz on Tort*, 16th edn, London: Sweet & Maxwell, p. 103.)

This definition of **negligence** can be broken down into the four component parts that a claimant must prove to establish negligence. The legal burden of proving each of these elements falls upon the claimant. See Figure 1.1.

Figure 1.1

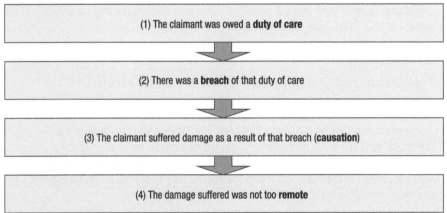

(1) The claimant was owed a **duty of care**

(2) There was a **breach** of that duty of care

(3) The claimant suffered damage as a result of that breach (**causation**)

(4) The damage suffered was not too **remote**

■ Duty of care

This chapter concerns the first element of negligence which is the legal duty of care. This concerns the relationship between the defendant and claimant, which must be such that there is an obligation upon the defendant to take proper care to avoid causing injury to the claimant in all the circumstances of the case.

There are two ways in which a duty of care may be established:

- the defendant and claimant are within one of the 'established duty situations'; or
- outside of these situations, according to the principles developed by case law.

Established duty situations

There are a number of situations in which the courts recognise the existence of a duty of care. These usually arise as a result of some sort of special relationship between the parties. Examples include:

- one road user to another;
- employer to employee;
- manufacturer to consumer (see *Donoghue* v *Stevenson* in the next section and also in Chapter 11);
- doctor to patient;
- solicitor to client.

■ The neighbour principle

Outside of these categories of established duty, a duty of care will be determined on the basis of individual circumstances. The 'neighbour principle' formulated by Lord Atkin in *Donoghue* v *Stevenson* [1932] AC 562 (HL) was initially used to determine whether a duty of care existed between defendant and claimant:

> **KEY CASE**
>
> *Donoghue* v *Stevenson* [1932] AC 562 (HL)
> *Concerning: duty of care; neighbour principle*
>
> **Facts**
>
> Mrs Donoghue and a friend visited a café. Mrs Donoghue's friend bought her a bottle of ginger beer. The bottle was made of opaque glass. When filling Mrs Donoghue's glass, the remains of a decomposed snail – which had somehow found its way into the bottle at the factory – floated out. Mrs Donoghue developed gastroenteritis as a result. ▶

Legal principle

Since Mrs Donoghue had not bought the bottle of ginger beer herself she could not make a claim in contract upon breach of warranty. She therefore brought an action against the manufacturer of the ginger beer. The House of Lords had to decide whether a duty of care existed as a matter of law.

The House of Lords held that the manufacturer owed her a duty to take care that the bottle did not contain foreign bodies which could cause her personal harm. This is known as the *narrow rule* in *Donoghue* v *Stevenson* – that a manufacturer of goods owes a duty of care to their ultimate consumer.

More importantly, the case establishes the *neighbour principle* which determines whether the defendant owes a duty of care in any situation. Lord Atkin stated:

> You must take reasonable care to avoid acts or omissions which you can reasonably foresee would be likely to injure your neighbour. Who, then, in law is my neighbour? The answer seems to be persons who are so closely and directly affected by my act that I ought reasonably to have them in my contemplation as being so affected when I am directing my mind to the acts or omissions which are called in question.

The neighbour principle is not limited in its application. As Lord Macmillan said in *Donoghue* v *Stevenson*: 'The categories of negligence are never closed.' This means that the courts can formulate new categories of negligence to reflect the current social view and make decisions based on consideration of public policy.

The basic concept of the neighbour principle was reformulated almost 60 years later in *Caparo Industries plc* v *Dickman* [1990] 2 AC 605 (HL).

KEY CASE

Caparo Industries plc v *Dickman* **[1990] 2 AC 605 (HL)**

Concerning: duty of care

Facts

The case considered the liability of an auditor for financial loss suffered by investors. However, it also set out the three points which a court must consider to establish whether a duty of care exists.

Legal principle

The three points are:

- reasonable foresight of harm;
- sufficient proximity of relationship;
- that it is fair, just and reasonable to impose a duty.

Caparo v *Dickman* effectively redefined the neighbour principle such that it adds the requirement that there must be a relationship of sufficient proximity and that the imposition of a duty of care must be fair, just and reasonable. The comparison can be seen in the following table:

Caparo v Dickman	Donoghue v Stevenson
Reasonable foresight of harm	Avoid acts or omissions which you can reasonably foresee would be likely to injure your neighbour
Sufficient proximity of relationship	Persons who are so closely and directly affected by my act that I ought reasonably to have them in my contemplation as being so affected when I am directing my mind to the acts or omissions which are called in question
Fair, just and reasonable to impose a duty	

> ✎ **EXAM TIP**
>
> When discussing the duty of care in your answers it is important to remember the third requirement imposed by *Caparo* v *Dickman*.

In *Caparo*, Lord Bridge endorsed the view of Brennan J in *Sutherland Shire Council* v *Heyman* (1985) 60 ALR 1 (High Court of Australia) in which he said that it was preferable:

that the law should develop novel categories of negligence incrementally and by analogy with established categories, rather than by a massive extension of a *prima facie* duty of care restrained only by indefinable 'considerations' which ought to negative, or to reduce or limit the scope of the duty or the class of person to whom it is owed.

In other words, the *Caparo* test should be used incrementally to determine duty of care and that each case should be considered by analogy to previous comparable duties. An example of this can be found in *Bhamra* v *Dubb* [2010] EWCA Civ 13 in which the defendant provided a wedding feast for a Sikh wedding, in which one dish contained eggs. The claimant was allergic to eggs and shortly after eating the dish became ill as a result of an anaphylactic reaction and died a few days later. The court held that the nature of the occasion was such as to extend the scope of the ordinary duty of care to encompass personal injury caused through the consumption of otherwise wholesome food containing eggs.

The House of Lords also commented on the *Caparo* test in *Sutradhar* v *National Environment Research Council* [2006] 4 All ER 490 (HL). Lord Hoffman stated that:

It has often been remarked that the boundaries between these three concepts [from *Caparo*] are somewhat porous but they are probably none the worse for that.

In particular, the requirement that the imposition of a duty should be fair, just and reasonable may sometimes inform the decision as to whether the parties should be considered to be in a relationship of proximity and may sometimes provide a special reason as to why no duty should exist, notwithstanding that the relationship would ordinarily qualify as proximate.

In particular, proximity remains a requirement for the existence of a duty of care even where the damage sustained takes the form of physical injury; foreseeability alone is not sufficient. In order to satisfy the requirement for proximity, the claimant must show that the defendant had a measure of control over and responsibility for the potentially dangerous situation.

The basic elements that need to be considered in establishing duty of care are illustrated in Figure 1.2.

Figure 1.2

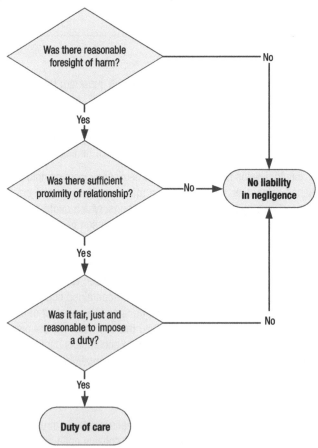

> **! Don't be tempted to . . .**
>
> Don't engage in a discussion of the elements of the duty of care if you are tackling a problem question that deals with an established duty situation. You will waste words and time going through the *Caparo* test if the problem involves, say, an incident between road users. You should simply say that there is an established duty situation and move on to the key issues raised by the question.

Having looked at the basic idea of the duty of care, the remainder of this chapter will consider the various restrictions and limitations on the basic test from *Caparo* in turn. These have developed in response to particular situations where the *Caparo* test needed modification, namely:

- omissions (failing to act);
- acts of third parties;
- misstatements;
- economic loss;
- nervous shock (or psychiatric harm);
- special claimants and defendants.

Omissions (failing to act)

As Lord Goff said in *Smith* v *Littlewoods; Maloco* v *Littlewoods* [1987] AC 241 (HL) 271, 'the common law does not impose liability for what are called pure omissions'. Similarly in *Stovin* v *Wise* [1996] AC 923 (HL) 943–4, Lord Hoffmann commented that:

> [It] is less of an invasion of an individual's freedom for the law to require him to consider the safety of others in his actions than to impose upon him a duty to rescue or protect . . . A duty to prevent harm to others or to render assistance to a person in danger or distress may apply to a large and indeterminate class of people who happen to be able to do something.

In other words, the law does not recognise a duty of care owed to the whole world to take positive action to prevent harm. In *Caparo* terms, it would not be fair, just or reasonable to impose such a general duty. So, if you see someone in peril, you are not obliged to try to rescue them, and if you fail to do so you cannot be liable in negligence for not acting positively. Therefore, if you see a stranger face down in a pond, you do not have any legal obligation to prevent them from drowning – even though you might feel a strong *moral* obligation to do so.

However, there are certain situations in which a duty to act positively is imposed. This can be based on the existence of a special relationship or a relationship of power or control between the parties. Examples include:

- prison officers and prisoners (*Home Office* v *Dorset Yacht Co. Ltd* [1970] AC 1004 (HL));

- employer and employee (*Hudson* v *Ridge Manufacturing Co.* [1957] 2 QB 348 (Manchester Winter Assizes));

- occupier and visitor (this relationship is imposed by statute; see Chapter 6 on occupiers' liability);

- parent and child (*Carmarthenshire County Council* v *Lewis* [1955] AC 549 (HL)).

✎ EXAM TIP

If you are faced with a problem question in which someone fails to act and loss or damage results, you should be careful to establish whether or not a special relationship exists. A good rule of thumb is whether it seems reasonable for the party in question to act. While there is no obligation to prevent a stranger from drowning in a pond, the situation would be quite different in the case of a parent who watched their child drown in a paddling pool and did nothing.

A positive duty can also arise as a result of a need to protect an individual from the acts of a third party. There is some overlap here – if you have a duty to protect someone against someone else's act, then it follows that you can potentially be liable for your omission to do so.

◼ Acts of third parties

In the same way that there is no general duty to act, there is no general duty of care in relation to the acts of third parties, unless there is a special relationship with that third party. For example, in *Stansbie* v *Troman* [1948] 2 KB 48 (CA), a decorator was entrusted with the key to a house that he was painting. He failed to secure the premises and the house was burgled. Tucker LJ stated that a duty of care existed where:

> . . . [T]he act of negligence itself consisted in the failure to take reasonable care to guard against the very thing that in fact happened.

This was in contrast to the position in *Perl (Exporters) Limited* v *Camden LBC* [1983] QB 342 (CA) and *King* v *Liverpool City Council* [1986] 1 WLR 890 (CA). Both of these cases involved loss or damage caused by burglars or vandals who gained entry to the property they damaged by first gaining entrance to an adjacent property. The distinction between these cases and *Stansbie* v *Trotman* is that there is no duty to secure your own property in order to protect another's, but there is a duty to protect another's if you have assumed the responsibility of taking care of it.

The House of Lords considered the duty of care to third parties further in *Smith* v *Littlewoods Organisation Ltd* [1987] AC 241.

KEY CASE

Smith v *Littlewoods Organisation Ltd* [1987] AC 241 (HL)
Concerning: duty of care; third parties

Facts

The defendants bought a cinema, intending to demolish it and replace it with a supermarket. However, the work was not completed and the cinema remained empty and unattended. Some children deliberately started a fire in it which burned the cinema down and badly damaged an adjacent café, billiard saloon and church. The claimants sued on the basis that their losses had been caused by the negligence of the defendants.

Legal principle

In this case, the appeal failed since the defendants had not known of the previous acts of vandalism in their cinema involving fire and since the cinema had not otherwise presented an obvious fire risk, then there was no duty to protect the claimants' property by securing the cinema. The House of Lords did say that the existence of a duty of care in such cases depended on all the circumstances of the case and on socially accepted standards of behaviour and that cases in which such a duty would exist were likely to be rare. However, it was held that the defendant could owe a duty in relation to the acts of third parties if the following 'special circumstances' existed:

- There was a 'special relationship' between claimant and defendant.

- The defendant negligently created a source of danger and it was reasonably foreseeable that a third party would interfere.

- The defendant either knew or was capable of knowing that a third party had created a danger or a risk of danger and had failed to take reasonable steps to abate it.

The House of Lords has also considered whether there may potentially be liability in negligence for the *criminal* acts of another:

KEY CASE

Mitchell v *Glasgow City Council* **[2009] UKHL 11**

Concerning: duty of care; criminal acts of third parties

Facts

M and D were neighbours in secure local authority housing. D had made numerous threats to kill M. The local authority had warned D that if he did not desist, they would take steps to evict him. They served a recovery notice which provoked D into further threats against M. The local authority had kept M informed of the steps they were taking. However, they then summoned D to a meeting at which he was again warned that if he continued such anti-social behaviour then he could be evicted. Around an hour after the meeting, D attacked M with a stick or iron bar about the head. M subsequently died.

M's widow and daughter claimed against the local authority in negligence on the basis that it had been under a duty to warn M that the meeting with D was to take place so that M would have known to take steps to avoid D afterwards.

Legal principle

The House of Lords held that there was nothing to show that the local authority had made itself responsible for protecting M from the criminal acts of D, so it was not fair, just or reasonable to infer a duty of care to warn M of the steps it was taking with regards to D. It went on to set out the situations in which there may be liability in negligence for the criminal acts of another:

■ where there is vicarious liability for the crimes of the third party (see Chapter 4);

■ where the defendant had an obligation to supervise the acts of the third party;

■ where the defendant created the risk of danger (the example given by Lord Brown mentions arming the third party with a weapon);

■ where there is an assumption of responsibility for the victim.

■ Misstatements

Liability for negligence in tort is generally based upon the defendant's conduct or occasionally, as seen above, their failure to act. It was long accepted that negligent or unintentional statements, however inaccurate or misleading, could not provide the basis for an action to recover financial loss caused by reliance on that statement. For example, in *Candler* v *Crane Christmas & Co* [1951] 2 KB 164 (CA), investors were not able to recover money lost as a consequence of their reliance on negligently prepared accounts.

Hedley Byrne v Heller

It was not until the landmark case of *Hedley Byrne* v *Heller* that the House of Lords established that liability in tort could be founded upon a negligent misstatement:

KEY CASE

Hedley Byrne & Co Ltd v *Heller and Partners Ltd* **[1964] AC 465 (HL)**

Concerning: liability for negligent misstatement

Facts

The claimant was an advertising company that was offered work by a small company with whom they had no previous dealings. It sought a reference from the company's bank which was prepared without any checks being made into the current state of its finances. In reliance upon the bank's reference, the claimant carried out work for the company which then went into liquidation before any payment was made. The claimant sought to recover its losses from the defendant bank on the basis of its negligent misstatement.

Legal principle

The House of Lords held that there were circumstances in which a person could be liable in tort for losses caused by a statement which he made if he did not take sufficient care to ensure that his statement was accurate or if he did not make it clear that he had taken no steps to ensure its accuracy.

As this opened a new area of **tortious** liability, the House of Lords imposed strict limitations upon the situations which would give rise to liability. As with liability for omissions, a special relationship must exist between the parties before there is a possibility of liability for negligent misstatement that causes economic loss; see Figure 1.3.

Examples of the 'special relationship' under *Hedley Byrne* v *Heller* include that between:

- an environmental health inspector and the owners of a guest house (*Walton* v *North Cornwall District Council* [1997] 1 WLR 570 (CA));

- a bank clerk advising on a mortgage (*Cornish* v *Midland Bank plc* [1985] 3 All ER 513 (CA));

- a friend (holding himself out as having some knowledge about cars) purchasing a car on his friend's behalf (*Chaudry* v *Prabhakar* [1989] 1 WLR 29 (CA)).

The criteria from *Hedley Byrne* v *Heller* were restated in *Caparo Industries plc* v *Dickman* which you have already encountered in relation to the general existence of the duty of care:

Figure 1.3

(1) The relationship will exist if one party exercises skill and judgement and the other party acts in reliance of this skill and judgement

(2) The person making the statement must possess skill in relation to the particular statement that is made and should realise that the other party will act in reliance upon the statement

(3) The party to whom the statement is made must have acted in reliance with that statement in circumstances where it was reasonable for him to rely upon the statement

KEY CASE

Caparo Industries plc v *Dickman* **[1990] 2 AC 605 (HL)**

Concerning: negligent misstatement

Facts

C, a company, owned shares in F plc. F's accounts were audited by D and published. C then purchased further shares in F, ultimately taking over F. They suffered a substantial financial loss. C sued D in negligence, claiming that the shares in F had been purchased in reliance on D's audit and that the financial position of F had been misstated (and was thus misleading): in particular that an apparent pre-tax profit of £1.3m should have been shown as a loss of over £400,000 and that had these accounts been correct, C would not have bought further shares in F.

The judge at first instance held that the D did not owe C a duty of care either as a shareholder of F or as an investor holding no shares. On appeal by C, the Court of Appeal, by a majority, held that a duty of care was owed to C as shareholders but not as investors. D appealed to the House of Lords.

Legal principle

The House of Lords allowed the appeal, holding that D had not owed a duty of care to C in respect of its purchase of F's shares (even though the affairs of the company were known to be such as to render it susceptible to an attempted takeover).

To establish a claim in negligent misstatement, particularly with regard to the 'special relationship', the claimant must prove that the defendant must have known that:

- the statement would be communicated to the claimant;
- the statement would be made specifically in connection with a particular transaction;
- the claimant would be very likely to rely upon it in deciding whether or not to proceed with the transaction.

In *Henderson* v *Merrett Syndicates* [1995] 2 AC 145 (HL), Lord Goff stated that the foundation of the duty of care in *Hedley Byrne* v *Heller* was the assumption of responsibility by the defendant to the claimant. If this was established, then it was also established that the third limb of *Caparo* would be satisfied: namely, that it was fair, just and reasonable to impose a duty of care. An example where the House of Lords did not find a special relationship or assumption of responsibility can be found in *Customs and Excise Commissioners* v *Barclays Bank plc* [2006] UKHL 28.

Liability to third parties

Where the defendant makes a statement which is communicated to the claimant by a third party and the claimant suffers loss, there still may be sufficient proximity for liability to arise for the defendant's negligent misstatement as long as there is a special relationship between defendant and claimant (*Spring* v *Guardian Assurance plc* [1995] 2 AC 296 (HL); *White* v *Jones* [1995] 2 AC 207 (HL)).

Economic loss

KEY DEFINITION: Economic loss

Financial losses which are not attributable to physical harm caused to the claimant or his property. It includes loss of profits, loss of trade and loss of investment revenue.

There is a separate set of rules relating to **economic loss** because the courts have felt the need to ensure that a defendant does not attract limitless liability as a result of his actions. Most conduct that amounts to a tort affects a finite number of people and gives rise to largely determinate harm. The sorts of situations that fall within pure economic loss tend to lack these limiting factors so a defendant could be liable to a large number of claimants on the basis of a single incident. For example, if a lorry crashes into an electricity substation as a result of negligent driving and the electricity supply to an industrial estate and shopping centre is cut off for eight hours, the extent of the financial losses would be immense. Such potentially limitless liability would make it impossible to obtain insurance to cover such losses, thus creating an even more difficult situation if all economic loss was actionable.

Pure economic loss which is not consequential on physical damage to the claimant's property is *not recoverable* in tort. Therefore, most cases turn on whether or not the particular loss suffered is pure economic loss. Economic losses can be caused by:

- damage to property;
- acquisition of defective goods or property.

! Don't be tempted to . . .

Don't conclude that an economic loss is not recoverable without considering the particular circumstances in which economic losses may be recovered. Students often stick with this general principle without demonstrating the depth of knowledge required to consider its exceptions, and thus miss out on valuable marks.

Damage to property

Economic loss which is a direct consequence of physical damage is an exception to the general rule that economic loss is not recoverable in tort.

KEY CASE

Spartan Steel and Alloys Ltd v *Martin & Co (Contractors) Ltd* **[1973] 1 QB 27 (CA)**
Concerning: consequential economic loss

Facts

The claimants manufactured stainless steel alloys at a factory 24 hours a day. The defendants' employees, who were working on a nearby road, damaged the electrical supply cable to the factory. The electricity board shut off the power supply to the factory for $14^{1}/_{2}$ hours until the cable was mended. The claimants scrapped a 'melt' in the furnace, reducing its value by £368. If the supply had not been cut off, they would have made a profit of £400 on the melt, and £1767 on another four melts, which would have been put into the furnace. They claimed damages from the defendants in respect of all three sums.

Legal principle

The claimants could recover the damage to the melt in progress and the loss of profit on that melt. They could not recover for the loss of profit during the time that the electricity was switched off. The damage to the melt in progress was physical damage and the loss of profit on it was a direct consequence of the physical damage. The further loss of profit was pure economic loss and not recoverable.

In *Spartan Steel and Alloys* Lord Denning said:

> I think the question of recovering economic loss is one of policy. Whenever the courts draw a line to mark out the bounds of duty they do it as to limit the responsibility of the defendant . . . It seems to me better to consider the particular relationship in hand and see whether or not, as a matter of policy, economic loss should be recoverable or not.

Acquisition of defective goods or property

The general position in relation to the claimant acquiring defective goods or property is the same as for other cases of economic loss: the loss is not recoverable in tort.

However, there has been a series of cases in which this position was relaxed.

KEY CASE

Anns v *Merton London Borough Council* **[1978] AC 728 (HL)**

Concerning: economic loss

Facts

The claimants were tenants of a block of flats built in accordance with plans approved by the council. The foundations were too shallow. The tenants sued for the cost of making the flats safe on the basis that the council either negligently approved inadequate plans or failed to inspect the foundations during construction.

Legal principle

A duty of care was owed by the council and that if their inspectors did not exercise proper care and skill then the council was liable even though the loss suffered was economic loss.

KEY CASE

Junior Books Ltd v *Veitchi Co Ltd* **[1983] 1 AC 520 (HL)**

Concerning: economic loss

Facts

The claimants were having a factory built. On the advice of their architect, they subcontracted the defendants to complete the work. The defendants laid an unusable floor which had to be replaced. The claimants sued for the costs of replacing the floor and the loss of profit while the floor was relaid.

Legal principle

Even though the claimants had suffered no physical damage, they successfully recovered all the heads of loss claimed, despite their all being economic loss. The court considered that, in all the circumstances, the proximity of the parties was only 'just short of a direct contractual relationship' and that, as such, a duty of care existed.

These decisions appeared to mark a significant departure from the general principle that economic loss was not recoverable in tort. The courts almost immediately tried to limit the effects of *Anns* and *Junior Books*. Although *Junior Books* has not yet been overruled, it has never been followed – the courts have always distinguished it on its particular facts. There are a number of examples where courts rejected claims for pure economic loss based on *Anns* (for example, *D & F Estates Ltd* v *Church Commissioners for England* [1989] AC 177 (HL)).

The House of Lords finally clarified the situation in *Murphy* v *Brentwood District Council* [1991] 1 AC 398 (HL).

KEY CASE

Murphy v *Brentwood District Council* **[1991] 1 AC 398 (HL)**
Concerning: economic loss

Facts
A council approved plans for a concrete raft upon which properties were built. The raft moved and caused cracks in the walls of a property which was sold for £35,000 less that it would have done had it not been defective.

Legal principle
The House of Lords overruled *Anns* and held that the council was not liable in the absence of physical injury.

In summary, then, *economic loss arising from a negligent act or omission is not recoverable.*

The House of Lords gave a useful overview of the scope of liability for economic loss and the various tests used by the courts in *Customs and Excise Commissioners* v *Barclays Bank plc* [2006] UKHL 28.

Psychiatric injury

The existence of the duty of care has also been examined in great depth in relation to psychiatric injury. Before considering this, it is first necessary to look at what is meant by psychiatric injury and the means by which it must be caused in order to give rise to a potential claim in negligence.

Definition of psychiatric injury

Psychiatric injury must be *medically recognised*. A number of different conditions have been tested by case law, as the table below shows.

Medically recognised	Not medically recognised
Post-traumatic stress disorder (*Leach* v *Chief Constable of Gloucestershire Constabulary* [1999] 1 WLR 1421 (CA))	Distress (*Kralj* v *McGrath* [1986] 1 All ER 54 (QBD))
Pathological grief (*Vernon* v *Bosley* (No 1) [1997] RTR 1 (CA))	Simple grief (*Vernon* v *Bosley* (No 1) (CA))
Personality disorder (*Chadwick* v *British Railways Board* [1967] 1 WLR 912 (QBD))	
Miscarriage (*Bourhill* v *Young*; *Hay* v *Young* [1943] AC 92 (HL))	

In addition, the psychiatric damage must be caused by a 'sudden event'.

KEY CASE

Alcock v *Chief Constable of South Yorkshire* **[1992] 1 AC 310 (HL)**
Concerning: psychiatric injury; sudden event

Facts

The police allowed a large crowd of football supporters into an already crowded stand which was surrounded by a high perimeter fence. In the chaos that followed, 95 people were crushed to death. A large number of claims were made by those present at the scene and those who had viewed the events on the television. Claims were made by various family members and friends of those present.

Legal principle

Lord Ackner stated that:

> Shock . . . involves the sudden appreciation by sight or sound of a horrifying sight or sound or a horrifying event, which violently agitates the mind. It has yet to include psychiatric illness caused by the accumulation over a period of time of more gradual assaults on the nervous system.

Duty of care

A duty of care is owed if the claimant is a *reasonably foreseeable victim*.

KEY CASE

Alcock v *Chief Constable of South Yorkshire* **[1992] 1 AC 310 (HL)**

Concerning: psychiatric injury claims

Facts

The facts are stated in the previous Key Case box.

Legal principle

The House of Lords laid down three factors to be considered in determining whether a duty of care is owed in psychiatric injury cases:

- *foreseeability* – it must be reasonably foreseeable that a person of normal fortitude in the position of the claimant would suffer illness due to his/her close ties of love and affection with the victim; *and*

- *proximity* – there must be temporal and spatial proximity of the claimant in relation to the accident; *and*

- *how the shock was caused.*

The definition of the reasonably foreseeable victim was subsequently considered by the House of Lords in *Page* v *Smith* [1996] AC 155 (HL).

KEY CASE

Page v *Smith* **[1996] AC 155 (HL)**

Concerning: psychiatric injury; reasonably foreseeable victim

Facts

The claimant was involved in a road accident with the defendant when the defendant failed to give way when turning out of a side road. The claimant was physically unhurt in the collision, but the accident caused him to suffer the onset of myalgic encephalomyelitis (ME) from which he had suffered for about 20 years but which was then in remission.

Legal principle

The House of Lords held that foreseeability of physical injury was sufficient to allow a claimant directly involved in the incident to recover in psychiatric injury even if physical harm does not occur. In doing so, they identified two types of victim – *primary* and *secondary* victims.

Primary victims

Primary victims are directly involved in the incident.

In *Alcock, rescuers* were also placed in the class of primary victims. However, in *White and Others* v *Chief Constable of the South Yorkshire Police* [1999] 2 AC 455 (HL), their Lordships modified the position with regard to rescuers such that they must show actual or apprehended danger – in other words, the rescuer must establish objective exposure to danger or a reasonable belief that there was an exposure to danger.

In *Dooley* v *Cammell Laird and Co Ltd* [1951] 1 Lloyd's Rep 271 (Liverpool Assizes) and *Wigg* v *British Railways Board* (1986) 136 NLJ 446 (QBD) a further category of primary victims was established in situations where the *claimant believes he has caused another's death or injury*. This would only succeed if the claimant was actually present when the death or injury occurred (*Hunter* v *British Coal* [1999] QB 140 (CA)). However, this category was removed in *White and Others* v *Chief Constable of South Yorkshire Police* [1999] 2 AC 455 (HL) where their Lordships held that only persons in *actual danger of physical harm* can be classified as primary victims.

Secondary victims

Secondary victims must satisfy the tests laid down in *Alcock*:

- There must be a close relationship of love and affection with the primary victim (there is a rebuttable presumption in favour of this in the case of parents and spouses).

- Ordinary passers-by *may* be able to claim if the incident witnessed was 'particularly horrific' (although this was unsuccessful in *McFarlane* v *E E Caledonia Ltd* [1994] 2 All ER 1 (CA)).

In certain circumstances it may be possible for a claimant to succeed in a psychiatric injury claim after witnessing destruction of property (*Attia* v *British Gas plc* [1988] QB 304 (CA)).

In *Rothwell* v *Chemical & Insulating Co Ltd: Re Pleural Plaques* [2007] 3 WLR 876 (HL), one of the claimants had suffered a recognised psychiatric illness from the fear that he would contract a serious asbestos-related illness in the future. However, the House of Lords refused to extend the principle from *Page* v *Smith* to apply to the facts of his claim. The Lords also held that the defendants could not have foreseen such psychiatric illness as the result of their breach of duty several years earlier.

Proximity

The issue of proximity was considered in *McLoughlin* v *O'Brian* [1983] 1 AC 410 (HL).

KEY CASE

McLoughlin v *O'Brian* **[1983] 1 AC 410 (HL)**

Concerning: psychiatric injury; spatial and temporal proximity

Facts

The claimant's husband and children were involved in a road accident. The claimant, who was two miles away at the time, was told of the accident about two hours later by a neighbour, who took her to hospital to see her family. There she learnt that her youngest daughter had been killed, and she saw her husband and the other children, and witnessed the nature and extent of their injuries. They were still in the same state as at the scene; covered in oil and mud. The claimant sued in nervous shock.

Legal principle

The nervous shock suffered was the reasonably foreseeable result of the injuries to her family caused by the defendant's negligence and she was entitled to recover damages.

To satisfy the requirement of proximity, the claimant need not be present at the time of the accident, but must come upon the *immediate aftermath*.

How the shock was caused

The claimant must see or hear the event *through unaided sight or hearing*. In *Alcock* it was held that shock communicated by live television broadcasts was not sufficient since it did not show recognisable or identifiable individuals suffering.

■ Special claimants and defendants

The law of negligence has no statutory basis. It has developed through a huge number of cases. This has meant that when considering whether a duty of care exists in any given situation, the courts have the flexibility to take public policy considerations into account and steer the evolution of the tort of negligence accordingly. This flexibility has also allowed the courts to protect certain classes of defendant from liability in negligence and also to provide additional help to certain classes of claimant in bringing an action.

Unborn children

The existence of a duty of care requires reasonable foresight of harm. However, in the case of unborn children, the defendant might not realise that the female claimant is pregnant, although it is quite possible that a person's negligence might harm an unborn child.

In *Burton* v *Islington Health Authority* [1993] QB 204 (CA) it was held that a duty of care is owed to an unborn child which becomes actionable on birth. In other words, a child can sue in negligence for events occurring during its time in its mother's womb. This common law position is only applicable to persons born prior to 22 July 1976 when the Congenital Disabilities (Civil Liability) Act 1976 came into force. This Act gives a right of action to a child who is born alive and disabled in respect of the disability, if it is caused by an occurrence which affected the mother during pregnancy or the mother or child during labour, causing disabilities which would not otherwise have been present. It extends to pre-conception torts, where the mother is harmed prior to conceiving and the harm suffered affects the health of the baby at birth.

Police, rescuers and public authorities

The courts have found that there is no general duty of care owed by the *police* to any particular individual. In *Hill* v *Chief Constable of West Yorkshire* [1989] AC 53 (HL) it was held that the duty of the police is to the public at large. This case involved Peter Sutcliffe, the 'Yorkshire Ripper' who murdered 13 women. The mother of his last victim sued the police for negligence for failing to catch him, alleging numerous missed opportunities. The House of Lords held that the police owed no duty of care towards Susan Hill to protect her from the Ripper on the basis that if such claims were allowed, the police would be inhibited in the exercise of their professional judgement and that a significant amount of police resource would be diverted from investigating crime to the defence of civil cases brought against them.

This approach has been extended to cases involving the *fire service* (*Capital and Counties plc* v *Hampshire County Council* [1997] QB 1004 (CA)) and the *coastguard* (*OLL Ltd* v *Secretary of State for Transport* [1997] 3 All ER 897 (QBD)). In respect of the *ambulance service*, there is no general duty to respond to a call, although once a call has been accepted, the service owes a duty to the named individual at a specific address (*Kent* v *Griffiths, Roberts and London Ambulance Service* [1999] PIQR P192 (CA)) provided that it is just, fair and reasonable to impose such a duty.

In respect of *public authorities*, it was held in *X (Minors)* v *Bedfordshire County Council* [1995] 2 AC 633 (HL), that in most instances an action in negligence against a public authority carrying out its delegated powers would fail. However, in *Connor* v *Surrey County Council* [2010] EWCA Civ 286, the Court of Appeal decided that the common law duty of care could be established in exceptional circumstances and held an education authority liable for psychiatric injury caused to one of its employees by its negligence.

□ REVISION NOTE

You may have covered the remedies available under judicial review where a public body acts beyond its authority (*ultra vires*) in constitutional and administrative (public) law. If so, it might be useful to refresh your memory as to how local authorities operate under powers delegated from the executive.

However, in *Barrett* v *Enfield London Borough Council* [2001] 2 AC 550 (HL), Lord Hutton disagreed with the decision in *X* v *Bedfordshire County Council*, considering that challenges based upon the careless exercise of discretionary powers by a public authority *could* be founded in negligence.

In both cases, though, the House of Lords was careful to limit the possible liability of public authorities in negligence. If every decision the Lords made was potentially actionable in tort, this would impose unworkable restraints on their ability to perform their functions and be contrary to public interest. The courts will attempt to balance the social need for the public authority to carry out its duties effectively and the need for an adequate remedy for the individual who suffers from the negligent exercise of the public authority's discretion.

This partial immunity has been subject to appeal in the European Court of Human Rights. In *Osman* v *UK* (2000) 29 EHRR 245 (ECtHR) the European Court of Human Rights held that police immunity violated the Article 6 right to a fair hearing. In *Z* v *UK* (2002) 34 EHRR 3 (ECtHR) it was held that the immunity applied in *X* subjected the claimants to 'inhuman and degrading treatment' (Article 3) and denied them an effective remedy (Article 13).

Other examples include *D* v *Bury Metropolitan Borough Council* [2006] 1 WLR 917 (CA) in which a local authority was held not to owe a duty of care to the parents of a child who was the subject of a child abuse investigation.

The House of Lords readdressed the extent of the duty of care owed by public authorities to the public in two conjoined appeals:

KEY CASE

Van Colle v *Chief Constable of Hertfordshire Police; Smith* v *Chief Constable of Sussex Police* [2009] 1 AC 225 (HL)

Concerning: duty of care owed of public authorities

Facts

In *van Colle*, a man named Brougham was arrested and charged with thefts from three sources: Giles van Colle and two companies called Southern Counties and Alpha Optical. Brougham offered money to Southern Counties and Alpha Optical to drop the charges. Giles van Colle's car was destroyed in a fire that was found to have been started deliberately and he was threatened with physical harm if he did not drop the charges against Brougham. Van Colle did not drop the charges and he was shot dead by Brougham before the trial commenced. Brougham was convicted of murder. Prior to these events, he had three convictions for common assault, disorderly behaviour and theft. The police officer in charge of the case, to whom the threats had been reported, was subject to internal disciplinary proceedings for failing to perform his duties conscientiously in relation to the threats and was fined five days' pay. Van Colle's parents issued proceedings against the police for failing to protect their son from the risk of serious harm of which they were, or should have been, aware. They claimed that this police failure amounted to a breach of Article 2 of the European Convention on Human Rights.

In *Smith*, Mr Smith lived with his partner, Gareth Jeffrey, but had suggested a break in the relationship following an argument. During the time they were apart, Jeffrey made attempts to resume the relationship but Mr Smith made it clear he considered it to be over. Jeffrey made threats against Mr Smith, including death threats, and Mr Smith eventually contacted the police but the officers who visited him did not take a statement or complete a crime form even though they were told of the history of violence. Mr Smith completed a form that would allow his telephone calls to be traced but was told this would take four weeks. The threatening messages continued, including one that said: 'I am close to you now and I am going to track you down and I'm not going to stop until I've driven this knife into you repeatedly.' Mr Smith contacted the police and told them that he believed his life was in danger but he was told that the investigation was proceeding and that he should call 999 if he was concerned about his safety. A few days later, Jeffrey attacked Mr Smith at his home with a claw hammer, fracturing his skull and causing brain damage. Jeffrey was arrested, charged, convicted and sentenced to 10 years' imprisonment for the attack. Mr Smith issued proceedings against the Chief Constable of Sussex for negligence in failing to protect him from the attack.

The claim brought by the parents of van Colle was based upon human rights rather than common law negligence as it seemed that previous case law ruled out any possibility of liability arising from a failing to protect a person from becoming the victim of a crime. However, Mr Smith was out of time to bring a human rights claim so pursued a claim in negligence.

Legal principle

In relation to *van Colle*, although the case had succeeded at the Court of Appeal, the House of Lords upheld the appeal by the police. The House of Lords acknowledged that Article 2 of the Convention could be violated if the police failed to protect a person from a 'real and immediate threat to life' but that in this instance there was an insufficient basis upon which the police could have reached a conclusion that violence would be used.

In relation to *Smith*, the House of Lords ruled that the imposition of liability would create a detrimental effect by encouraging the police to engage in defensive policing rather than investigating crime.

In essence, then, the House of Lords upheld the approach taken in *Hill* in 1989 in relation to both of these appeals and thus seem to have closed the door upon any possibility of holding the police liable in negligence for failing to protect an individual from becoming the victim of a crime. However, the case does more than simply affirm the position stated in *Hill* because both *van Colle* and *Smith* involved a far more specific threat against a named individual. In *Hill* there was no basis upon which the police could have believed that Mrs Hill's daughter was at any greater risk than many other potential victims so it would have been unrealistic to expect them to undertake measures to protect her. Although the majority of the House of Lords did not allow this factor to alter their approach to the general principle, the dissenting judge, Lord Bingham, thought different. He said that:

> If a member of the public furnishes a police officer with apparently credible evidence that a third party whose identity and whereabouts are known presents a specific and imminent threat to his life or physical safety, the police owes a duty to that member of the public to take reasonable steps to assess the threat and, if appropriate, take reasonable steps to prevent it being executed.

✎ EXAM TIP

When writing an essay on this topic, it will be important to point out the difference in the facts of *van Colle* and *Smith* and that of the previous case of *Hill* as this acknowledges that there was potential to depart from the previous position or at least to modify the principle in *Hill*. Equally, awareness of the dissenting view and the ability to use it to argue for an alternative outcome to the cases would be valuable. Finally, these cases have attracted a great deal of academic comment so be sure to research the views expressed and seek to incorporate them into your work.

■ Putting it all together

Answer guidelines

See the problem question at the start of the chapter. A diagram illustrating how to structure your answer is available on the companion website.

Approaching the question

This is a broad question that requires you to think about the policy considerations behind the case law that has defined the scope of the duty of care in negligence. As such, you need to know both *what* the duty of care is in a range of situations and, more importantly, *why* it has developed in that way.

Important points to include

There are several points that an answer to this question could include:

- The basic idea of the duty of care and a statement of the general duty from *Donoghue* as restated in *Caparo*;
- The established duty situations – such as between road users, employers/ employees, doctors/patients, solicitor/client – what do these have in common?
- A discussion on the duty of care for failing to act and how the duty to act positively can arise in certain relationships of power/control;
- How individuals can be protected against the negligent acts of third parties in 'special circumstances';
- The evolution of the duty of care in negligent misstatement and the 'special relationships' within which it can arise;
- The operation of the duty rules relating to pure economic loss;
- The existence of the duty of care in relation to psychiatric injury/nervous shock and the limitations on the existence of the duty.

 Make your answer stand out

The key to success in this question is to relate each of the duty situations that you have considered in the main body of your essay to the point raised in the question: that is, how each of the cases reflects the court assessing the need to protect society from loss or harm caused by the carelessness of others. Do not simply describe a range of relevant case authorities without commenting on how they protect individuals in particular situations: it is the depth of analysis that will make your answer stand out.

READ TO IMPRESS

Arden, M. (2010) Human rights and civil wrongs: tort law under the spotlight. *Public Law*, p. 140.

Hogg, K. (1994) Negligence and economic loss in England, Australia, Canada and New Zealand. 43, *International & Comparative Law Quarterly*, p. 116.

Morgan, J. (2009) Policy reasoning in tort law: the courts, the Law Commission and the critics. 125, *Law Quarterly Review*, p. 215.

Norris, W. (2009) The duty of care to prevent personal injury. 2, *Journal of Personal Injury Law*, p. 114.

Perry, S. (1992) Protected interests and undertakings in the law of negligence. 42, *University of Toronto Law Journal*, p. 247.

Steele, I. (2008) Negligence liability for failing to prevent crime. 67, *Cambridge Law Journal*, p. 239.

Voyiakis, E. (2009) The great illusion: tort law and exposure to danger of physical harm. 72, *Modern Law Review*, p. 909.

Witting, C. (2001) Distinguishing between property damage and pure economic loss in negligence: a personality thesis. 21, *Legal Studies*, p. 481.

www.pearsoned.co.uk/lawexpress

 Go online to access more revision support including quizzes to test your knowledge, sample questions with answer guidelines, podcasts you can download, and more!

Negligence:
breach of duty

Revision checklist

Essential points you should know:

- [ ] The concept of the 'reasonable man'
- [ ] How to determine the standard of care for particular defendants
- [ ] The factors which the courts consider in determining the standard of care
- [ ] The availability and operation of *res ispa loquitur*

■ Topic map

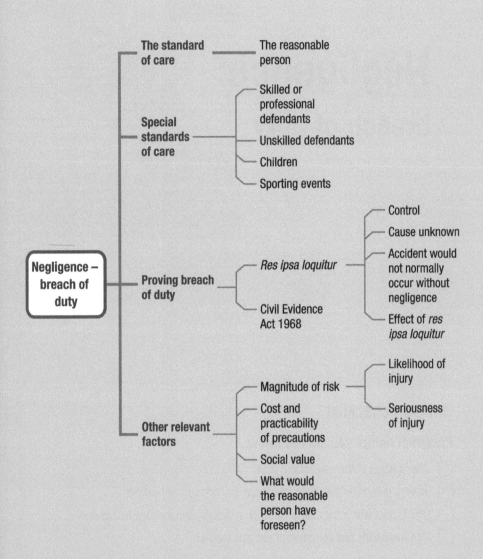

■ Introduction

Once it has been established that a duty of care exists, the next element in establishing negligence is demonstrating that the duty has been breached.

In other words, breach of duty is concerned with whether an individual has fulfilled their duty of care or not. This is closely related to the idea of the standard of care, which, as its name suggests, is the degree of 'carefulness' that the law expects an individual to take to avoid causing harm or injury to another. As you might expect, the concept of the standard of care has been developed by case law to cover a range of different situations that have arisen as the tort of negligence has evolved since *Donoghue* v *Stevenson*.

ASSESSMENT ADVICE

Essay questions

Essay questions on breach of duty/standard of care could be set to be quite wide, covering a variety of situations, or quite narrow, focusing on, say, the standard of care in medical negligence, or that owed to children. If you are revising for an essay question on breach of duty, you should make sure that you understand not only the current relevant case law that applies to the various special standards of care, but also the principles and reasoning of the courts behind the decisions and any previous cases that have led to the current position. Your analytical skills will be demonstrated by showing *how* and *why* the law has taken a particular approach, rather than simply describing *what* the law happens to be or what it has been.

Problem questions

Problem questions on negligence will invariably contain a section involving breach of duty. Without breach of duty, there can be no negligence, so it would be hard to devise a meaningful problem question on this key area of tort law without involving a discussion as to whether or not a particular defendant had breached their duty of care (assuming, of course, that you have already established that one exists – see Chapter 1). Remember that the facts of a problem question could – and often will – involve one or more of the novel duty situations, so look for clues in the facts that will steer you towards the correct area of law. Examples that should give you a steer could be that the defendant is a child, or a junior doctor on their first day at work. To approach a problem question with confidence will require you to know all of the special standards of care and how they apply.

■ Sample question

Could you answer this question? Below is a typical essay question that could arise on this topic. Guidelines on addressing the question are included at the end of the chapter, whilst a sample problem question and guidance on tackling it can be found on the companion website.

ESSAY QUESTION

'The standard of care in negligence is that of the reasonable person.'

Discuss the accuracy of this statement using examples and cases to support your answer.

■ Breach of duty

The second element of negligence is *breach of duty*. Having established that a duty of care exists in law and in the particular situation, the next step in establishing liability is to decide whether the defendant is in breach of that duty – in other words, whether the defendant has not come up to the *standard of care* required by law. See Figure 2.1.

Standard of care

The standard of care was (generically) defined in *Blyth* v *Birmingham Waterworks* (1856) 11 Exch 781.

KEY CASE

Blyth v *Birmingham Waterworks* **(1856) 11 Exch 781**
Concerning: standard of care

Facts

A wooden plug in a water main became loose in a severe frost. The plug led to a pipe which in turn went up to the street. However, this pipe was blocked with ice, and the water instead flooded the claimant's house. The claimant sued in negligence.

Legal principle

Alderson B defined negligence as:

The omission to do something which a *reasonable man* guided upon those considerations which ordinarily regulate the conduct of human affairs, would do, or doing something which a *prudent and reasonable man* would not do (emphasis added).

Figure 2.1

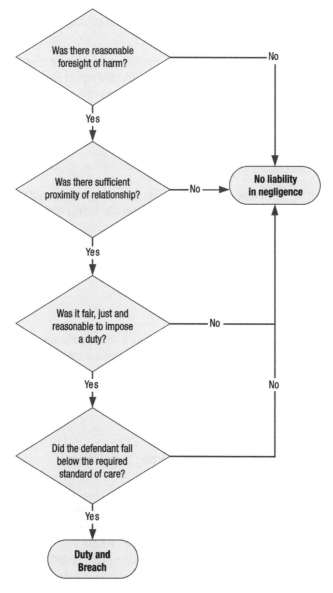

The reasonable person

The conduct of the defendant will be measured against that of the reasonable person. What are the characteristics of such a person? In *Hall* v *Brooklands Auto-Racing Club* [1933] 1 KB 205 (CA), Greer LJ described such a person as:

- 'the man in the street'; or
- 'the man on the Clapham omnibus'; or
- 'the man who takes the magazines at home, and in the evening pushes the lawn mower in his shirt sleeves'.

The reasonable person, therefore, is 'average', not perfect. In deciding whether a defendant has breached the duty of care, the court applies an *objective* test. In other words, the general question is 'what would a reasonable person have foreseen in this particular situation?' rather than 'what did this *particular* defendant foresee in this particular situation?'.

❗ Don't be tempted to . . .

Don't confuse the terms duty of care and standard of care. The standard of care determines whether a particular duty of care has been breached. You should always consider the existence of the duty itself before discussing whether or not a particular defendant has reached the appropriate standard required to absolve him or her from liability.

Special standards of care

There are certain situations in which the courts apply a different standard of care from that of the reasonable person since the application of the general standard of care as that of the reasonable person would not be suitable:

- where the defendant has a particular skill or profession;
- where the defendant has a particular *lack* of skill;
- where the defendant is a child;
- where the defendant is competing in or watching a sporting event.

Skilled or professional defendants

The standard of care applied to professionals with a particular skill or expertise is that of the reasonable person with the same skill or expertise. For instance, a doctor would be expected to show a greater degree of skill and care to a patient than 'the man on the Clapham omnibus'. This test was established in *Bolam* v *Friern Hospital Management Committee* [1957] 1 WLR 582 (QBD).

KEY CASE

Bolam v *Friern Hospital Management Committee* [1957] 1 WLR 582 (QBD)

Concerning: medical negligence; standard of care

Facts

The claimant underwent a course of electro-convulsive therapy in hospital as treatment for severe depression. This involves the application of electrical current to the patient's head with the aim of causing seizures. The doctor failed to provide the claimant with any muscle relaxants or any physical restraint. The claimant suffered dislocation of both hip joints with fractures of the pelvis on each side. The court had to decide whether it was negligent not to provide relaxants or restraints.

Legal principle

The standard of care for doctors is 'the standard of the ordinary skilled man exercising and professing to have that special skill'. There were conflicting views from practitioners on the use of relaxants and restraints. As there were therefore doctors who *would* have acted in the same way, the doctor treating the claimant had acted in accordance with a competent body of medical opinion and was therefore not negligent.

The decision in *Bolam* has been approved by the House of Lords in subsequent cases (e.g. *Sidaway* v *Bethlem Royal & Maudsley Hospital Governors* [1985] AC 871 (HL)).

The *Bolam* test has also been held to apply to other professionals in general. This has included such diverse professions as:

- auctioneers (*Luxmoore-May* v *Messenger May Baverstock* [1990] 1 WLR 1009 (CA));
- double glazing window designers (*Adams* v *Rhymney Valley DC* (2001) 33 HLR 41 (CA)).

However, the *Bolam* test has also been criticised for being too protective of professionals. In medical negligence cases in particular, it has been argued that the test allows practitioners to set their own standards, rather than having those standards set by the courts. The House of Lords clarified the situation in *Bolitho* v *City and Hackney Health Authority* [1998] AC 232 (HL).

KEY CASE

Bolitho v *City and Hackney Health Authority* [1998] AC 232 (HL)

Concerning: medical negligence; standard of care

Facts

The claimant suffered brain damage as a result of a doctor's failure to attend to clear a child's blocked airways by intubation. There was a difference of medical opinion as to whether intubation was necessary in the particular circumstances. ▶

> **Legal principle**
>
> Although there was a recognised body of medical opinion in accordance with the doctor's practice, the House of Lords held that a doctor *could* be liable in negligence despite the presence of a body of medical opinion in favour of their actions. The court can decide that a body of opinion is not reasonable or responsible if it can be demonstrated that the professional opinion is not capable of withstanding logical analysis.

Despite *Bolitho*, it remains the case that it is very difficult to prove professional negligence where there is a body of opinion which agrees that the defendant has followed an accepted practice.

Unskilled defendants

The general standard of care in negligence is an objective test, judged against the standards of the reasonable person. This means that no allowance is made for the inexperience or lack of skill of the defendant.

> **KEY CASE**
>
> *Nettleship* v *Weston* [1971] 2 QB 691 (CA)
>
> *Concerning: negligence; unskilled defendants*
>
> **Facts**
>
> A learner driver crashed into a lamp post and injured her instructor.
>
> **Legal principle**
>
> The driver was liable despite her inexperience. The standard of care required of all motorists is the same: that of the reasonably competent driver.

The same principle has been held to apply in relation to junior doctors such that they are required to reach the standard of the reasonable competent doctor of the same rank (*Wilsher* v *Essex Area Health Authority* [1987] QB 730 (CA)).

Where a person undertakes an activity requiring specialist skills, they are required to reach the standard of a person reasonably competent in that skill (*Wells* v *Cooper* [1958] 2 QB 265 (CA)).

Children

Child defendants are expected to reach the standard of care reasonably expected of ordinary children of the same age.

Mullin v *Richards* **[1998] 1 WLR 1304 (CA)**

Concerning: negligence; children

Facts

Two 15-year-old schoolgirls were fencing with plastic rulers during a class when one of the rulers snapped and a fragment of plastic caused one of them to lose all useful sight in one eye.

Legal principle

As Hutchison LJ stated:

> the question for the judge is not whether the actions of the defendant were such as an ordinarily prudent and reasonable adult in the defendant's situation would have realised gave rise to a risk of injury, it is whether an ordinary, prudent and reasonable 15-year-old schoolgirl in the defendant's situation would have realised as such.

Therefore, since such games were common and rarely led to injury, the injury in question was unforeseeable to 15-year-old schoolgirls, and there was no liability in negligence.

Very young children are, of course, less likely to foresee that their acts might cause harm to others. If so, they will not owe a duty of care and cannot therefore be liable in negligence.

Older children may be judged against the adult standard of care (*Gorely* v *Codd* [1967] 1 WLR 19 (Lincoln Assizes)). The courts will consider all the circumstances, including the nature of the activity pursued.

Sporting events

Spectators and competitors in sporting events may be owed a *lower* standard of care than the general standard.

Wooldridge v *Sumner* **[1963] 2 QB 43 (CA)**

Concerning: standard of care owed to spectators

Facts

An experienced rider at an equestrian event galloped his horse around a corner so quickly that the horse went out of control, plunged off the track and injured a photographer in the ensuing chaos.

▶

Legal principle

This was held to be 'an error of judgement' on the part of the rider rather than actionable negligence; furthermore, the Court of Appeal held that the duty of care would only be breached where a competitor demonstrated a 'reckless disregard' for the safety of the spectator.

This test of 'reckless disregard' was extended to fellow competitors in *Harrison* v *Vincent* [1982] RTR 8 (CA). Referees may also owe a duty of care to participants (*Smoldon* v *Whitworth and Nolan* [1997] PIQR 133 (CA)).

 Make your answer stand out

For a more detailed discussion of the operation of negligence in relation to sporting events see:

Fafinski, S. (2005) 'Consent and the rules of the game: the interplay of civil and criminal liability for sporting injuries', 69 *Journal of Criminal Law* 414.

Other relevant factors

When determining the standard of care, the courts will take all the circumstances of the case into account. This will possibly involve consideration of a number of other relevant factors including:

- the magnitude of the risk;
- the cost and practicability of precautions;
- the social value of the defendant's activities;
- what the reasonable person would have foreseen.

✎ EXAM TIP

Many students fail to consider all the circumstances when deciding whether there has been a breach of duty. Therefore, if the facts of the question present an opportunity for you to discuss their possible effects on the standard of care, you should do so.

Magnitude of risk

The magnitude of the risk is determined by the *likelihood* of it occurring and the *seriousness* of the potential injury.

Likelihood of injury

KEY CASE

Bolton v *Stone* [1951] AC 850 (HL); *Miller* v *Jackson* [1977] QB 966 (CA)
Concerning: standard of care; likelihood of injury

Facts

Both cases involved damage caused by cricket balls which had been hit out of the ground. In *Bolton* v *Stone* the ground had been occupied and used as a cricket ground for about 90 years, and there was evidence that on some six occasions in a period of over 30 years a ball had been hit into the highway, but no one had been injured. In *Miller* v *Jackson* cricket balls were hit out of the ground eight or nine times a season.

Legal principle

A greater risk of damage than normal increases the standard of care required of a potential defendant. Negligence was not found in *Bolton* v *Stone* but was in *Miller* v *Jackson*.

 Make your answer stand out

Lord Denning provided an entertaining and eloquent counter-argument by way of dissenting judgment in *Miller* v *Jackson*. It is worth reading to see the difference in view between Lord Denning and the other judges. It demonstrates the amount of discretion judges can have in determining the relevant standard of care 'in all the circumstances'. Such commentary may be useful in an essay.

A further example of a situation in which it was held that the defendant should have reached a higher standard of care where there was an increased likelihood of injury was *Haley* v *London Electricity Board* [1965] AC 778 (HL). Here a blind claimant fell down a hole dug in the pavement. Given that it is reasonably foreseeable that a blind person could be walking along a pavement, the defendants had a duty to take extra precautions to ensure safety.

Seriousness of injury

If the defendant knows that a specific individual is at risk of suffering greater damage than normal, the defendant may be required to reach a higher standard of care.

KEY CASE

Paris v *Stepney Borough Council* [1951] AC 367 (HL)
Concerning: standard of care; seriousness of injury

Facts

The claimant was a mechanic. His employers knew that he was blind in one eye. While the claimant was using a hammer to remove a bolt on a vehicle, a chip of metal flew off and entered his good eye, so injuring it that he became totally blind. The defendants did not provide goggles for him to wear, and there was evidence that it was not the ordinary practice for employers to supply goggles to men employed in garages on the maintenance and repair of vehicles.

Legal principle

The defendants owed a higher standard of care to the claimant because they knew that an injury to his good eye would cause him much more serious consequences than the same injury to a worker with two good eyes.

Cost and practicability of precautions

The court will also take into account what (if any) measures the defendant could have taken to avoid the risk of injury, the cost of those measures and the ease with which they could have been implemented.

KEY CASE

Latimer v *AEC Ltd* **[1953] AC 643 (HL)**

Concerning: standard of care; cost and practicability of precautions

Facts

Owing to an exceptionally heavy storm of rain, a factory was flooded with surface water which became mixed with an oily liquid used as a cooling agent for the machines, which was normally collected in channels in the floor. When the water drained away from the floor, which was level and structurally perfect, it left an oily film on the surface which was slippery. The defendants spread sawdust on the floor, but owing to the unprecedented force of the storm and consequently the large area to be covered, there was insufficient sawdust to cover the whole floor. In the course of his duty the claimant slipped on a portion of the floor not covered with sawdust, fell, and was injured.

Legal principle

The only way to remove the risk would have been to close the affected part of the factory until it had dried out. This would have been expensive and disproportionate to the relatively small risk of injury.

Therefore, the greater the risk of injury, the more a defendant has to do to reduce or eliminate that risk, even if it is costly. The defendant will not generally be able to rely on the fact that the cost of precautions was too expensive to excuse their breach of duty.

For example, in *Palmer* v *Cornwall County Council* [2009] EWCA Civ 456, the Court of Appeal held that one person was not adequate to supervise 300 schoolchildren.

Social value

Where the defendant's behaviour is in the public interest, it is likely to require the exercise of a *lower* standard of care. In *Daborn* v *Bath Tramways Motor Co Ltd* [1946] 2 All ER 333 (CA), Asquith LJ stated that 'the purpose to be served, if sufficiently important, justifies the assumption of abnormal risk'.

Where human life is at risk, a defendant may also justifiably take abnormal risks (*Watt* v *Hertfordshire County Council* [1954] 1 WLR 835 (CA)). However, this does not mean that the defendant is justified in taking *any* risk. Emergency services, for example, must still take care in passing red traffic signals and remember to use their sirens and lights to alert other road users to their presence. Section 1 of the Compensation Act 2006 allows the court to consider whether precautionary or defensive measures might prevent a socially desirable activity.

What would the reasonable person have foreseen?

The standard of care is predicated upon what the reasonable person would have foreseen. This depends upon the probability of the consequence. A defendant must take care to avoid 'reasonable probabilities, not fantastic possibilities' (*Fardon* v *Harcourt-Rivington* [1932] All ER Rep 81 (HL)).

A good example of this can be found in *Harris* v *Perry* [2009] 1 WLR 19 (CA). Here, the Court of Appeal held that the Divisional Court imposed an unreasonably high standard of care in holding that children playing on a bouncy castle hired by parents for a children's party required uninterrupted supervision. It was impossible to preclude all risk that, when playing together, children might injure themselves or each other, and minor injuries must be commonplace.

It was quite impractical for parents to keep children under constant surveillance or even supervision and it would not be in the public interest for the law to impose a duty upon them to do so. The defendant could not reasonably have foreseen that, in turning to help strap in another child on the bungee run, she would expose the children playing on the bouncy castle to an unacceptable risk.

Proving breach of duty

The legal burden of proving breach of duty is on the claimant. This must be established 'on balance of probabilities'. However, there are certain circumstances in which the claimant may have some assistance. These are:

- where the maxim *res ipsa loquitur* applies;
- where section 11 of the Civil Evidence Act 1968 applies.

Res ipsa loquitur

KEY DEFINITION: *Res ipsa loquitur*

This is a Latin phrase which means 'the thing speaks for itself'.

In certain circumstances courts will be prepared to find a breach of duty against the defendant without hearing detailed evidence and therefore *prima facie* negligence. There are three conditions which must be satisfied for the claimant to be able to use *res ipsa loquitur.*

KEY CASE

***Scott* v *London & St Katherine Docks Co* (1865) 3 H&C 596**

Concerning: proof of breach of duty; availability of res ipsa loquitur

Facts

The claimant was injured by a sack of sugar which fell from a crane operated by the defendants.

Legal principle

A claimant will be assisted by *res ipsa loquitur* if:

■ the thing causing the damage is under the control of the defendant or someone for whose negligence the defendant is responsible;

■ the cause of the accident is unknown;

■ the accident is such as would not normally occur without negligence.

Control

The event which causes the damage must be within the control of the defendant. In *Easson* v *LNER* [1944] 2 KB 421 (CA) a four-year-old child fell through the door of a long distance express train while the train was in motion some seven miles from the previous station, and was injured. There was no evidence as to how the door was opened. It was held that the mere fact that the door was opened was not of itself *prima facie* evidence of negligence against the railway company since the railway company could not be expected to be in continuous control of the train doors. A passenger might have been the cause of the accident.

Cause unknown

If the cause of the accident is known, *res ipsa loquitur* cannot apply. The facts do not 'speak for themselves'. Instead, the court must decide on all the facts whether negligence is established (*Barkway* v *South Wales Transport* [1950] AC 185 (HL)).

Accident would not normally occur without negligence

The accident must be such as would not normally occur without negligence. Examples include situations where:

- a large bag of sugar fell from a hoist onto the claimant (*Scott* v *London and St Katherine Docks Co*);

- a customer slipped on yogurt on a supermarket floor that had not immediately been cleaned up (*Ward* v *Tesco Stores Ltd* [1976] 1 WLR 810 (CA));

- a patient went into hospital with two stiff fingers and came out with four stiff fingers (*Cassidy* v *Ministry of Health* [1951] 2 KB 343 (CA)).

Res ipsa loquitur was held to apply to a plane crash by the Privy Council in *George* v *Eagle Air Services* [2009] 1 WLR 2133 (PC) since planes do not normally crash, the defendant (company) had control of the plane, its flight and its pilot, and there was no explanation that was consistent with the absence of fault.

▮ The effect of *res ipsa loquitur*

If *res ipsa loquitur* is available, then it raises a *prima facie* presumption of negligence against the defendant. The defendant must then explain how the accident could have occurred without negligence. If the defendant succeeds, then the claimant must try to prove the defendant's negligence. This will be difficult, since, if negligence could be proved it is unlikely that the claimant would have relied on *res ipsa loquitur* in the first place. The burden of proof does not shift from the claimant (*Ng Chun Pui* v *Lee Cheun Tat* [1988] RTR 298 (PC)).

✎ EXAM TIP

It is a common mistake to state that *res ipsa loquitur reverses* the legal burden of proof, such that the defendant must show that the damage was not caused by failure to reach the required standard of care. This is not so. The burden remains on the claimant throughout. This was made clear by the decision of the Privy Council in *Ng Chun Pui*.

Civil Evidence Act 1968

Claimants in negligence proceedings may also be assisted by section 11 of the Civil Evidence Act 1968.

Civil Evidence Act 1968, section 11

11 Convictions as evidence in civil proceedings

. . .

(2) In any civil proceedings in which by virtue of this section a person is proved to have been convicted of an offence by or before any court in the United Kingdom or by a court-martial there or elsewhere –

(a) he shall be taken to have committed that offence unless the contrary is proved.

Therefore, if the defendant has been convicted of a criminal offence by a UK court, this is taken as proof that the defendant *did* commit it in any associated civil proceedings unless the contrary is proved. If the defendant has been convicted of an offence which includes negligent conduct, then the burden of proof shifts to the defendant to prove that there was no negligence. Examples of such offences include:

- careless, and inconsiderate, driving (section 3, Road Traffic Act 1998, as substituted);
- gross negligence manslaughter.

■ Putting it all together

Answer guidelines

See the essay question at the start of the chapter.

Approaching the question

This is a typical essay question on the standard of care in negligence. As this is such a broad topic area, spend some time planning the different areas that you are going to discuss rather than just jumping straight in.

Important points to include

1 This question deals with the standard of care in negligence. You should start by explaining that the *general* standard of care in negligence was defined in *Blyth* v

Birmingham Waterworks as 'doing something which a prudent and reasonable man would not do' or 'the omission to do something which a reasonable man . . . would do'. This will then lead in to a discussion of the exceptions to these principles – the special situations in which the courts apply a different standard of care.

2 The main part of this essay should involve an explanation of the situations in which the standard of care in negligence is *not* that of the reasonable person:

- where the defendant has a particular skill;
- where the defendant has a particular lack of skill;
- where the defendant is a child;
- where the defendant is involved in a sporting event (either as competitor or spectator).

3 For each of these situations you should explain why the application of the general standard of care would not be suitable before going on to address the actual standard of care that is applied in each of the situations.

4 Your answer should also include a brief discussion of other relevant factors which the courts might take into account in deciding whether to apply a different standard of care to that of the reasonable person. This will possibly involve the consideration of a range of other factors, such as:

- the magnitude of the risk;
- the cost and practicability of precautions;
- the social utility of the defendant's activities;
- what the reasonable person would have foreseen.

5 Your conclusion should summarise the main points raised and relate them back to the statement provided in the question.

 Make your answer stand out

The question asks you to use examples and cases to support your answer. Don't forget to do so! Each of the points you make should be supported by a case authority, a (very) brief summary of the facts insofar as they are relevant to the legal principle which you are trying to establish and a concise statement of the legal principle itself.

READ TO IMPRESS

Arden, M. (2010) Human rights and civil wrongs: tort law under the spotlight. *Public Law*, p. 140.

Hogg, K. (1994) Negligence and economic loss in England, Australia, Canada and New Zealand. 43, *International & Comparative Law Quarterly*, p. 116.

Morgan, J. (2009) Policy reasoning in tort law: the courts, the Law Commission and the critics. 125, *Law Quarterly Review*, p. 215.

Norris, W. (2009) The duty of care to prevent personal injury. 2, *Journal of Personal Injury Law*, p. 114.

Perry, S. (1992) Protected interests and undertakings in the law of negligence. 42, *University of Toronto Law Journal*, p. 247.

Steele, I. (2008) Negligence liability for failing to prevent crime. 67, *Cambridge Law Journal*, p. 239.

Voyiakis, E. (2009) The great illusion: tort law and exposure to danger of physical harm. 72, *Modern Law Review*, p. 909.

Witting, C. (2001) Distinguishing between property damage and pure economic loss in negligence: a personality thesis. 21, *Legal Studies*, p. 481.

www.pearsoned.co.uk/lawexpress

 Go online to access more revision support including quizzes to test your knowledge, sample questions with answer guidelines, podcasts you can download, and more!

Negligence:

causation and remoteness of damage

3

Revision checklist

Essential points you should know:

- [ ] Explain factual causation and apply the 'but for' test
- [ ] Identify and address the problems posed by multiple causes
- [ ] Appreciate the difficulties of establishing a 'lost chance'
- [ ] The meaning of *novus actus interveniens* and its impact on causation
- [ ] The principles and policies involved in remoteness of damage

■ Topic map

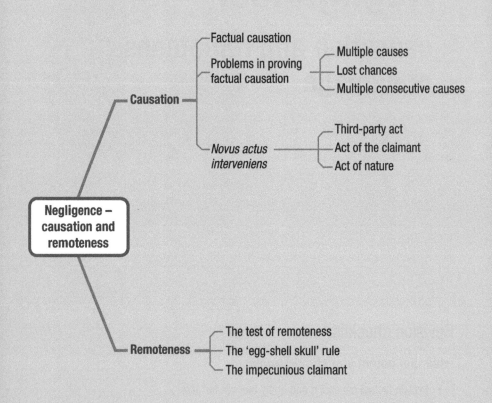

■ Introduction

Causation and remoteness provide the link between the defendant's negligent conduct and the harm suffered by the claimant.

The previous chapters covered duty of care and breach of duty whilst this chapter focuses on causation and remoteness. Students tend to find duty and standard of care relatively straightforward but often struggle with principles of causation and remoteness. This means that these topics are frequently ignored by students and left out of both revision and exam answers, which leads to an inevitable loss of marks. It may help to focus on causation and remoteness in very simple terms and gradually build upon your understanding as you work through the chapter. Causation requires that there is a link between the defendant's negligence and the claimant's injury (did the defendant cause the harm?), whilst remoteness eliminates causes that are too distant from the original negligence to be recoverable (is there a strong enough link between the negligence and the damage?).

ASSESSMENT ADVICE

Causation and remoteness are topics which are often overlooked by students.

Essay questions

Essay questions on causation and remoteness are not popular topics, so students tend to avoid questions involving these issues. It is often the case that when essays on these topics appear in examinations as the only essays on negligence, students who have revised duty and breach tackle the questions on the basis of this revision and skirt over, or ignore altogether, issues of causation and remoteness. This is an extremely poor strategy; you *must* answer the question that appears on the exam paper, not the question that you hoped would appear. To adapt the question to the material that you have revised does not attract any credit; you would be better placed answering an entirely different question. However, the problem can be avoided with careful revision of causation and remoteness.

Problem questions

Problem questions will often involve issues of causation and remoteness which are frequently ignored or dealt with at only a superficial level. To do so deprives you of a whole section of marks. Any answer to a problem question on negligence must cover all four elements on the tort, so it is essential that you are able to demonstrate an understanding of causation and remoteness, in addition to duty and breach. It is worth the effort to get to grips with these topics; negligence is a favourite topic with examiners and the ability to address aspects of the tort that are neglected by other students will set your answer apart from the others.

■ Sample question

Could you answer this question? Below is a typical essay question that could arise on this topic. Guidelines on addressing the question are included at the end of the chapter, whilst a sample problem question and guidance on tackling it can be found on the companion website.

ESSAY QUESTION

'Causation and remoteness provide the link between the defendant's negligent conduct and the harm suffered by the defendant.'

Discuss.

■ Causation

The claimant must show a causal link between the defendant's act or omission and the loss or damage suffered. This is often referred to as the 'chain of causation'.

Factual causation

The breach of duty must be the factual cause of the damage. The general test used by the courts to determine factual causation is known as the 'but for' test.

KEY CASE

Cork v Kirby MacLean Ltd [1952] 2 All ER 402 (CA)
Concerning: causation; 'but for' test

Facts

A workman, an epileptic, was set to work painting the roof inside a factory, which necessitated his doing the work from a platform some 23 feet above the floor of the factory. The platform was around 27 inches wide and was used for the deposit of the workman's bucket and brush. There were no guard-rails or toe-boards. The workman fell from the platform and was killed.

> **Legal principle**
>
> Lord Denning stated that:
>
> ... if the damage would not have happened *but for* a particular fault, then that fault is the cause of the damage; if it would have happened just the same, fault or no fault, the fault is not the cause of the damage.

The question to be asked as a starting point in establishing factual causation is 'but for the defendant's breach of duty, would the loss or damage have occurred?'. The facts of the case often mean that the application of the test is straightforward:

KEY CASE

Barnett v *Chelsea and Kensington Hospital Management Committee* [1969] 1 QB 428 (QBD)

Concerning: causation; 'but for' test

Facts

A patient was turned away from a casualty department by a doctor who refused to examine him. He later died of arsenic poisoning. It was shown that the man would not have recovered even if the doctor had treated him.

Legal principle

The hospital was not liable for the clear breach of duty in failing to treat the patient. The failure to treat was not the cause of death. The patient would have died just the same.

Proof of damage is an essential element of negligence. In *Rothwell* v *Chemical & Insulating Co Ltd: Re Pleural Plaques* [2007] 3 WLR 876 (HL), the court considered a number of conjoined appeals in which the claimants had been exposed to asbestos dust. This led to the claimants:

- developing pleural plaques (areas of fibrosis present on the inner surface of the ribcage and the diaphragm). These were invisible and caused no adverse medical symptoms;

- being exposed to a risk of developing an asbestos-related disease in the future; and

- anxiety that they may develop an asbestos-related disease in the future.

The House of Lords held that symptomless plaques were not compensatable damage and that neither the risk of future illness nor anxiety about the possibility of that risk materialising amount to damage for the purposes of creating a cause of action. Moreover, it was not possible to establish a viable claim in negligence by aggregating three heads of damage, none of which were actionable in themselves.

> ! **Don't be tempted to . . .**
>
> Be careful not to assume that the 'but for' test of factual causation is so straightforward or obvious in a problem scenario that it is not worth mentioning. Factual causation is a key part of negligence and you will lose marks if your analysis is not complete and thorough.

Problems in proving factual causation

Although the 'but for' test might seem straightforward, there are situations in which proving factual causation is more difficult. This can occur in cases involving:

- multiple causes of damage;
- a 'lost chance' of recovery/avoiding injury;
- multiple *consecutive* causes of damage.

Multiple causes of damage

Where there is more than one possible cause of harm to the claimant, the claimant does not have to show that the defendant's breach of duty was the *only* cause of damage or even the *main* cause of damage.

KEY CASE

Bonnington Castings Ltd v *Wardlaw* [1956] AC 613 (HL)

Concerning: causation; multiple causes of damage

Facts

The claimant contracted pneumoconiosis after working for years in dusty conditions. There were two main causes of dust in the foundry, one of which was required by law to be extracted. It was impossible to prove which dust the claimant had inhaled.

Legal principle

Since the dust which should have been extracted was at least a partial cause of the damage, the defendant was liable in negligence. The claimant therefore only needs to show that a defendant's breach of duty '*materially contributed*' to the damage.

This was relatively straightforward, since there were only two possible causes of damage. However, particularly in medical negligence cases, there may be too many possible causes for the claimant to discharge the burden of proof on balance of probabilities.

KEY CASE

Wilsher v *Essex Area Health Authority* [1988] AC 1074 (HL)

Concerning: causation; multiple causes of damage; balance of probabilities

Facts

The claimant was born prematurely and needed extra oxygen to survive. A junior doctor inserted a catheter into a vein rather than an artery. As a result, the baby received too much oxygen, which caused damage to the retina and consequent blindness.

There were five possible causes of the baby's blindness. It was impossible to say which of the five competing and different scenarios had actually happened.

Legal principle

Causation was not established. Since none of the potential causes was more likely to have happened than any of the others the balance of probabilities was not satisfied.

Therefore, taking *Bonnington Castings* and *Wilsher* together, where there is more than one cause, the defendant's breach must be the *substantial cause* of the damage.

The defendant may also be liable if the breach of duty materially increases the risk of damage.

KEY CASE

McGhee v *National Coal Board* [1973] 1 WLR 1 (HL)

Concerning: causation; multiple causes of damage; material increase of risk

Facts

The claimant was employed to clean out brick kilns. The working conditions were hot, dirty and dusty, but the defendants provided no adequate washing facilities. After some days working in the brick kilns the claimant was found to be suffering from dermatitis. The evidence also showed that the fact that after work the claimant had had to exert himself further by bicycling home with brick dust adhering to his skin had added materially to the risk that he might develop the disease.

Legal principle

Although the employer was not liable for injury resulting from the claimant's exposure to dust in the normal course of his work, it had materially increased his risk of doing so, since the failure to provide washing facilities meant the claimant was caked in dust for longer than required as he cycled home. The employer was found liable in negligence for materially increasing the risk.

The *McGhee* test was used in favour of the claimant by the House of Lords in *Fairchild* v *Glenhaven Funeral Services Ltd* [2003] 1 AC 32 (HL). In *Fairchild*, the claimant had worked for several different employers, all of whom had exposed him to asbestos. The (late) claimant contracted mesothelioma (a form of cancer that is almost always caused by exposure to asbestos) and died. His wife sued the employers on his behalf in negligence. However, since a single fibre of asbestos can trigger mesothelioma, it was impossible for the cause of death to be attributed to any single employer on balance of probabilities. The House of Lords held that the appropriate test in this situation was that from *McGhee*: whether the defendant had materially increased the risk of harm towards the claimant. Therefore, the employers were jointly and severally liable.

The situation in *Fairchild* was further considered by the House of Lords in *Barker* v *Corus UK Ltd* [2006] 2 AC 572 (HL). Here the claimant's husband, who died of mesothelioma, had been exposed to asbestos during three periods in his working life: first while working for a company which had since become insolvent, secondly while working for the defendant and thirdly while self-employed. On the claimant's claim in negligence the judge decided that the defendant was jointly and severally liable with the insolvent company for the deceased's mesothelioma but that damages should be subject to a 20% reduction for the deceased's contributory negligence while self-employed.

One distinction from *Fairchild* was that *all* the possible defendants in that case had wrongly exposed the deceased to asbestos. The House of Lords held that this wrongful exposure by all defendants was not a necessary criterion for liability. Therefore, a defendant who wrongly exposed the deceased to the risk may still be liable even though the other exposures either occurred naturally or resulted from the deceased's own acts.

However, the main question in this case that had not arisen in *Fairchild* was whether the solvent employers should bear the additional proportion of the damage for which the insolvent employers were responsible. The House of Lords accepted the argument that the solvent employer should not, Lord Hoffman stating that:

> In my opinion, the attribution of liability according to the relative degree of contribution to the chance of the disease being contracted would smooth the roughness of the justice which a rule of joint and several liability creates. The defendant was a wrongdoer, it is true, and should not be allowed to escape liability altogether, but he should not be liable for more than the damage which he caused and, since this is a case in which science can deal only in probabilities, the law should accept that position and attribute liability according to probabilities. The justification for the joint and several liability rule is that if you caused harm, there is no reason why your liability should be reduced because someone else also caused the same harm. But when liability is exceptionally imposed because you may have caused harm, the same considerations do not apply and fairness suggests that if more than one person may have been responsible, liability should be divided according to the probability that one or other caused the harm.

Thus, following *Barker*, where defendants are being held liable on the *Fairchild* basis, each defendant is only liable to the extent to which they increased the risk to the claimant. This concept has been referred to as 'proportionate liability'.

However, this notion has been reversed by section 3 of the Compensation Act 2006 which specifically refers *only* to cases of mesothelioma caused by exposure to asbestos. This provides in section 3(2)(b) that *all* defendants are jointly and severally liable, so a person who contracts the disease after being exposed to asbestos is able to recover full damages even if they can only establish a case against one of several possible defendants. In *Sienkiewicz* v *Greif* [2011] UKSC 10, the Supreme Court held that a claimant could establish liability by demonstrating that the defendant had been in breach of duty by exposing him to asbestos fibres and had thereby materially increased the risk that he would develop mesothelioma.

Note that other diseases are left to be decided on the common law alone. In *Ellis* v *Environment Agency* [2008] EWCA Civ 1117 the Court of Appeal refused to extend the *Fairchild* approach to ordinary industrial injuries.

In cases where a medical professional has been negligent in explaining fully the risks of treatment, it is for the claimant to establish that, had those risks been explained, then they would not have given consent (and the injury at risk would not have happened) (*Chester* v *Afshar* [2004] UKHL 41).

'Lost chance' cases

If a claimant cannot establish that 'but for' the defendant's actions they would not have suffered loss, can they instead argue that the defendant's breach has lowered their chances of a more desirable outcome? This logic suggests that a 'chance' has some value in itself and that losing a chance through the breach of another is a sufficient loss to give rise to a claim in negligence.

The courts have, however, been extremely reluctant to impose liability where the negligence of the defendant caused the claimant to lose a chance of avoiding physical injury.

KEY CASE

Hotson v *East Berkshire Area Health Authority* **[1987] AC 750 (HL)**

Concerning: causation; lost chance

Facts

A boy fractured his hip when he fell from a tree. The hospital made a misdiagnosis and the boy developed a hip deformity. Experts confirmed that he would have had a 75% chance of developing the deformity even if the diagnosis had been made correctly. The Court of Appeal upheld the decision of the trial judge who awarded the boy 25% of the damages that were considered appropriate for his injury for his lost chance of recovery. The Health Authority appealed to the House of Lords.

Legal principle

The decision of the Court of Appeal was reversed. The House of Lords took a traditional 'all or nothing' approach and considered that, since there was only a 25% chance that the hospital's negligence had caused the boy's injuries, this did not satisfy the balance of probabilities.

KEY CASE

Gregg v *Scott* [2005] UKHL 2; [2005] 2 AC 176

Concerning: causation; lost chance

Facts

The claimant consulted his doctor about a lump under his arm. The doctor should have referred the claimant to the hospital, but instead misdiagnosed the lump as benign fatty tissue. In fact, a cancerous lymphoma was developing. It was only when the claimant was admitted to hospital nine months later that the cancer was discovered and treatment commenced. At the time of the initial misdiagnosis, the claimant's chance of surviving for 10 years was 42%; at the time that treatment commenced it was 25%. At neither time was survival for over 10 years probable (on the balance of probabilities). The trial judge considered himself bound by *Hotson* and dismissed the claim. The Court of Appeal also dismissed the appeal by a majority. The claimant appealed further to the House of Lords.

Legal principle

The decision of the Court of Appeal was upheld by a 3–2 majority.

The House of Lords considered this more recently in the important case of *Gregg* v *Scott.*

Each of the judgments given in *Gregg* v *Scott* employs very different reasoning as shown in Figure 3.1.

Multiple consecutive causes of damage

Where there are consecutive causes of damage, the application of the 'but for' test is applied to the *original defendant.*

KEY CASE

Performance Cars Ltd v *Abraham* [1962] 1 QB 33 (CA)

Concerning: multiple consecutive causes

Facts

The first defendant negligently drove into a Rolls-Royce. The Rolls-Royce was later negligently struck by another car, driven by the second defendant.

Legal principle

The first defendant remained liable. The second defendant was not liable for the cost of the respray since the car already needed a respray at the time of the collision with the second defendant.

Figure 3.1

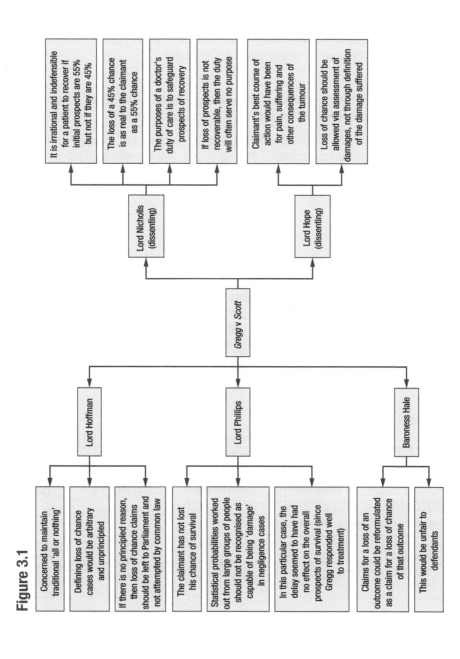

Novus actus interveniens

KEY DEFINITION: *Novus actus interveniens*

This is a Latin phrase which means 'a new act intervenes'.

An intervening act may break the chain of causation between the defendant's breach of duty and the loss or damage suffered by the claimant (see Figure 3.2).

If the *novus actus interveniens* is sufficient to break the chain, then the defendant may not be liable despite being in breach of the duty of care. The intervening act may be:

- a third-party act;
- an act of the claimant; or
- an act of nature.

Third-party act

For a third-party act:

- The original defendant will be liable where the intervening act does not cause the loss. The original defendant will be responsible for 'injury and damage which are the natural and probable results of the [initial] wrongful act (*Knightley* v *Johns* [1982] 1 WLR 349 (CA)).

- The original defendant will be liable where the intervening act is one that should have been foreseen (*Lamb* v *Camden London Borough Council* [1981] QB 625, (CA)).

Figure 3.2

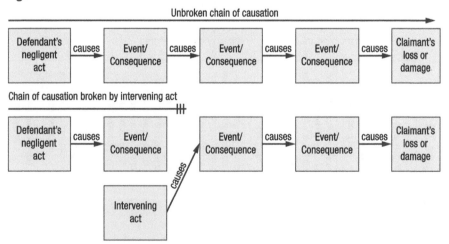

The question of whether an intervening event will break the chain of causation is one for the courts to decide in all the circumstances.

KEY CASE

***Baker* v *Willoughby* [1970] AC 467 (HL); *Jobling* v *Associated Dairies Ltd* [1982] AC 794 (HL)**

Concerning: novus actus interveniens; *third-party acts*

Facts

In *Baker* v *Willoughby* the claimant was knocked down by a car due to the negligent driving of the defendant. He suffered a permanent stiff leg as a result. After the accident, but before the trial, he was shot in the injured leg during a robbery at work. As a result, his leg was amputated.

In *Jobling* v *Associated Dairies* the claimant was injured at work due to his employer's negligence. He slipped and injured his back and lost 50% of his earning capacity as a result. Three years later, he developed spondylotic myelopathy, a spinal disease. This had not been brought about by the accident. He was consequently unable to work.

Legal principle

In *Baker* the court held that the gunman's act was not a *novus actus interveniens* and the defendant remained liable. The claimant's loss of earnings was a result of the original injury. The later robbery and consequent amputation did not change this, even though the eventual damage was different and more severe.

In *Jobling* the disease of the spine *was* held to be a *novus actus interveniens* which did break the chain of causation.

Act of the claimant

In this case, the *novus actus interveniens* will mean that the claimant is responsible for his own damage.

KEY CASE

***McKew* v *Holland & Hannen & Cubitts (Scotland) Ltd* [1969] 3 All ER 1621 (HL)**

Concerning: novus actus interveniens; *act of the claimant*

Facts

As a result of the defendants' negligence, the claimant suffered a leg injury. This left his leg seriously weakened. He later fell when attempting to descend a steep flight of steps with no handrail, suffering further serious injuries. He did not seek assistance in climbing the stairs. ▶

Legal principle

The claimant's act in attempting to descend a steep staircase without a handrail in the normal manner and without adult assistance when his leg had previously given way on occasions was unreasonable. The court held that his act was a *novus actus interveniens* which had broken the chain of causation. As a result, the defendants were not liable in damages for his second injury.

In order for the act of a claimant to be a *novus actus interveniens*, it must be entirely unreasonable in all the circumstances. This was considered in *Corr* v *IBC Vehicles* [2008] 2 WLR 499 (HL). In this case, the deceased had suffered a serious accident at work, which his employer admitted had been caused by its breach of duty. As a result of the accident, he had become depressed. His depression worsened until, six years after the accident, he died by suicide by jumping from the top of a multi-storey car park. His wife claimed damages for the physical and psychological injuries that he had suffered. The employers were held liable and his deliberate act in taking his own life was not a *novus actus interveniens*. The House of Lords pointed out that the rationale of the principle that a *novus actus interveniens* broke the chain of causation was fairness: it was not fair to hold a tortfeasor liable for damage caused by some independent, supervening cause for which he was not responsible.

However, in this case, the deceased had not taken a voluntary, informed decision as an adult of sound mind. The suicide was the response of a man suffering from a severely depressive illness which arose as a consequence of his employer's tort that had impaired his capacity to make reasoned and informed judgements about his future. Therefore, it was not unfair to hold IBC responsible for the consequences of its breach of duty.

□ REVISION NOTE

If the claimant partially contributes to his or her own damage or injury, this may raise issues of contributory negligence which is covered in Chapter 13. This will generally lead to a reduction in the claimant's damages.

Act of nature

Intervening acts of nature will not generally break the chain of causation. However, the defendant will not normally be liable where the intervening act of nature is unforeseeable and separate from the initial negligent act or omission.

KEY CASE

Carslogie Steamship Co Ltd v *Royal Norwegian Government* [1952] AC 292 (HL)

Concerning: novus actus interveniens; *act of nature*

Facts

The claimant's ship was damaged following a collision. After temporary repairs, the ship then set off on a voyage to a port in the United States where permanent repairs could be carried out. During her voyage across the Atlantic the ship sustained further heavy weather damage during a storm.

Legal principle

The defendants were not liable for the damage caused by the storm. The court held that the storm could have happened on any voyage and therefore the storm damage was not a consequence of the collision. It was unforeseeable and quite separate.

■ Remoteness

The final element required in establishing negligence is the extent of the damage suffered by the claimant which should be attributable to the defendant. In other words, for how much of the claimant's loss should the defendant be responsible?

□ REVISION NOTE

Remoteness is sometimes referred to as 'legal causation' or 'causation in law'.

The test of remoteness

KEY CASE

Re Polemis and Furness, Withy & Co Ltd [1921] 3 KB 560 (CA)

Concerning: remoteness of damage

Facts

The charterers of a ship filled the hold with a cargo including a number of containers of petrol. These filled the hold with petrol vapour which ignited when a heavy plank was dropped into the hold by a stevedore whilst the ship was unloading, destroying the ship.

Legal principle

The defendants were liable for *all* damage which resulted from the breach of duty, regardless of whether that damage was foreseeable by the defendant. As Scrutton LJ stated:

> . . . if the act would or might probably cause damage, the fact that the damage it in fact causes is not the exact kind of damage one would expect is immaterial, so long as the damage is in fact directly traceable to the negligent act.

The test in *Re Polemis* does not limit liability for the direct consequences of a negligent act, however severe or unforeseeable those consequences may be. It has been criticised for its unfairness in that respect. Similar circumstances arose in *Overseas Tankship (UK) Ltd* v *Morts Dock and Engineering Co Ltd (The Wagon Mound) (No 1)* [1961] 1 All ER 404 (PC).

KEY CASE

Overseas Tankship (UK) Ltd v *Morts Dock and Engineering Co Ltd (The Wagon Mound) (No 1)* [1961] AC 388 (PC)

Concerning: remoteness of damage

Facts

The defendants negligently leaked a quantity of bunkering oil into Sydney Harbour from a tanker. This oil drifted into the claimant's wharf where it mixed with assorted detritus including cotton wadding. Welding was taking place in the wharf. The claimants sought (and received) assurances that it was safe for them to continue welding. However, sparks from the welding ignited the oily wadding which caused fire to spread to two ships, damaging them. The wharf was also fouled.

Legal principle

At first instance, the trial judge applied the principles from *Re Polemis*, finding that the defendants were liable for the fire damage, since the fouling to the wharf was a foreseeable consequence of the leakage. On appeal, the Privy Council reversed the decision, holding that the correct test for remoteness is reasonable foreseeability of the kind or type of damage in fact suffered by the claimant.

The tests in *Re Polemis* and *The Wagon Mound (No 1)* cannot be reconciled. The decision in *Re Polemis* was taken by the Court of Appeal and has never been overruled, since *The Wagon Mound (No 1)* was heard by the Privy Council. As such, both cases remain good law. However, *The Wagon Mound (No 1)* is now accepted by the courts (including the Court of Appeal) as the relevant test to follow in questions of remoteness.

✎ EXAM TIP

The names of the two key cases on remoteness are extremely long. It is perfectly acceptable to refer to them in an exam as *Re Polemis* and *The Wagon Mound*.

Remoteness in psychiatric injury cases

The degree of foreseeability required depends on whether or not the claimant is a primary or secondary victim (see Chapter 1).

Primary victims	Secondary victims
Defendant must or should have foreseen some physical injury to claimant	Psychiatric injury must be foreseeable in a person of reasonable fortitude in the circumstances
Even if no physical injury occurs, but psychiatric injury does, defendant is still liable	

The 'egg-shell skull' rule

If the type of injury is foreseeable, but the severity of the injury is not, due to some pre-existing special condition on the part of the claimant, then the defendant remains liable for *all* the losses.

KEY CASE

Smith v *Leech Brain & Co Ltd* [1962] 2 QB 405 (CA)

Concerning: remoteness; the 'egg-shell skull' rule

Facts

The claimant was splashed by molten metal as a result of his employer's negligence and suffered a burn to his lip. This burn triggered cancer, from which the claimant died. The claimant's lip was pre-malignant at the time of the incident.

Legal principle

Some form of harm from the burn was foreseeable although the particular type of harm in the particular circumstances was not. However, despite the fact that death from cancer was not a foreseeable consequence of the burn, the employers remained liable in negligence for the full extent of the damage.

In essence, the 'egg-shell skull' rule means that defendants must take their victims as they find them. Note that it also applies in cases of psychiatric damage. Therefore, defendants must also take their victims as they find them in respect to psychiatric injury, even if the victims suffer greater injury than a person of reasonable fortitude (*Brice* v *Brown* [1984] 1 All ER 997 (QBD)).

📖 REVISION NOTE

The 'egg-shell skull' rule also applies in cases of psychiatric harm. See Chapter 1.

The impecunious claimant

One particular situation where the 'egg-shell skull' rule had been held *not* to apply is in cases where the losses result from the claimant's lack of means. In *Liesbosch Dredger* v *SS Edison* [1933] AC 449 (HL), the claimant's dredger sank due to the defendant's negligence. The claimant could not afford to replace the lost dredger. In order to fulfil its contractual obligations, the claimant hired a dredger at an exorbitant rate. The House of Lords held that the claimant could not recover the high rental charges since these were a result of its own lack of means and not 'immediate physical consequences' of the negligent act.

The *Liesbosch* was distinguished by the Court of Appeal in cases relating to **mitigation of loss** (*Perry* v *Sidney Phillips & Son* [1982] 1 WLR 1297 (CA)) and subsequently only considered to apply in 'exceptional circumstances' (*Mattocks* v *Mann* [1993] RTR 13 (CA)).

It was finally put to rest in *Lagden* v *O'Connor* [2004] 1 AC 1067 (HL).

KEY CASE

Lagden v *O'Connor* [2004] 1 AC 1067 (HL)

Concerning: remoteness; the impecunious claimant

Facts

The defendant struck the claimant's car. The impecunious claimant had to hire a car from a car hire company that charged more for the credit involved because the claimant could not afford to pay in advance.

Legal principle

The defendant was liable for the costs incurred. The observations of the House of Lords in the *Liesbosch Dredger*, despite the eminence of their source, can no longer be regarded as authoritative. They must now be regarded as overtaken by subsequent developments in the law.

◼ Putting it all together

Answer guidelines

See the essay question at the start of the chapter.

Approaching the question

This question invites a wide-ranging discussion of the role of causation and remoteness in negligence. As such, you should put together a well-balanced essay that covers both causation and remoteness. Too much focus on one area will prevent you from gaining the credit available for the other.

Important points to include

- You could start by explaining the purpose of causation and remoteness as a means of both apportioning and limiting liability. Causation requires that there is a link between the defendant's negligence and the claimant's injury (essentially asking whether the defendant caused the harm) and remoteness requires that there is a strong enough link between the negligence and the damages to eliminate causes that are too distant from the original negligence to be recoverable.

- In causation, you should discuss the 'but for' test in factual causation before deepening your discussion with an analysis of why proving factual causation proves difficult in practice. This will lead on to a discussion of situations in which there are multiple causes of damage (either occurring concurrently or consecutively) and cases in which the negligence of the defendant caused the claimant to 'lose a chance'.

- You should also discuss the concept of *novus actus interveniens* as a means of breaking the chain of causation and consider intervening acts by third parties, by the claimant themselves or by an act of nature.

- The discussion of remoteness should include both tests from *Re Polemis* and *The Wagon Mound (No 1)* with an explanation of why they cannot be reconciled and why they both remain good law. You should also explain that *The Wagon Mound (No 1)* is followed in practice. Remember that remoteness is also affected by the 'egg-shell skull' rule. ▶

Make your answer stand out

The law of negligence is primarily derived from case law. As such you should always seek to provide case authority for each of the main points that you make in your essay.

It is quite easy in a broad question such as this to drift off point, or to produce an explanation of the topic without engaging fully with the question. At the end of each paragraph, you should ask yourself 'why is this paragraph relevant to the answer is this question?' and make sure that you refer back to the question where appropriate. This will naturally lead to a more focused answer.

READ TO IMPRESS

Cartwright, J. (1996) Remoteness of damage in contract and tort: a reconsideration. 55, *Cambridge Law Journal*, p. 488.

Weir, T. (2002) Making it more likely v making it happen. 61, *Cambridge Law Journal*, p. 519.

Wright, R. (1985) Causation in tort law. 73, *California Law Review*, p. 1735.

www.pearsoned.co.uk/lawexpress

 Go online to access more revision support including quizzes to test your knowledge, sample questions with answer guidelines, podcasts you can download, and more!

Vicarious liability

4

Revision checklist

Essential points you should know:

☐ The requirements that must be satisfied for vicarious liability to arise

☐ The tests used to distinguish between an employee and an independent contractor

☐ The meaning of, course of employment, and the relevance of 'a frolic of one's own'

☐ The implications of failure to obey instructions or the commission of an intentionally wrongful act

☐ The ways in which an employer may recover the cost of paying damages to the claimant from the employee

■ Topic map

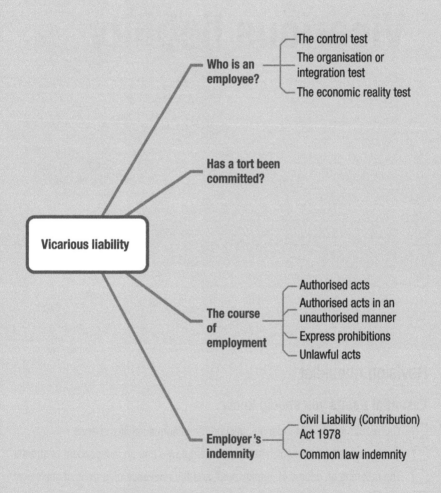

■ Introduction

Vicarious liability is a term used to explain the liability of one person for torts committed by another person.

The general rule is that a person who commits a tort will be personally liable: the claimant brings an action against the person who has caused harm/damage or otherwise fulfilled the requirements of one of the torts that are actionable *per se*. Vicarious liability is an exception to this rule and it gives the claimant the ability to hold someone other than the person who commits the tort liable. It arises most usually in relation to employers and employees and this chapter will focus primarily on that relationship to explain the principles of vicarious liability. It is often advantageous for a claimant to bring an action against an employer on the basis of vicarious liability because there is more likelihood that the employer will be able to pay damages, either personally or under an insurance policy. Vicarious liability is an important revision topic due to the unique way in which it imposes secondary liability on someone not directly involved in the tort. This means that it can combine with any of the other torts covered in this guide.

ASSESSMENT ADVICE

Essay questions

Essay questions focusing on vicarious liability are popular. They require students to demonstrate that they have grasped a complicated way of imposing liability on third parties. As vicarious liability is a strict liability tort, there is scope for essays to require a consideration of the fairness of imposing liability on employers for torts which they did not commit themselves and which they could not have prevented their employees from committing. Add balance to your essay by balancing arguments about unfairness against the rationale for imposing vicarious liability.

Problem questions

Problem questions involving vicarious liability are common. Vicarious liability could be combined with any other tort, i.e. an employee could commit any of the torts in the course of employment and their employer would be vicariously liable. It is often overlooked in problem questions as students tend to focus on the most direct cause of the tort as being the potential defendant. Remember that any tort committed during the course of employment should trigger a discussion of vicarious liability, so look out for this in the facts.

■ Sample question

Could you answer this question? Below is a typical essay question that could arise on this topic. Guidelines on answering the question are included at the end of the chapter, whilst a sample problem question and guidance on tackling it can be found on the companion website.

> ### ESSAY QUESTION
>
> Vicarious liability represents 'a compromise between two conflicting principles: on the one hand, the social interest in furnishing an innocent tort victim with recourse against a financially responsible defendant; on the other, a hesitation to foist any undue burden on business enterprise'. (Fleming, J.G. (1998) *The Law of Torts*, 9th edn, Sydney: LBC Information Services, pp. 409–410.)
>
> Discuss the extent to which the case law has maintained a balance between these conflicting principles.

■ Vicarious liability

Vicarious liability arises as a result of the relationship between the person who commits the tort and a third party. Although the most common relationship which gives rise to vicarious liability is the employer/employee relationship, there are other relationships of which you should be aware:

- principal and agent;
- business partners;
- vehicle owners and delegated drivers.

There are three essential components that must be satisfied in order that a third party can be held liable for the torts committed by another. These components are outlined in general terms in Figure 4.1 and also in relation to the employer/employee relationship that forms the main focus of this chapter.

Who is an employee?

An employer is only liable for torts committed by his employees and not those committed by an independent contractor, so the distinction between these two is important. Many working relationships fall clearly into the employer/employee relationship such as sales

Figure 4.1

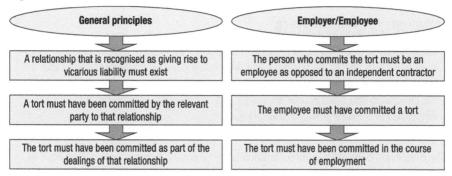

assistants, solicitors and university lecturers, whilst others, such as landscape gardeners and electricians, are independent contractors who provide their services to a range of people. However, the distinction is not always clear-cut:

- A lecturer may be an independent contractor if, rather than working for a particular university, they provide personal tuition services to students on an individual basis.

- An electrician may be an employee if, rather than working on his or her own account doing lots of different jobs for different people, they work exclusively within one organisation.

The central feature that distinguishes employees and independent contractors is not the type of work that they do but the way in which the work is done. The courts have formulated a number of different tests that seek to get to the heart of this distinction.

The control test

KEY DEFINITION: Control test

The control test distinguishes an employee and an independent contractor on the basis of whether the employer had the right to control the nature of the work done and, most importantly, how it must be done: *Yewen* v *Noakes* (1880) 6 QBD 530 (CA).

This is the oldest test that was used to determine whether a person was an employee and it has its origins in the 'master and servant' nature of the employment relationship. It is an unrealistic way of distinguishing employees and independent contractors in modern employment situations where many employers do not have the expertise or knowledge to supervise the way in which skilled employees carry out their work: imagine a hospital manager telling a surgeon how to perform an operation!

The organisation or integration test

KEY DEFINITION: Organisation test

The organisation test makes a distinction between a *contract of service* whereby 'a man is employed as part of the business and his work is done as an integral part of the business' and a *contract for services* whereby 'work, although done for the business, is not integrated into it but is only accessory to it': *Stevenson, Jordan and Harrison Ltd* v *McDonnell and Evans* [1952] 1 TLR 101 (CA).

The distinction between a contract *of* service and a contract *for* services can be hard to grasp. The explanation and example given in the table below may help you to understand the difference.

Contract of service	Contract for services
An organisation engages a person to carry out various tasks within the organisation that are integral to its core purpose	An organisation requires a particular service to be supplied and seeks out a person who can provide that service, which is supplementary to the core purpose of the organisation
E.g. an organisation that produces components for domestic electrical goods employs an electrician to carry out safety checks on the finished products	E.g. an organisation that produces double glazing products engages an electrician to rewire the factory

The economic reality test

In recognition that the control and organisation/integration tests do not cover all situations in which it is necessary to determine whether someone is an employee or an independent contractor, the courts developed the economic reality test (sometimes called the 'multiple test' or the 'pragmatic test'):

KEY CASE

Ready Mixed Concrete Ltd v *Minister of Pensions* **[1968] 2 QB 497 (DC)**

Concerning: employees; economic reality test

Facts

Drivers were hired by the claimant organisation to deliver concrete using vehicles owned by the drivers which they purchased from the claimant and which had to be painted the company colours and carry the company logo. Drivers were responsible for the

---

maintenance of the vehicles and had flexible hours of work. It was held that the drivers were not employees, thus the claimant was not liable for their National Insurance contributions.

Legal principle

It was held that there were three conditions that had to be met before a worker would be considered to be an employee:

1 The employee must provide work or skill for the employer in return for payment of a wage or some other remuneration.

2 The employee agrees, expressly or impliedly, that they will work under the control of the employer.

3 All other circumstances are consistent with the situation being characterised as a contract of employment.

The first two requirements should be relatively easy to ascertain, whereas the third is an extremely open provision that could cover the following points:

- **Method of payment:** Employees tend to receive regular payments (weekly, monthly), whereas contractors are more likely to receive a lump sum for a particular piece of work.

- **Tax and National Insurance:** Employees usually have deductions made at source, i.e. by the employer, whereas independent contractors are responsible for their own contributions.

- **Working hours:** Employees often have fixed or regulated hours of work whereas independent contractors are more likely to set their own schedule of work.

- **Provision of equipment:** An employee will expect an employer to provide an equipped working environment with the tools needed to complete their duties, whereas an independent contractor will usually provide their own tools and equipment.

- **Level of independence:** Employees are generally quite constrained in the scope of their duties, whilst independent contractors have more control, particularly in terms of working for more than one person and in being able to refuse to carry out certain tasks or to reject work altogether.

In *Viasystems Ltd* v *Thermal Transfer Ltd* [2006] QB 510 (CA), the Court of Appeal held that in cases where employees are 'borrowed' then, in principle, there is no reason why both 'employers' should not be vicariously liable. The court considered that the concept of 'transference' of employment was misleading and it was more appropriate to concentrate on the relevant negligent act and whose responsibility it was to prevent it. Employers must now monitor carefully their supervision of the work of anyone else's employees. Following *Viasystems*, both they and any other individual who could (and should) have prevented the negligent act carry potential vicarious liability.

No single test is accepted as authoritative by the courts, although it is the economic reality test that tends to be applied as it covers aspects of both of the other tests. In any essay, you might want to consider how these tests have evolved and address whether they provide a reliable means for distinguishing employees and independent contractors. In a problem question, you will need to apply the economic reality test to determine whether someone is an employee, remembering to take into account the factors listed above in deciding the third limb of the *Ready Mixed Concrete* test.

Has a tort been committed?

This second requirement for vicarious liability is often overlooked. This is essential as there can be no vicarious (secondary) liability if there is no direct (primary) liability. In other words, if the employee does not satisfy the requirements of a tort, the employer cannot be held vicariously liable.

📖 REVISION NOTE

It is often the case that the relevant tort is negligence so make sure that you have a good grasp of this topic. However, vicarious liability can apply to any tort, so it might be useful to remind yourself of the key principles of the various torts that you have studied and think about how these could occur in an employer/employee relationship.

If the employee has committed a criminal offence, this may give rise to liability if the elements of a tort were also satisfied. For example, an employee who attacks a customer will also have satisfied the requirements of the tort of battery, so the situation may give rise to vicarious liability.

! Don't be tempted to . . .

Remember that there has to be a tort committed for an employer to be **vicariously liable**. Students often fail to consider fully the tortious liability of an employee before concluding that the employer is vicariously liable. Look to see particularly if there are any particular defences open to the employee.

The course of employment

An employer is not liable for all torts committed by an employee, only those which take place during the course of employment.

KEY DEFINITION: Frolic of his own

This is a phrase used to describe conduct that falls outside of the course of employment because it is something that the employee has done within working time that is unrelated to his work and is undertaken on his own account: *Joel* v *Morison* (1834) 172 ER 1338. For example, a delivery driver who deviates from his authorised route to visit a friend in hospital will be on a frolic of his own as this is a 'new and independent journey . . . entirely for his own business': *Storey* v *Ashton* (1869) LR 4 QB 476 (DC).

Rather than the timing or location of the employment, it is accepted that course of employment is more concerned with the duties of the employment: what the employee is employed to do. There are two situations which are accepted as falling within the scope of course of employment:

- acts by the employee that are authorised by the employer;
- acts which, although not authorised by the employer, are so closely connected with what the employee was supposed to be doing that they can be considered as carrying out an authorised act in an unauthorised, or wrongful, manner.

Authorised acts

This category is straightforward. If the employee is following his employer's instructions and commits a tort in doing so, the employer will be vicariously liable.

For example, if a security guard is told to detain a suspected shoplifter, the employer will be vicariously liable if this results in unlawful battery or false imprisonment (see Chapter 10).

Authorised acts in an unauthorised manner

This covers a range of situations such as acting contrary to instructions or performing an authorised task in a negligent manner.

KEY CASE

Century Insurance v *NI Road Transport Board* [1942] AC 509 (HL)

Concerning: authorised acts in an unauthorised manner

Facts

The driver was employed to deliver petrol which involved transferring the petrol from his lorry to a storage tank at his destination. Whilst doing so, he lit a cigarette and threw the match on the ground, causing an explosion.

Legal principle

It was held that the driver was acting in the course of his employment. He was doing exactly what he was supposed to be doing (delivering petrol) albeit in a woefully careless manner.

This can be distinguished from situations in which the employee does something which is beyond the scope of his employment responsibilities, even if he is acting from good motives:

KEY CASE

Beard v *London Omnibus Co* [1900] 2 QB 530 (CA)

Concerning: acts beyond the scope of employment

Facts

A bus conductor drove a bus around the front of the bus depot as he knew that it was needed urgently for its next journey and the driver could not be found. Whilst manoeuvring the bus, the conductor injured a mechanic.

Legal principle

It was not part of the conductor's duties to drive the bus, thus in doing so he was outside of the course of his employment. As such, the employer was not vicariously liable for the injury caused to the mechanic.

✎ EXAM TIP

A useful way to identify whether the employee is acting within the course of employment is to ask the question, 'What is this person employed to do?' As you see in *Century Insurance*, doing the tasks that you are supposed to do, even to a poor standard or in a dangerous manner, will usually fall within the course of employment.

Express prohibitions

If an employer has explicitly prohibited an employee from acting in a particular manner or taking on a certain task, you might expect that acting contrary to these instructions would take the employee outside of the course of employment. However, this is not always the case as the courts have made a distinction between prohibitions relating to the *manner* (how the employee should do the job) and *scope* (what the employee should do) of employment. See Figure 4.2.

Figure 4.2

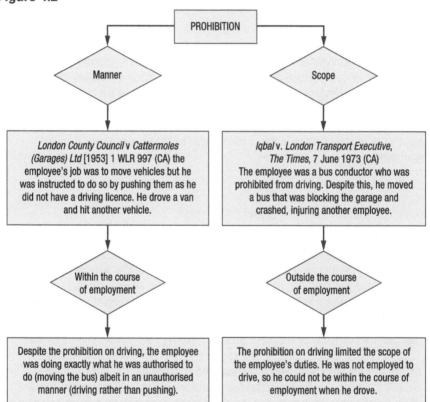

Unlawful acts

You might expect that the deliberate commission of a criminal act by an employee would automatically take him outside the course of his employment but this is not necessarily the case. The courts have developed a test to determine whether an employer will be vicariously liable for intentional wrongful acts of employees:

KEY CASE

Lister and Others v *Hesley Hall Ltd* [2002] 1 AC 215 (HL)

Concerning: intentional wrongful acts

Facts

The claimants were residential students at a school for difficult children owned by the defendant. One of the wardens employed by the defendant was sexually abusing the children in his care and was eventually subjected to criminal proceedings. The claimants sought to hold the defendant vicariously liable for the harms they suffered as a result of the abuse.

Legal principle

The House of Lords adopted the 'closeness of connection' test to determine whether an intentionally wrongful act by an employee would fall within the course of employment. Here, the sexual abuse occurred on the employer's premises whilst the employee was engaged in performing his duties of caring for the children. As such, there was a close connection between the employment and the abuse so the employer would be vicariously liable. This was particularly so as there was an obvious risk of sexual abuse in the circumstances so the employer should have been alert for it.

Examples of vicarious liability for unlawful acts include:

- *Gravil* v *Carroll* [2008] ICR 1222 (CA), in which the Court of Appeal held that a rugby club was vicariously liable for its (semi-professional) player's tortious assault against a member of the opposing team (fracturing his eye-socket) after the whistle had been blown to stop play following an altercation. The court did make it expressly clear, however, that nothing in the judgment was relevant to the playing of rugby or any other game otherwise than under a contract of employment.

- *Majrowski* v *Guy's and St Thomas's NHS Trust* [2007] 1 AC 224 (HL), in which the House of Lords held that an employer could be vicariously liable for an employee's breach of a statutory obligation which sounded in damages. This case concerned breach of section 1 of the Protection from Harassment Act 1997 where the claimant alleged that he had been unlawfully harassed by his departmental manager. Section 3 of the Act created a civil wrong whereby a breach of section 1 gave rise to the ordinary remedies for civil wrongs, including damages.

- *Maga* v *The Trustees of the Birmingham Archdiocese of the Roman Catholic Church* [2010] EWCA Civ 256, in which the Court of Appeal held that an archdiocese was vicariously liable for sexual abuse committed by a priest since his role and work gave him authority and opportunity to commit that abuse and consequently there was a sufficiently close connection for liability to arise.

The closeness of connection test requires an assessment of the link between the employee's wrongful act and the tasks that he was supposed to be carrying out. This picks up on the established position of finding vicarious liability if the situation can be characterised as an unauthorised way of carrying out an authorised task.

Close connection	No connection
An employee responsible for conveyancing in a firm of solicitors fraudulently induces an elderly client to sign documents that pass ownership of her properties to him (*Lloyd* v *Grace Smith & Co* [1912] AC 716). This was within the course of employment as it was a dishonest way of doing the tasks that the employee was engaged to carry out.	A secretary employed by a firm of solicitors took advantage of the knowledge she had picked up to pose as a solicitor to a new client. She prepared papers for him to sign, one of which gave her authority to access his bank account. She transferred £100,000 to her own account. This would not fall within the course of employment as there was no connection between her actions and her responsibilities as a secretary.
A security guard rugby-tackles a shoplifter to stop them leaving the supermarket with stolen goods. In doing so, he is performing the task that he is engaged to do, i.e. protect the employer's property, so is acting within the course of his employment.	An estate agent punches a colleague upon discovering he has been having an affair with his wife. This has no link with his employment as an estate agent so will not give rise to vicarious liability.

 Make your answer stand out

The test formulated in *Lister* has implications for vicarious liability in that it imposed liability on an 'innocent' employer for the intentional criminal acts of an employee. You might find it useful to read the House of Lords decision for insight into the policy underlying the decision. Roe's (2002) article also provides a detailed analysis of the decision and Glassbrook's (2005) article considers how *Lister* has been applied in subsequent cases.

Employer's indemnity

As vicarious liability only arises if the employee has committed a tort, the employer and employee are regarded as joint tortfeasors. This means that the employer may be able to recover some of the cost of paying damages to the claimant from the employee. There are two ways in which this could occur, detailed in the sections that follow.

Civil Liability (Contribution) Act 1978

Section 1(1) allows a defendant who has paid damages to a claimant to recover a contribution from any other defendant who is responsible for the harm or loss caused (whether liability is joint or several).

The quantification of the contribution is decided on the basis of what is 'just and equitable' in the circumstances of the case, section 2(1), but could cover the whole amount of damages paid to the claimant if the court felt that the employer, although vicariously liable for the employee's tort, was entirely blameless.

KEY DEFINITION: Joint liability and several liability

Joint liability arises if two or more people cause harm/damage to the same claimant when they are (1) engaged in a joint enterprise (the author and publisher of a defamatory article); (2) one party authorises the tort of the other (A tells B to park his car on C's land); and (3) one party is vicariously liable for the torts of the other (employer/employee).

Several liability occurs in all other cases that do not fall within these three categories but where more than one defendant has caused harm/damage to the claimant. For example, if a collision between two vehicles damaged the claimant's wall, the drivers would be severally liable.

Common law indemnity

In *Lister* v *Romford Ice & Cold Storage Co Ltd* [1957] AC 555 (HL), the House of Lords held that an employer could obtain an indemnity (the full cost of the damages paid to the claimant) if the loss or injury had been caused by the employee's breach of contract (in this case, breach of the implied duty to exercise reasonable care and skill).

An employer cannot claim an indemnity at common law unless he is in no way to blame for the employee's conduct: *Jones* v *Manchester Corporation* [1952] 2 QB 852 (CA).

✎ EXAM TIP

In a question involving vicarious liability, do not forget to consider whether the employer can recover some or all of the damages paid to the claimant from the employee. It is worth mentioning the possibility of indemnity under *Lister* but requirement of faultlessness is likely to make recovery under the statutory scheme preferable.

■ Putting it all together

Answer guidelines

See the essay question at the start of the chapter.

Approaching the question

This is a typical essay question dealing with vicarious liability. The quotation from Fleming outlines the two opposing perspectives of the employer's position if he is held vicariously liable for the torts of his employees: (1) it provides fair outcome for the victim as the employer is more likely to be able to compensate him and (2) it is an unfair outcome as it holds the blameless employer financially responsible for the torts committed by employees. The question requires you to consider how far the case law has managed to achieve an acceptable balance between these two positions.

Important points to include

- Start by explaining vicarious liability to demonstrate your understanding of the basic concept. This will form the basis of the rest of the essay. Do simple things well.

- Engage with the quotation. Explain its meaning and set out the two positions identified in the quotation in your own words. Remember that vicarious liability is a means of determining which of two innocent parties (the victim and the employer) should suffer.

- Make sure that you are able to use the case law in the way required by the question. It is no good to tackle this question by describing the facts of all the cases that you can remember as this will attract little credit. Think about each case and consider whether it found in favour of the employer (no vicarious liability) or the victim (vicarious liability) and consider whether this seems like a fair outcome.

- Think also about what it was that the employee did that caused harm to the victim and consider whether it is reasonable to hold the employer responsible for those acts. If you deal with the cases in this way, you will be slanting them towards the issue raised by the question and this will attract credit from your examiner.

- Consider which of the two positions outlined in the question are most favoured by case law, i.e. do the courts tend to find for the employer or the victim, and consider the implications of this position. ▶

Make your answer stand out

Make sure that you do not lose focus on the question. It is always tempting to throw other points that you can remember about vicarious liability into your essay but remember that this will not attract any credit if it is not relevant to the question. For example, a discussion of the distinction between an employee and an independent contractor has no place in this essay.

Remember that evidence of wide reading will attract credit from the examiners so include journal articles on key issues in your revision and incorporate references to these into your essay. Bear in mind that case notes will be published about important cases and these can be an excellent source of information about the implications of case law.

READ TO IMPRESS

Douglas, W. (1928–9) Vicarious liability and administration of risk. 38, *Yale Law Journal*, p. 584.

Glassbrook, A. (2005) You're only supposed to blow the bloody doors off: employer's vicarious liability for the torts of violent employees. *Journal of Personal Injury Law*, p. 240.

McKendrick, E. (1990) Vicarious liability and independent contractors: a re-examination. 53, *Modern Law Review*, p. 770.

Roe, R. (2002) *Lister* v *Hesley Hall*. 65, *Modern Law Review*, p. 270.

www.pearsoned.co.uk/lawexpress

 Go online to access more revision support including quizzes to test your knowledge, sample questions with answer guidelines, podcasts you can download, and more!

Employers' liability

Revision checklist

Essential points you should know:

- [ ] The scope of the common law duty to ensure the safety of employees
- [ ] The operation of the law in relation to safety of premises, plant, system of work and competency of staff
- [ ] The elements of the tort of breach of statutory duty
- [ ] The tests used to determine whether a breach is actionable

Topic map

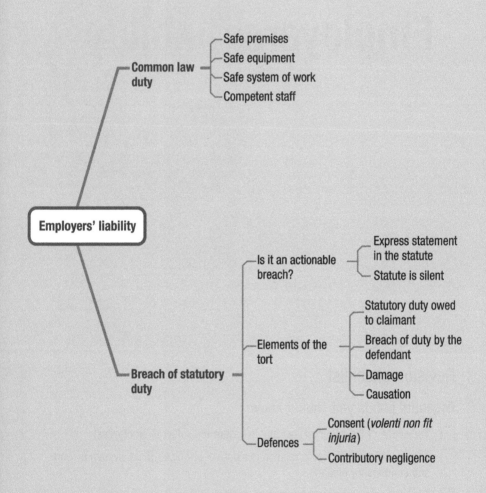

■ Introduction

Employers' liability covers a range of statutory and common law duties placed upon an employer in order to protect employees against injury at work.

There is a fair degree of overlap between the common law protection which has developed over many years and the statutory protection introduced by key legislation such as the Health and Safety at Work Act 1974. An employer may also be vicariously liable for an injury caused by one employee to another (see Chapter 4). This is an area of law that has been strongly influenced by an influx of European law aimed at ensuring that all member states have high levels of industrial safety.

There are approximately 500,000 injuries in the workplace every year and around 10% of those injured at work attempt to rely on tort law to obtain compensation.

ASSESSMENT ADVICE

Essay questions

Essay questions on employers' liability are not popular with students, probably due to the range of sources of this complex area and the difficulty of seeing a coherent pattern to the law. Its popularity with examiners varies, so it would be sensible to check your own syllabus to see how much attention was paid to this topic.

Problem questions

Problem questions often combine issues of vicarious liability and employers' liability, so it is sensible to ensure that you are familiar with both topics. It would limit the potential for success of your answer if you tackled a question that raised both issues but you were only able to deal with vicarious liability. This is not a difficult area of law – it just has some overlap between statute and common law provisions – so taking a methodical approach will pay dividends.

■ Sample question

Could you answer this question? Below is a typical problem question that could arise on this topic. Guidelines on answering the question are included at the end of the chapter, whilst a sample essay question and guidance on tackling it can be found on the companion website.

PROBLEM QUESTION

Christine was employed by FruitInc, a company specialising in the canning of fresh fruit, as a canning machine operator. The machine had sharp moving parts which are required to be fenced by section 14(1) of the Factories Act 1961:

> Every dangerous part of any machinery . . . shall be securely fenced.

FruitInc had secured a guard fence around the moving parts of the canning machine with a sign stating that 'This guard must not be removed except by a Manager'.

Christine (who was not a manager) removed the guard. David, the manager, noticed that the guard had been removed but did nothing. That afternoon, Christine caught her hair in the machine and was scalped, suffering severe head injuries as a result.

Advise Christine if she has any claims in tort against FruitInc.

■ Common law duty

An employer has a common law duty to take reasonable care to ensure the safety of his employees. This is a personal and non-delegable duty which means that the employer cannot escape liability by claiming to have passed the responsibility for the employee's safety to another party, i.e. an independent contractor. For example, if an employee was injured in a workplace fire caused by faulty wiring that had been installed by an independent contractor, the employer would not be able to pass liability on to them.

Employers' liability reflects the ordinary principles of negligence in that only injuries that have been sustained by a failure to take reasonable care will give rise to liability. The duty was said in *Wilsons & Clyde Coal Co Ltd* v *English* [1938] AC 57 (HL) to cover four key elements:

- the duty to provide safe premises and a safe place to work;
- the duty to provide safe plant, materials and equipment;
- the duty to provide a safe system of work and safe working practices;
- the duty to provide a competent staff as colleagues.

📖 REVISION NOTE

The common law duty does not extend to independent contractors. The distinction between independent contractors and employees was covered earlier (in Chapter 4). It would be useful to refresh your memory of the distinction as part of your revision of employers' liability.

Safe premises

The duty to provide safe premises is concerned with the building itself and structural aspects of it such as the floors (*Latimer* v *AEC*) below and windows (*General Cleaning Contractors* v *Christmas* [1953] AC 180 (HL)) so as to distinguish it from the plant and machinery within the building (safe equipment) and the way that the work is done within the building (safe system of work). The employer must take reasonable steps to ensure that the employee is not injured by defective premises:

KEY CASE

Latimer v *AEC Ltd* [1953] AC 643 (HL)

Concerning: reasonable care

Facts

A factory floor was dangerously slippery following flooding. The employer put down sawdust but did not have enough to cover the whole floor. The employee was injured when he slipped on an uncovered patch.

Legal principle

There would be no liability as the employer had done what was reasonable in the circumstances to protect against the particular risk.

If the employee's work takes him onto premises owned by others, the employer must take reasonable steps to ensure that these are safe and will not injure his employee. In *Cook* v *Square D Ltd* [1992] ICR 262 (CA), the Court of Appeal identified the factors that an employer must consider when determining whether a workplace is safe for an employee:

- the location where the work is required to be done;
- the nature of the building;
- the nature of the work required from the employee;
- the employee's expertise and experience;
- the degree of control that it is reasonable to expect the employer to exercise;
- whether the employer is aware that the premises are dangerous.

Safe equipment

The employer must provide safe and appropriate equipment and ensure that it is properly maintained. This duty is supplemented by the Employers' Liability (Defective Equipment) Act 1969 which defines 'equipment' as 'any plant and machinery, vehicle, aircraft and clothing' and expands the duty upon the employer to include liability for equipment that is defective due to the negligence of third parties, i.e. the manufacturer.

KEY CASE

Knowles v *Liverpool County Council* [1993] 1 WLR 1428 (HL)

Concerning: liability for existing defects

Facts

The claimant injured his finger when a flagstone that he was carrying broke due to an inherent defect in its manufacture. The employer argued (1) that he could not have known about the defect so should not be liable and (2) that a flagstone was not equipment.

Legal principle

The House of Lords held that section 1(1)(b) of the Employers' Liability (Defective Equipment) Act 1969 made it clear that the employer would be liable for defects that were not obvious or visible and which were caused by a third party such as a manufacturer. Further, the broad definition of 'equipment' would encompass 'any article of whatever kind furnished by the employer for the purposes of his business'.

Although the duty is broad, liability may be avoided (as with all categories of duty) if the employer can establish that the defective equipment did not cause the employee's injury. For example, if the employer can establish that the employee would not have used safety equipment even if it had been provided, he will not be liable: *McWilliams* v *Sir William Arrol & Co Ltd* [1962] 1 WLR 295 (HL).

Safe system of work

This is the area that gives rise to the greatest number of claims. Case law has elaborated on the elements covered by a safe system of work:

KEY CASE

Speed v *Thomas Swift & Co Ltd* [1943] 1 KB 557 (CA)

Concerning: safe system of work

Facts

The claimant was injured during the loading of a ship because there were several deficiencies with the system used to do so and the ship in question was not suited to the usual routine used for loading.

Legal principle

The court considered that the duty to provide a safe system of work included four features:

(1) the physical layout of the job;

(2) the sequence by which the work is carried out;

(3) the provision of warnings and notices and the issue of special instructions where necessary;

(4) the need to modify or improve the system to respond to particular circumstances.

The following situations are covered by the requirement to provide a safe system of work:

- Failing to warn employees of the dangers associated with their work: *Pape* v *Cumbria County Council* [1992] ICR 132 (QBD): the employer did not tell cleaners that failing to use gloves when handling chemicals could lead to dermatitis.

- Failing to ensure that safety measures provided were used: *Bux* v *Slough Metals* [1973] 1 WLR 1358 (CA): the employer knew that the employee refused to wear safety goggles provided but did nothing, thus was liable when his eyes were injured by molten metal.

- Failing to take action to guard against known risks: *Rahman* v *Arearose Ltd* [2001] QB 351 (CA): the employer was liable when his employee was attacked by a customer as he had taken no action to introduce a system to prevent this despite attacks against other members of staff in the past.

- Failure to protect against psychiatric injury: *Walker* v *Northumberland County Council* [1995] 1 All ER 737 (DC): the employer did nothing to alter an employee's workload after he returned to work following a nervous breakdown, thus was liable when he suffered a second breakdown as they were aware he was susceptible to stress.

Competent staff

The employer must ensure that he recruits competent staff and that an appropriate level of training and supervision is provided to ensure that employees do not pose a threat to the safety of their colleagues.

This category of duty overlaps with vicarious liability (Chapter 4) thus giving an employee injured by a colleague two potential ways of holding the employer liable (in addition to the personal liability of the colleague responsible); see Figure 5.1.

Figure 5.1

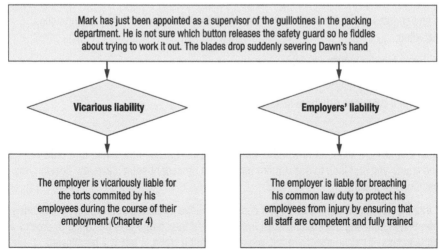

> ! **Don't be tempted to . . .**
>
> When analysing an employer's liability to provide competent staff who do not endanger the safety of others, also consider the potential overlap with vicarious liability. Often one particular set of circumstances can give rise to multiple torts and it is important to identify all which may apply (unless the question specifically restricts you from mentioning certain torts or only requires you to consider liability for particular torts).

■ Breach of statutory duty

The common law duty is supplemented by statute law which imposes further duties on employers. The most commonly encountered **statutory duties** arise from the Health and Safety at Work etc. Act 1974, although there are others. Claims for breach of statutory duty therefore most commonly arise in the context of employment. If an employer breaches his statutory duty and this results in injury to the employee, then this may give rise to a civil claim.

Is it an actionable breach?

Not all statutes give rise to a civil claim if breached.

Express statement in the statute

A few statutes expressly state that a claim in tort will be allowed if they are breached including:

- Consumer Protection Act 1987;
- Misrepresentation Act 1967;
- Mineral Workings (Offshore Installations) Act 1971.

Statute is silent

Most statutes are silent as to whether an action in tort arises in the event of a breach. The courts will first look to see if there has been a precedent set in case law deciding the issue of civil liability.

If there is no precedent, the court will consider a range of factors in deciding Parliament's intention in enacting the statute. Most importantly, if the statute was designed to protect a limited class of individuals, then it is more likely that a claim in tort will be allowed.

Lonrho Ltd v *Shell Petroleum Co Ltd (No 2)* [1982] AC 173 (HL)

Concerning: breach of statute giving rise to civil liability

Facts

A sanctions order made under the Southern Rhodesia Act 1965 prohibited anyone from supplying or delivering any crude oil or petroleum products to Southern Rhodesia on a penalty of a fine or imprisonment. The appellants argued that contravention of the sanctions order would amount to breach of statutory duty by the respondents giving the appellants a right of action in tort.

Legal principle

Lord Diplock stated that the test for deciding whether a statute gives rise to civil liability is that:

> ... the court should presume that if the Act creates an obligation which is enforceable in a specific manner then it is not enforceable in any other manner. In this way if the Act was intended for the general benefit of the community rather than for the granting of individual rights then it will not usually be possible to use the Act to bring an action in tort.

The exceptions to this rule are:

- where the Act benefits a particular class of individuals;
- where the claimant suffered damage which was particular, direct and substantial and different from that suffered by the rest of the public.

The courts will also look to see whether the statute provides a remedy for its breach. If the statute providing protection to a limited class of individuals provides no remedy for its breach then the courts are likely to infer that Parliament intended for a civil claim to lie – otherwise, those protected by the statute would have no remedy at all in respect of the protection that the statute offered (*Cutler* v *Wandsworth Stadium Ltd* [1949] AC 398 (HL)).

Where the statute provides for compensation, this does not automatically mean that this is the only remedy available (*Groves* v *Lord Wimborne* [1898] 2 QB 402 (CA) 147).

In essence there are many factors which allow the courts discretion in determining whether a right of action in tort will lie for breach of statutory duty. As Lord Simonds said in *Cutler* v *Wandsworth Stadium Ltd* [1949] AC 398 (HL):

> The only rule which in all circumstances is valid is that the answer must depend on a consideration of the whole Act and the circumstances, including the pre-existing law, in which it was enacted.

❗ Don't be tempted to . . .

Don't assume that all breaches of statutory duty are actionable. If the statute is silent, remember to apply the common law tests to determine whether it is likely that the courts would allow a tortious claim for breach of statutory duty. You should then make sure that you cover the elements of the tort in turn.

Elements of the tort

Assuming that the statute allows a civil claim, the claimant must establish the elements of the tort as follows:

- statutory duty owed to the claimant;
- breach of duty by the defendant;
- damage;
- causation.

Statutory duty owed to the claimant

If the statute protects a limited class of people, then the claimant must establish that they are a member of that class.

KEY CASE

Hartley v *Mayoh & Co* [1954] 1 QB 383 (CA)

Concerning: existence of statutory duty

Facts

The defendants were in breach of the Factory and Workshop Acts 1901, 1907 and 1908 by negligently miswiring electrical switches at a factory. A fireman, called to a fire at the factory, was electrocuted.

Legal principle

The claim, brought by the deceased fireman's widow, failed. The fireman was outside the protected class, since the statutes protected factory workers, not visitors to the factory.

Breach of duty by the defendant

The claimant must establish that the defendant was in breach of duty. This is determined by the wording of the relevant statute.

Some statutes impose *strict liability*. That is to say that the statute will impose an absolute requirement which, if unmet, will be a breach of duty even if the breach is not the defendant's fault.

KEY CASE

John Summers & Sons Ltd v *Frost* [1955] AC 740 (HL)

Concerning: breach of statutory duty; strict liability

Facts

The claimant, a maintenance fitter, was employed by the defendants in a steel works. While working on a power-driven grinding machine, his thumb came into contact with the revolving grindstone and he was injured. He brought an action for damages for breach of statutory duty under section 14(1) of the Factories Act 1937.

Legal principle

The Act provided that 'Every dangerous part of any machinery, other than prime movers and transmission machinery, shall be securely fenced . . .' The defendants argued that it would be impracticable to fence their machinery. However, the House of Lords refused to accept this. Liability was strict.

However, the required standard of care may not be stated so precisely. For instance, in *Brown* v *NCB* [1962] AC 574 (HL) the duty imposed was 'to take such steps as may be necessary for keeping the road or working place secure'.

Employers need to appreciate and take into account the risks of accidents occurring. In *Robb* v *Salamis (M & I) Ltd* [2007] 2 All ER 97 (HL), the ladder which led to the claimant's bunk bed on an offshore platform was loose, causing the claimant to fall and injure himself. In the lower courts it was held that the accident was not reasonably foreseeable and that the claimant was to blame, either fully or partially, as he knew that the ladders were portable and were often removed. He, therefore, should have checked that the ladder was stable. However, the House of Lords held that the defendant's obligations under the Use of Work Equipment Regulations 1998 were continuous. Therefore, they should not have waited for an accident to happen but should instead have anticipated that ladders which were not affixed to the bunk beds could cause injury. The fact that the claimant was careless was immaterial to the employer's liability for breach of statutory duty. The finding of 50% contributory negligence, however, was upheld.

✎ EXAM TIP

Problem questions involving breach of statutory duty will usually provide statements from the statute at issue. If liability is not strict, remember to argue both for and against liability being imposed and identify the strengths and weaknesses of both sides. The best answers always show a balanced understanding of all potential outcomes.

Damage

The damage suffered by the claimant must be of the type which the statute was intended to protect.

> **□ REVISION NOTE**
>
> This requirement is similar to that of remoteness in negligence. Refer back to Chapter 3 to refresh your memory.

> **KEY CASE**
>
> ***Gorris* v *Scott* (1874) LR 9 Exch 125**
>
> *Concerning: breach of statutory duty; type of damage*
>
> **Facts**
>
> The defendant, a ship-owner, undertook to carry the claimant's sheep from a foreign port to England. On the voyage some of the sheep were washed overboard by reason of the defendant's failure to take a precaution made under section 75 of the Contagious Diseases (Animals) Act 1869.
>
> **Legal principle**
>
> The Act was designed to prevent the loss of livestock through contagious diseases. Since the loss suffered was different, the claim did not succeed.

Causation

The final element in the tort is that there must be a causal link between the defendant's breach of duty and the claimant's loss. Where the breach of statutory duty is not the only cause of the defendant's injuries, it is enough that it materially contributed to it (*Bonnington Castings* v *Wardlaw* [1956] AC 613 (HL)).

> **□ REVISION NOTE**
>
> *Bonnington Castings* v *Wardlaw* was covered earlier (in Chapter 3). It involved a breach of the statutory duty under the Grinding of Metals (Miscellaneous Industries) Regulations 1925 to keep the ducts of dust-extraction plants free from obstruction.

Defences

An employer could seek to limit or avoid liability by relying on the defences of:

- consent (*volenti non fit injuria*);
- contributory negligence.

Consent

The defence of **consent** is not available to an employer who is in breach of his own statutory duty. This is a matter of public policy (*Wheeler* v *New Merton Board Mills Ltd* [1933] 2 KB 669 (CA)).

However, consent *is* available where an employee sues an employer for being vicariously liable for a colleague's breach of statutory duty (*ICI Ltd* v *Shatwell* [1965] AC 656 (HL)).

With the exceptions above in mind, the defence of consent will be generally available where there has been a breach of statutory duty (Lord Reid in *ICI Ltd* v *Shatwell*).

Contributory negligence

Contributory negligence is generally available. However, in relation to factory workers, the courts are more reluctant to find contributory negligence against an employee (*Caswell* v *Powell Duffryn Associated Collieries Ltd* [1940] AC 152 (HL)).

📖 **REVISION NOTE**

Contributory negligence and *volenti non fit injuria* (consent) are general defences which are available to most torts. You will find a more detailed outline of the elements of these defences and their operation in Chapter 13.

■ Putting it all together

Answer guidelines

See the problem question at the start of the chapter. A diagram illustrating how to structure your answer is available on the companion website.

Approaching the question

This is a problem question that raises a number of potential claims against FruitInc by Christine. You, therefore, should begin by thinking about what those claims might be so that you can structure your answer accordingly. Don't be tempted to start immediately – a question which has multiple claims requires you to identify them all, so a few moments planning will help prevent you missing one altogether, especially in the pressure of an exam. ▶

Important points to include

There are three potential claims against FruitInc. You should deal with them in turn.

Common law negligence – FruitInc has a common law duty to take reasonable care of its employees. It covers four key elements: safe premises/workplace; safe plant, materials and equipment; safe system of work; competent colleagues (*Wilsons & Clyde Coal*). Consider each of these elements in turn.

- Safe workplace? More concerned with building. Probably does not apply here (*Latimer* v *AEC Ltd*).
- Safe plant? Again, the machine was not unsafe *per se* (*Knowles* v *Liverpool County Council*).
- Safe system of work? FruitInc has a duty to ensure that the safety measures provided were used (*Speed* v *Thomas Swift& Co Ltd*; *Bux* v *Slough Metals*) – probable breach here.
- Competent staff? David was incompetent in not requiring Christine to use the guard.

FruitInc appears to be in breach of its common law duty of care. Causation is established via the 'but for' test. Christine's injury is a reasonably foreseeable type and therefore not too remote.

- Defences? Consent may work since Christine deliberately removed the guard. If this fails, then contributory negligence is likely to succeed (see Chapter 13).

Breach of statutory duty – will be allowed if the Factories Act 1961 allows a civil claim. This will be established by reading the Act. If it is silent, as most are, then the next step is looking to see if there is decided case law on the issue. If none, then the court will look at the Act as a whole and decide (*Cutler* v *Wandsworth Stadium*). This Act appears to protect a limited class of individuals and seems to provide no remedy for its breach. The courts also tend to allow civil claims for breaches of health and safety legislations. It is likely that the Act will allow a claim in tort for a breach of section 14(1).

- Is Christine a member of the protected class? She is a factory worker and is therefore protected (*Hartley* v *Mayoh & Co*).
- Has there been a breach of duty by FruitInc? Section 14(1) imposes strict liability; hence FruitInc is in breach (*John Summers & Sons Ltd* v *Frost*).
- Has Christine suffered the type of injury the Act was designed to prevent? Clearly (*Gorris* v *Scott*)!
- Is there a causal link? But for FruitInc's breach, Christine would not have been scalped.

- Defences? (see Chapter 13). Consent will not be available to FruitInc for a breach of its own statutory duty (*Wheeler* v *New Merton Board Mills Ltd*). Contributory negligence is likely to succeed as Christine seemed to recklessly disregard her own safety (but see *Caswell* v *Powell Duffryn Associated Collieries Ltd*).

Vicarious liability – (see Chapter 4). FruitInc may be vicariously liable for David's negligence committed in the course of employment which caused Christine's injury of a reasonable foreseeable type. Consent will again be unlikely to succeed, but contributory negligence will be applicable as in the other heads of claim.

 Make your answer stand out

Remember to cover all three potential claims. Don't be misled by the fact that the problem states a statute into only covering breach of statutory duty.

Take each of the claims in turn and analyse them methodically. Remember to relate each point back to the facts and provide supporting case authority for each point of law you make.

READ TO IMPRESS

Allen, S. (2009) The complexity of employers' liability law: interpretation and proving fault. 4, *Journal of Personal Injury Law*, p. 243.

Tomkins, N. (2007) Misleading reports? 2, *Journal of Personal Injury Law*, p. 150.

www.pearsoned.co.uk/lawexpress

 Go online to access more revision support including quizzes to test your knowledge, sample questions with answer guidelines, podcasts you can download, and more!

Occupiers' liability

Revision checklist

Essential points you should know:

☐ The meaning of key terms such as occupier, visitor, premises and trespasser

☐ The scope of the duty established under the Occupiers' Liability Act 1957

☐ The implications of the Occupiers' Liability Act 1984 in relation to liability for trespassers

☐ The defences available to an occupier and the ability to limit or exclude liability

☐ Liability for dangers created by independent contractors on land occupied by others

■ Topic map

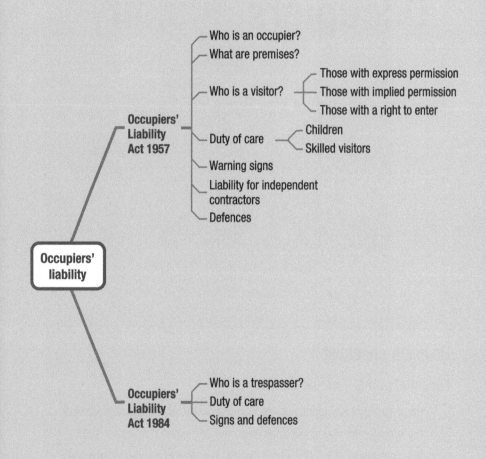

Occupiers' liability

Occupiers' Liability Act 1957
- Who is an occupier?
- What are premises?
- Who is a visitor?
  - Those with express permission
  - Those with implied permission
  - Those with a right to enter
- Duty of care
  - Children
  - Skilled visitors
- Warning signs
- Liability for independent contractors
- Defences

Occupiers' Liability Act 1984
- Who is a trespasser?
- Duty of care
- Signs and defences

A printable version of this topic map is available from **www.pearsoned.co.uk/lawexpress**

▉ Introduction

Occupiers have an obligation to ensure that their land is not hazardous to others.

This obligation is governed by statute law as the Occupiers' Liability Act 1957 (OLA 1957) was introduced to clarify the common law position. It was supplemented by the Occupiers' Liability Act 1984 (OLA 1984) which covers injuries caused to trespassers. Occupiers' liability is an important topic because the scope of the tort is so immense; think of all the situations in which you enter land or premises belonging to others: shops, university, pubs, the gym and even friends' houses. All occupiers have a duty to ensure that you are not injured on their land and that your property is not damaged. The statutes should form the central focus of your revision and it is essential that you are able to identify and explain the key provisions that govern liability in this area.

ASSESSMENT ADVICE

Essay questions

Essay questions on occupiers' liability often focus on whether or not the law has achieved its purpose, i.e. whether the statutes offer an appropriate level of protection to visitors and trespassers without unduly burdening the occupier of land. Alternatively, essays may require an exploration of whether the legislation is necessary in light of the protection offered by other areas of tort law such as negligence, trespass and nuisance.

Problem questions

Problem questions on this topic are popular with examiners. A very common error occurs when students fail to recognise that the question is dealing with occupiers' liability and deal with the facts on the basis of negligence. Avoid this by remembering that injury caused on another's land should trigger a discussion of occupiers' liability. It is also essential that the correct statute be applied so pay careful attention to the distinction between lawful visitors and trespassers.

Sample question

Could you answer this question? Below is a typical problem question that could arise on this topic. Guidelines on answering the question are included at the end of the chapter, whilst a sample essay question and guidance on tackling it can be found on the companion website.

PROBLEM QUESTION

Omar runs a small museum specialising in agricultural artefacts. There are several signs displayed prominently that read 'please do not touch the exhibits' and two of the rarest machines are also roped off to protect them from the public. Lewis (aged four) climbs on an antique plough whilst his mother is queueing in the tea shop. He slips and sustains a deep laceration to his leg from the exposed blades. There is an exhibition of dairy equipment in the cellar which attracts Aggie. She sees that there is a sign at the top of the step but does not put on her glasses to read what it says so she is not aware that part of the handrail is missing. She starts to descend the stairs, slips and falls, breaking her leg. Lucy works in the newly refurbished tea shop, which was fitted by Bob, a local handyman. Bob struggled with some of the wiring, not being experienced with electrical work, and this causes a power surge during which the coffee machine explodes, causing Lucy to suffer severe burns.

Advise Omar as to the strength of the possible claims against him in tort.

Occupiers' Liability Act 1957

Prior to this statute, the extent of liability owed by an occupier depended upon the nature of the relationship with the person injured. The OLA 1957 abolished this in favour of two categories:

- lawful visitors, who were protected by the Act;
- all others, who were not protected (most of these are now protected by OLA 1984).

KEY STATUTE

Occupiers' Liability Act 1957, section 1(1)

The purpose of the Act is to 'regulate the duty which an occupier of premises owes to his visitors in respect of dangers due to the state of the premises or to things done or omitted to be done on them'.

Who is an occupier?

There is no statutory definition of '**occupier**', thus recourse must be made to the common law which has taken a broad view of the issue:

KEY DEFINITION: Occupier

A person who exercises an element of control over premises: *Wheat* v *E. Lacon & Co Ltd* [1966] AC 552 (HL).

- As there are varying degrees of control that can be exercised, this means that there can be more than one occupier.

- This includes physical control of premises and legal control of premises; in *Harris* v *Birkenhead Corporation* [1976] 1 WLR 279 (CA), the council was the occupier of an empty house even though it had not taken physical possession as it had served a notice of compulsory purchase on the owner thus was in legal control of the property.

✎ EXAM TIP

Remember that liability falls upon the *occupier* of land and that this may not necessarily be the person who owns the land. The central question is 'who has control of these premises?' and you should also keep in mind that there may be more than one occupier simultaneously.

What are premises?

The definition of premises is wide and covers not only land and buildings but also 'any fixed or moveable structure, including any vessel, vehicle or aircraft': section s1(3)(a), OLA 1957. This has covered:

- a ship in dry dock: *London Graving Dock* v *Horton* [1951] AC 737 (HL);

- aircraft: *Fosbroke-Hobbes* v *Airwork Ltd* [1937] 1 All ER 108 (DC);

- scaffolding and ladders (moveable structures): *Wheeler* v *Copas* [1981] 3 All ER 405 (DC).

Who is a visitor?

There are three categories of people that are considered lawful visitors, as described below.

Those with express permission

This is a relatively straightforward category although it can be complicated if the visitor behaves in a way that exceeds the extent of the permission that has been granted. The occupier has the right to limit the way in which a visitor behaves whilst on his premises, and a visitor who deviates from this will be a **trespasser** (covered by OLA 1984), not a lawful visitor.

> **✎ EXAM TIP**
>
> The distinction between lawful visitor and trespasser is an important one as it determines which statute is relevant as the basis for liability. This makes it a popular issue in problem questions. Make sure that you can distinguish between the two by identifying what permission has been granted to the visitor and making reference to specific facts that suggest that this permission has been exceeded.
>
> ■ Where was the visitor entitled to go?
>
> ■ What was the visitor entitled to do?
>
> ■ When was the visitor required to leave?

Remember this useful quotation: 'When you invite a person into your house to use the staircase, you do not invite him to slide down the banisters', *The Calgarth* [1927] P 93 (CA).

Those with implied permission

This is a slightly more problematic category as it involves those who have not been prohibited from entering the premises but have not been explicitly invited and who are assumed not to be objectionable to the occupier. For example, it is accepted that a person who enters premises wishing to speak to the occupier or to make a delivery has implied permission to do so.

Implied permission is also subject to limitations which, if exceeded, render the person a trespasser but it can be more complicated to determine the boundaries of implied permission. It would be likely to include such situations as entry into parts of property that have no relation to the purpose of his visit: for example, a delivery person may have implied permission to enter the reception area but not to wander around the gardens.

In *Harvey* v *Plymouth City Council* [2010] EWCA Civ 860, [2010] PIQR P18, it was held that any implied permission to enter must be exercised properly: the duty to ensure that land is safe for visitors to enter is limited to the ordinary use of the land. As Carnwarth LJ commented:

> An implied licence for general recreational activity cannot, in my view, be stretched to cover any form of activity, however reckless.

If an occupier knows that his land is used by trespassers but does nothing to prevent them from entering his land, this may amount to implied permission to enter:

KEY CASE

Lowery v *Walker* **[1911] AC 10 (HL)**

Concerning: trespassers; implied permission

Facts

A path across the defendant's field was used as a short cut to the railway station by several people. The defendant was aware of this and objected to it but had never taken active steps to prevent its occurrence. Without warning, the defendant put a wild horse in the field which attacked the claimant.

Legal principle

It was held that the defendant's awareness of the presence of people on his land and his failure to stop or limit their actions amounted to an implied licence to enter the property.

Those with a right to enter

The law gives rights of entry to certain categories of people which render them within the definition of lawful visitor irrespective of the wishes of the occupier of the land, e.g. police officers entering under warrant.

Those who enter premises pursuant to a contract are also deemed to be entitled to entry thus are regarded as visitors.

Duty of care

KEY STATUTE

Occupiers' Liability Act 1957, section 2(2)

The common duty of care is . . . to take such care as in all the circumstances of the case is reasonable to see that the visitor will be reasonably safe in using the premises for the purposes for which he is invited or permitted by the occupier to be there.

⬚ REVISION NOTE

The standard of care expected resembles that applied in negligence so it would be useful to review the more detailed consideration of liability for foreseeable risks that can be found in Chapters 1, 2 and 3.

Note the following points regarding the duty of care:

- Although there is similarity with the standard of care in negligence, there is also an important distinction as an occupier is empowered by statute to determine the boundaries of his liability. Section 2(1), OLA 1957 provides that an occupier may extend, restrict, modify or exclude his duty to visitors by agreement or otherwise.

- As the occupier controls the extent of the permission to enter, a visitor who acts in a manner contrary to that permission becomes a trespasser (see above).

- The duty is to ensure that the visitor is not injured whilst on the premises. This is not the same as a duty to ensure that the premises are safe so the duty may be satisfied if the occupier displays warning signs or cordons off areas that are dangerous.

- There are situations in which the common duty of care differs, as illustrated in Figure 6.1.

Figure 6.1

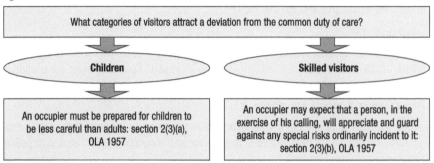

Children

Although section 2(3)(a) warns that children are less careful than adults, implying that greater care may be needed to protect them from harm, case law has sought to balance responsibility between occupiers and parents.

KEY CASE

Phipps v Rochester Corporation [1955] 1 QB 450 (DC)

Concerning: child visitors

Facts

A five-year-old child played on land under development by the local council. On one occasion, he fell down a trench dug by the council.

Legal principle

The court held that the defendant was entitled to assume that parents would take primary responsibility for the safety and control of their children. As a prudent parent would not have allowed a child of that age to play on a building site unattended, there was no liability as the defendant could not have been expected to protect against unforeseeable risks.

The policy behind this decision was that it was not socially desirable for parents to shift the burden of protecting their children from harm from themselves to landowners. Similarly in *Bourne Leisure v Marsden* [2009] EWCA Civ 671 the Court of Appeal held that there was no breach of duty by the occupiers of a holiday park in which a two-year-old drowned in a pond (even though the fence around the pond was not high enough to prevent the child climbing in), since the danger would have been obvious to adults and it was reasonable to expect a child of that age to have been supervised by an adult.

It is likely, however, that a duty will exist if land holds concealed dangers or allurements that tempt children into danger:

KEY CASE

Glasgow Corporation v *Taylor* [1922] 1 AC 44 (HL)

Concerning: child visitors

Facts

A seven-year-old child died after eating poisonous berries in a public park. The plants were fenced off but there were no notices warning that the berries were poisonous.

Legal principle

It was held that the plants did not present an obvious risk of danger so the council should have taken measures to draw attention to the concealed danger that they represented. The court also commented that an occupier who is aware that something on his land would act as an allurement to children (such as berries that look edible) must take greater care to protect against this risk involved.

The level of care expected will depend upon the nature of the risk and the age and awareness of the child. For example, in *Titchener* v *BRB* [1983] 1 WLR 1427 (HL), no duty was owed to a 15-year-old boy who was struck by a train whilst walking on a railway line at night as he was aware of the dangers posed by his activity.

Skilled visitors

The law expects skilled visitors whose expertise gives them greater awareness of risks of harm than the ordinary visitor to take precautions to protect themselves. This does not mean that occupiers have no duty towards skilled visitors; it depends on the nature of the risk. See Figure 6.2.

! Don't be tempted to . . .

Don't assume that a skilled visitor to premises is not owed a duty by the occupier. While it is true that skilled visitors are not owed a duty in relation to the sorts of risk of which they would be especially aware by virtue of their expertise, it does not follow that they are not owed a duty in relation to any risk. Look at the particular skills of the visitor and see if they are related to the manner in which the visitor suffers injury before deciding on liability.

Figure 6.2

Danny is an electrician employed to fit a power shower in Mary's bathroom

Danny injures his back when he trips over a loose floorboard in the hallway

Danny is badly burnt after receiving an electric shock. He realised that Mary's wiring was faulty, but decided to carry on working without turning the electricity off at the mains

This would not be covered by section 2(3)(b) because this was not a risk that was in any way associated with Danny's work as an electrician. The common duty of care will apply

The risks of electricity are those which are ordinarily incidental to the work of an electrician thus Mary could expect Danny to protect himself against the risk of such harm, thus section 2(3)(b), applies

Warning signs

KEY STATUTE

Occupiers' Liability Act 1957, section 2(4)(a)

Where damage is caused to a visitor by a danger of which he had been warned by the occupier, the warning is not to be treated without more as absolving the occupier from liability, unless in all the circumstances it was enough to enable the visitor to be reasonably safe.

The following factors should be taken into account when considering whether a warning sign was 'enough to enable the visitor to be reasonably safe':

- How specific was the warning? For example, consider the difference between 'Caution' and 'Caution: slippery surface'; the warning should be sufficiently precise so that the visitor knows what risk he is facing.

- How obvious was the danger? Hidden dangers necessitate greater efforts to call attention to them than readily apparent risks. In *Staples* v *West Dorset District Council* [1995] 93 LGR 536 (CA), it was held that the risks posed by wet algae on a high wall were so obvious that there was no need for a warning sign.

- Is the sign combined with other safety measures? The use of fencing or barriers emphasises the need for safety.

- What sort of visitor is targeted? Something more than a sign may be needed to guard against risks that are linked to children.

Make your answer stand out

An occupier may try to avoid liability by using an exclusion notice rather than a warning sign. A detailed consideration of exclusion clauses is beyond the scope of this book, being an issue covered in the law of contract. Mesher (1979) summarised the position in relation to exclusion clauses and occupiers' liability.

Liability for independent contractors

Section 2(4)(b), OLA 1957 specifies three circumstances in which an occupier is liable for harm caused to a visitor by the work of an independent contractor:

- If it was unreasonable to entrust the work to an independent contractor, i.e. if it was work that the occupier could, in the circumstances, have carried out himself;
- If the occupier failed to take reasonable steps to ensure that the contractor was competent;
- If the occupier failed to take reasonable care to ensure that the work was carried out to an appropriate standard.

Maguire v *Sefton Metropolitan Borough Council* [2006] 1 WLR 2550 (CA) includes a discussion of the ability of an occupier to rely on the work done by an independent contractor.

> **✎ EXAM TIP**
>
> If you encounter issues relating to an independent contractor in a problem question, consider the following:
>
> *What did the occupier do to check the competence of the contractor?*
>
> - Did he take up references?
> - Did he check that the contractor was qualified or registered with a trade association?
> - Did he ask to see examples of his work?
>
> *What did the occupier do to check the quality of the work?*
>
> - Did he make periodic inspections when the work was in progress?
> - Did he ask for progress reports?
> - Did he inspect the finished work?

The occupier is only expected to do what is reasonable to check the quality of the work and this will vary according to the complexity and technical intricacy of the work. See Figure 6.3.

Figure 6.3

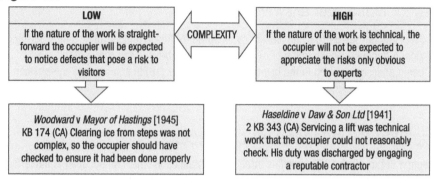

Defences

The following are ways in which an occupier could seek to limit or avoid liability:

- ■ *Volenti non fit injuria*: this asserts that the visitor consented to the risk of injury as he knew of and understood and accepted the risk of injury: section 2(5), OLA 1957.
- ■ Reliance on exclusion or limitation of liability by the use of notices (see above).
- ■ Contributory negligence: under the Law Reform (Contributory Negligence) Act 1945, damages awarded to the claimant will be reduced to the extent that the court accepts that he is responsible for his own injuries or loss.

📖 REVISION NOTE

Contributory negligence and *volenti non fit injuria* (consent) are general defences which are available to most torts in addition to occupiers' liability. You will find a more detailed outline of the elements of these defences and their operation in Chapter 13. You may find it useful to take a look at these defences and consider how they would operate in relation to occupiers' liability.

■ Occupiers' Liability Act 1984

OLA 1984 extended the protection of the law to cover:

- ■ trespassers;
- ■ people lawfully exercising private rights of way;
- ■ visitors to land covered by section 60 of the National Parks and Access to the Countryside Act 1949 and 'right to roam' legislation.

The scope of the protection is narrower than OLA 1957 in relation to lawful visitors as, according to section 1(1), OLA 1984, an occupier may be liable for injuries only and not damage to property. Other than this and its application to trespassers, the provisions of OLA 1984 mirror OLA 1957.

Who is a trespasser?

There is no statutory definition but case law has formulated a definition which has been generally accepted. Do not be concerned that the definition pre-dates the relevant legislation; this often happens when the common law has defined a term in a way that needs no amendment.

KEY DEFINITION: Trespasser

A trespasser is 'someone who goes on the land without invitation of any sort and whose presence is either unknown to the proprietor or, if known, is practically objected to': *Robert Addie & Sons (Collieries) Ltd* v *Dumbreck* [1929] AC 358 (HL).

Duty of care

Section 1(3) OLA 1984 outlines three conditions that must be satisfied for a duty to arise:

- The occupier must be aware of the danger or have reasonable grounds to believe that it exists (subjective).
- He knows or has reasonable grounds to believe that a trespasser is in the vicinity of the danger (subjective).
- The risk is one against which, in all the circumstances, he may reasonably be expected to offer some protection (objective: based on the reasonable occupier).

✎ EXAM TIP

The first two aspects of section 1(3) are based upon the occupier's actual knowledge of the risk and the presence of trespassers. Look for evidence of this in the facts. For example:

- Is there evidence that the land is used as a short cut?
- Is there a secure and undamaged boundary fence?
- Has the occupier noticed risks on his land?
- Is the occupier aware of previous accidents?

The third element is based upon the reasonableness of imposing liability. Factors to take into account include:

- The nature and extent of the risk, i.e. whether it was obvious or hidden and the severity of the harm that it posed;
- What sort of trespassers are involved? An occupier may be expected to take greater precautions to protect against harm to child trespassers than to adults.
- Could the danger have been reduced or negated by precautions? Did any precautions taken meet the standards of the reasonable occupier?

The approach taken by the courts to determining liability towards trespassers based upon these factors can be seen in *Young* v *Kent County Council* [2005] EWHC 1342 (QB) where it is interesting to note that the court commented that if the claimant had been an adult, rather than a 12-year-old child, the claimant would have received nothing. This demonstrates the variable standard of care in operation. The child was injured falling through a skylight. The County Council that owned the premises was found liable on the basis that it was aware that the skylight was flimsy and brittle and that children habitually used the roof as a meeting place. Its liability was reduced by 50% following a finding of contributory negligence by the claimant (see Chapter 11). The issues of liability for injuries caused to child trespassers was further explored by the Court of Appeal in *Keown*:

***Keown* v *Coventry Healthcare NHS Trust* [2006] 1 WLR 953 (CA)**
Concerning: child trespassers, state of the premises

Facts

The claimant was an 11-year-old child who was seriously injured falling from the fire escape that ran up three storeys of a hospital building. At trial, the claimant accepted that he was aware that the fire escape was dangerous and that he should not have been climbing on it. The trial judge found that the NHS trust was liable on the basis that the state of the premises posed a danger; the respondent was aware that children played in the hospital grounds and so should have guarded against the danger posed by the fire escape.

Legal principle

The Court of Appeal overturned the finding at first instance on the basis that the Occupiers' Liability Act 1984 required that injury be caused by the danger presented by the state of the building, not that injury be caused by the state of the building. In other words, there was nothing wrong with the fire escape and it would not have caused injury to anyone had it been used in a proper manner.

The *Keown* case makes an important distinction between injury caused by the danger presented by the state of the building (such as the defective condition of the skylight in *Young* v *Kent County Council*) and the dangerous use of perfectly well maintained premises. Reference was made in *Keown* to the House of Lords decision in *Tomlinson* v *Congleton Borough Council* [2004] 1 AC 46 where Lord Hoffmann held that 'the risk arose out of what [the claimant] chose to do and not out of the state of the premises'. These cases make it clear that injuries arising from the claimant's dangerous use of otherwise safe premises will not give rise to liability under the Occupiers' Liability Acts. *Tomlinson* was a landmark case that was regarded as an attempt to stem the development of a 'compensation culture' in the UK. As Lord Hobhouse commented:

The pursuit of an unrestrained culture of blame and compensation has many evil consequences and one is certainly the interference with the liberty of the citizen. Of course there is some risk of accidents arising out of the *joie de vivre* of the young, but that is no reason for imposing a grey and dull safety regime on everyone.

The approach in *Tomlinson* has since been reflected in section 1 of the Compensation Act 2006 which provides that:

A court considering a claim in negligence or breach of statutory duty may . . . have regard to whether a requirement to take [particular steps to meet an appropriate standard of care] might –

(a) prevent a desirable activity from being undertaken at all, to a particular extent or in a particular way, or

(b) discourage persons from undertaking functions in connection with a desirable activity.

Section 2 goes on to provide that an apology, an offer of treatment or other redress, shall not of itself amount to an admission of negligence or breach of statutory duty. In other words, even if the occupier takes steps to remedy an injury suffered on their premises, this will not automatically determine either negligence or a breach of statutory duty.

Signs and defences

In this respect, there is no distinction with the provisions outlined in relation to OLA 1957.

■ Putting it all together

Answer guidelines

See the problem question at the start of the chapter. A diagram illustrating how to structure your answer is available on the companion website.

Approaching the question

This is a typical example of a problem question involving occupiers' liability. Make sure that you follow the instructions: you are asked to advise Omar on the strength of his position rather than to advise the various claimants. Work through each claim separately to ensure that your answer is clear. There are some issues common to each claim, such as the meaning of 'occupier' and 'premises' but there is no need ▶

to repeat these points in relation to each claim: simply refer back to your previous discussion with clear signposting. For example, 'Omar is the occupier of premises as previously discussed' or 'Lucy is a lawful visitor as defined previously as she has permission to enter the premises in the course of her employment.'

Important points to include

- Take some time to plan your answer before you start writing. Identify how many claims there are in the question and try to work out what the key issue is in each case before you start.

- Lewis (aged four) is injured on the antique plough. Is he a visitor or a trespasser? Does his age make any difference to the imposition of liability?

- Aggie falls on the stairs and breaks her leg. Was the warning sign sufficient? Does it matter that she could not read it?

- Lucy was scalded by the exploding urn. Is it relevant that she is an employee? How does Bob's status as an independent contractor affect liability?

- You will need to be more detailed in working through the elements of occupiers' liability on the first occasion, so you will need to establish that Omar is the occupier of premises; explain the distinction between a visitor and a trespasser and outline the nature of the duty of care in relation to Lewis's claim. Reference can be made back to these explanations when dealing with the other parties. The key issue here is the modified duty in relation to children so make sure that you are able to list relevant statutory provisions and key cases on this issue.

- Omar will be able to resist Aggie's claim if he provided adequate warning of the risk to enable her to be 'reasonably safe' on the premises. You should make reference to section 2(2), OLA 1957. Much will depend on the wording of the sign and you will need to discuss whether her failure to read the sign alters the outcome of a claim.

- Lucy is a visitor to the premises as she had cause to be there as an employee. She was injured due to faulty work carried out by an independent contractor. Consider whether (a) Omar engaged a competent contractor (unlikely – Bob is a handyman without experience in electrical work so Omar should have engaged someone with experience in electrical wiring), and (b) whether Omar did enough to check the quality of the work (you would expect him to have tested to see whether the equipment was working properly as this is not a technical job but actually checking the wiring would have been too complicated). Ultimately, Omar's liability is likely to be based on Bob's lack of competence to carry out the work in question.

Make your answer stand out

Make sure that you pay close attention to the facts provided and think about how they might affect liability. For example, Lewis is four years old but has been left unsupervised whilst his mother is in the tea shop, so you could make an argument that Omar's precautions in roping off the machines would have been adequate if Lewis had been under adequate parental supervision. Remember that you are asked to advise Omar about the strength of the claims against him, so it would be useful to point out ways that he can oppose the claims.

It is also useful to consider the impact of facts that have not been provided. For example, in relation to Aggie, you should speculate on the wording of the sign at the top of the stairs. Again, your brief is to advise Omar on the strength of his position so you could suggest wording that would be adequate for him to avoid liability (for example, 'WARNING: part of the handrail is missing so visitors are advised to exercise extreme caution when using these stairs') and what sort of wording would not be sufficient (for example, a general 'Caution' sign would not give adequate information about what the risk is so that Aggie could avoid it).

READ TO IMPRESS

Bundock, M. and Farrelly, M. (2001) Dangerous premises and liability for trespassers. 151, *New Law Journal*, p. 309.

Mesher, J. (1979) Occupiers, trespassers and the Unfair Contract Terms Act 1977. *Conveyancer*, p. 58.

www.pearsoned.co.uk/lawexpress

 Go online to access more revision support including quizzes to test your knowledge, sample questions with answer guidelines, podcasts you can download, and more!

Nuisance

Revision checklist

Essential points you should know:

- [ ] The elements of private nuisance and its role in protecting rights in land including key concepts concerning the unreasonable use of land, such as malice, the sensitivity of the claimant and the character of the neighbourhood

- [ ] The role of public nuisance and the relevance of key concepts, such as the class of people affected and the requirement for special damage

- [ ] The distinction between private and public nuisance and their relationship with other property torts, such as trespass to land

- [ ] The nature and operation of defences and the availability of remedies

◼ Topic map

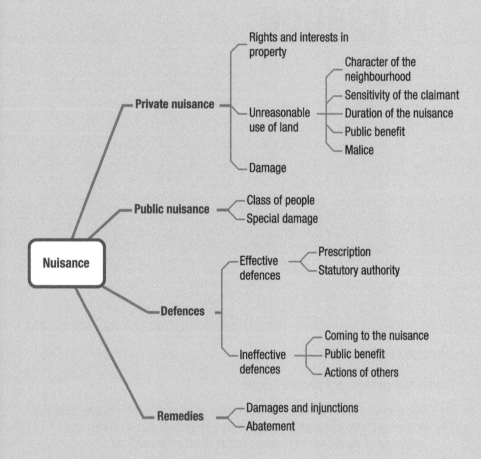

◼ Introduction

Nuisance may be private (affecting a particular individual or property) or public (impacting on a wider group of people).

Private nuisance is concerned with the protection of proprietary rights and interests; hence, its essence is to uphold the right to quiet enjoyment of one's own land. By contrast, it is a requirement of public nuisance that a section of the public is affected and it lacks any requirement for a nexus between the nuisance and property. Both torts raise issues of environmental protection as they cover topics such as noise and pollution but this is just a side effect of the scope of nuisance; remember that it is a tort aimed at protecting individuals not the environment generally.

Nuisance is one of the key ways in which individuals can secure a peaceful existence free from external interference. Given the premium placed on freedom from aggravation in today's society, nuisance has a key role to play in upholding an individual's interest in a quiet life. This is a very popular examination topic and thus should play a central role in your revision strategy.

ASSESSMENT ADVICE

Essay questions

Essay questions focusing on nuisance are relatively common. They may deal with private or public nuisance or a combination of the two, in which case an awareness of the relationship between them and any overlap is necessary. An essay could take a broader focus on the way that tort law protects property rights, in which case an ability to comment on nuisance and other torts, such as negligence and trespass to land, is essential.

Problem questions

Problem questions on nuisance are also common. Again, public and private nuisance may combine to test the student's ability to differentiate between the two torts. The same applies to trespass to land (mutually exclusive with private nuisance) and negligence so it could be beneficial to regard these torts as a useful group of revision topics.

◼ Sample question

Could you answer this question? Below is a typical problem question that could arise on this topic. Guidelines on answering the question are included at the end of the chapter, whilst a sample essay question and guidance on tackling it can be found on the companion website.

PROBLEM QUESTION

Beth owns a house that adjoins a field in which cows are kept. She runs her own business from a room in her house. Recently, the owners of the field have increased the number of cows kept there and have commenced construction of a barn near the boundary with Beth's house. The noise from the construction disturbs Beth during the day as her office overlooks the field and the mooing of the cows disturbs her sleep. Other people in the neighbourhood have also complained about the noise from the cows and the building work. During the construction, a large crane used to move building materials into the field dropped a pallet of bricks, sending debris into Beth's garden and injuring her gardener, Rhys, who was working there at the time. Beth is also aggrieved because the trees in the field are overhanging her driveway, making it difficult for her to park her car without scratching the paintwork.

Discuss claims that Beth may bring in tort. Do not discuss any liability in negligence.

■ Private nuisance

KEY DEFINITION: Private nuisance

'The very essence of private nuisance . . . is the unreasonable use of man of his land to the detriment of his neighbour': *Miller* v *Jackson* [1977] QB 966 (CA).

The definition makes it clear that **private nuisance** focuses around interference with land or property that stems from neighbouring land or property. This can take several forms, as illustrated in Figure 7.1.

This emphasises that the two central characteristics of private nuisance are:

■ protection of land or property and

■ protection from unreasonable interference.

Rights and interests in property

As private nuisance is concerned to protect interests in and enjoyment of land, it was considered fundamental that a person could only enjoy the protection of this tort if he had the right to exclusive possession of the land, e.g. the owner or leaseholder. This placed limitations on the availability of an action in private nuisance as visitors, lodgers and family members were not entitled to claim, so the principle was challenged in the courts. See Figure 7.2.

Figure 7.1

House House

Nuisance may emanate from one residential property and affect another. Remember that there is no requirement for them to be adjoining properties, provided that they are close enough to be affected by the nuisance

Flat

There is no requirement for different buildings, provided there is a separation of exclusive possession. In other words, a nuisance could emanate from one flat and affect another

House Tree

Nuisance must come from land rather than buildings, so it is possible for natural features such as trees to amount to nuisance. It also covers activities that take place on land. Remember that the nuisance may emanate from the house and affect the activity as well as the other way round

House Factory

Nuisance may emanate from commercial or industrial properties but these may also be the subject of nuisance. It is not only residential rights that are protected, so if, for example, subsidence of the residential property affects the commercial property, this may be an actionable nuisance

Park Stadium

Nuisance may involve land with no residential premises. Consider the nature and purpose of the land, for example, the noise from the stadium may be a nuisance in relation to the park, whilst trees from the park could encroach on the stadium

Figure 7.2

Is a proprietary right in the land required for an action in private nuisance?

──── Yes ────   ──── No ────

Malone v *Laskey* [1907] 2 KB 141 (CA)

The claimant was the wife of the leaseholder so was not entitled to exclusive possession in her own right. She was injured when the vibrations from a neighbouring property caused a toilet cistern to fall on her head. Her claim was rejected as she lacked a proprietary interest in the land

Khorasandjian v *Bush* [1993] QB 727 (CA)

The daughter of the property owner was harassed by the defendant. Her action in private nuisance succeeded despite the lack of proprietary interest in the property, probably because there was no clear need for an injunction to protect her and no other basis upon which this could be issued (as the case occurred prior to the Protection from Harassment Act 1997: see Chapter 10)

Hunter v Canary Wharf [1997] AC 655 (HL)

Concerning: interest in land

Facts

Residents in the area of the Canary Wharf development experienced interference with the television signals due to the construction of an 800-foot metal-plated tower. Some of the claimants were homeowners whilst others were family members, lodgers and others without a proprietary interest in the property affected.

Legal principle

The Court of Appeal had ruled that occupation of a home was a sufficient basis for a claim but this was reversed by the House of Lords who reinstated the requirement of a proprietary interest stated in *Malone* v *Laskey* (with the amendment that a wife's beneficial interest in the family home conferred a proprietary right upon her).

This decision restated private nuisance as a tort concerned with property rights and not one which protected against nuisance caused to individuals independently as it can only be brought by a person with rights to exclusive possession of the property such as an owner or tenant (or non-resident landlord if the nuisance is likely to cause permanent damage to his property).

Unreasonable use of land

An actionable nuisance requires that the use of the land which is the source of the nuisance is unreasonable. Remember that foreseeability is an element of reasonableness so that interference with the claimant's quiet enjoyment of land that is a foreseeable result of the defendant's use of his/her own land will be unreasonable. The courts have taken the following factors into account when determining whether or not particular use of land is unreasonable:

- character of the neighbourhood;
- sensitivity of the claimant;
- duration of the nuisance;
- public benefit;
- malice of the defendant.

Character of the neighbourhood

What is reasonable depends upon the location in which it takes place. It might be reasonable to operate a steelworks in an industrial area but not in the midst of a housing development.

The character of the neighbourhood is only a consideration if the nuisance complained of concerns inconvenience to the claimant, e.g. loss of sleep, or loss of enjoyment of property, such as smells that make it unpleasant to sit in the garden. If the nuisance causes physical damage, the character of the neighbourhood is irrelevant: *St Helen's Smelting Co* v *Tippings* (1865) 11 HL Cas 642 (HL) (where acid smuts from the smelting works damaged trees and plants on the claimant's land).

✎ EXAM TIP

Remember that whether something amounts to a nuisance will depend on a range of factors, including the location where it takes place. Examiners may test this knowledge by including an example of a nuisance from case law but varying the nature of the area in which it takes place.

The key point to note here is that 'what would be a nuisance in Belgrave Square would not necessarily be so in Bermondsey' (*Sturges* v *Bridgeman* (1879) 11 Ch D 852 (CA)). Demonstrate understanding by reformulating this principle in contemporary terms: e.g. the noise from factories may be tolerated in a heavily industrial area but not in the countryside.

Sensitivity of the claimant

The existence of nuisance is determined by considering its effect on a reasonable person and ordinary land use. If the claimant was unusually sensitive or was using his own land for an unusual purpose that made it particularly sensitive to disruption, he will not be able to rely on nuisance unless the action complained of would have disturbed a reasonable person.

KEY CASE

Robinson v *Kilvert* (1889) 41 Ch D 88 (CA)

Concerning: sensitivity of the claimant

Facts

The claimant carried out a trade involving heat-sensitive paper. He sought to bring an action in private nuisance against the occupier of the cellar in the same building as the heat from the defendant's trade damaged his paper.

Legal principle

It was held that the reasonable use of land would not become unreasonable merely because it affected someone with a particular sensitivity unless 'it interferes with the ordinary enjoyment of life, or the ordinary use of property for the purposes of residence or business' (*per* Cotton LJ).

Figure 7.3

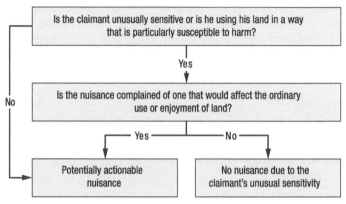

Figure 7.3 demonstrates the questions that need to be addressed to determine whether the claimant fails for unusual sensitivity.

Duration of the nuisance

To be actionable, a nuisance must be continuous. This does not mean that it has to occur all the time without interruption, merely that there must be some continuity to the disturbance; for example, noise from building works every night or smell from a weekly market.

Public benefit

The greater the general utility of the defendant's actions, the less likely it is that it will amount to an actionable nuisance. For example, building works that benefit the community may disturb residents in the immediate vicinity but the public benefit of the work will outweigh the inconvenience to individuals unless other factors make the nuisance unreasonable, such as a failure to take reasonable measures to minimise the interruption to others.

Malice

This is one of the rare occasions in law where malice on the part of the defendant contributes to liability. If the defendant acts out of hostility or spite, his actions are likely to fall within private nuisance even though they would not otherwise amount to an unreasonable use of land. It has been held that it is not 'a legitimate use of the defendant's house to use it for the purpose of vexing and annoying his neighbour' (*Christie* v *Davey* [1893] 1 Ch 316: the defendant banged metal trays and hammered on the wall to disrupt music lessons given by his neighbour).

KEY CASE

Hollywood Silver Fox Farm Ltd v *Emmett* **[1936] 2 KB 468 (DC)**

Concerning: malicious interruption

Facts

The defendant persistently fired his shotgun on his own land in order to disrupt the breeding of foxes on a neighbouring farm as he felt that the fur farm devalued his own land which he was trying to sell.

Legal principle

Whilst it was not unreasonable for a farmer to fire a shotgun on his own land, the fact that the defendant did so with the aim of disrupting the lawful activities of his neighbour changed the character of his actions and rendered them unreasonable and an actionable nuisance.

✎ EXAM TIP

Look out for evidence of ill-will or malice that motivates the defendant's actions. If there is no express motive stated, try to infer one from the surrounding facts. If the facts are ambiguous, remember to present both sides of the argument and note the difference in outcome raised by an adverse motive.

Damage

Private nuisance is not actionable *per se*, thus the claimant must suffer some harm, injury or damage in order to succeed with a claim. In *Hunter* v *Canary Wharf* [1997] 2 All ER 426, Lord Lloyd identified three categories of damage that give rise to an actionable private nuisance; see Figure 7.4.

! Don't be tempted to . . .

Remember to consider all the potential categories of damage that can give rise to actionable private nuisance. In the everyday sense of the word, a 'nuisance' is something that causes irritation or annoyance; in law, a nuisance can result from encroachment, physical injury to land or interference with its enjoyment. Categorise the particular nuisance into one of the *Hunter* categories to demonstrate whether the claimant has suffered some harm, injury or damage sufficient to allow his or her claim to continue.

Figure 7.4

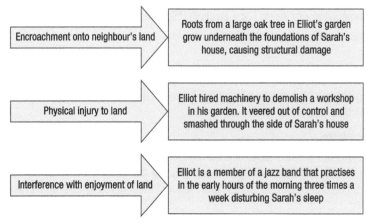

▮ Public nuisance

KEY DEFINITION: Public nuisance

Public nuisance 'materially affects the reasonable comfort and convenience of life of a class of Her Majesty's subjects' (*A-G* v *PYA Quarries Ltd* [1957] 2 QB 169 *per* Romer LJ).

There are two requirements that must be satisfied:

- the nuisance has affected a class of people; and
- the claimant has suffered special damage.

Class of people

There is a fair level of overlap between the sorts of conduct that may be actionable as private and **public nuisance**. The distinction between the torts is based upon the effect of the nuisance, not the nature of the nuisance itself. See Figure 7.5.

It is because a class of people is affected that public nuisance overlaps in terms of civil and criminal activity, hence, many actions are initiated by the Attorney-General. This element of injury and/or disturbance to a group is the key feature that characterises public nuisance.

Figure 7.5

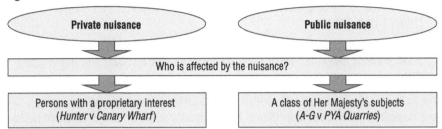

Attorney-General v *PYA Quarries* [1957] 2 QB 169 (CA)

Concerning: class of people

Facts

The process of quarrying was disrupting the local community both in terms of the dust and vibrations caused and also the scattering of splinters of rock and stone around the neighbourhood.

Legal principle

The argument that the nuisance only affected some local people and so lacked a sufficiently public nature was rejected. Lord Denning stated that a public nuisance was one which was so:

> widespread in range or so indiscriminate in its effect that it would not be reasonable to expect one person to take proceedings . . . to put a stop to it but that it should be taken on the responsibility of the community at large.

In *PYA Quarries*, Romer LJ stated that it was a question of fact in each case whether a sufficient number of people were affected by the nuisance to amount to a class of people. The following are examples that have been held to amount to a class of people:

- **local communities,** e.g. the organisation of an 'acid house party' in a field which disturbed local residents: *Ruffell* (1991) 13 Cr App R (S) 204 (CA);

- **groups of individuals with a common interest,** e.g. thousands of spectators at a football match whose enjoyment was impaired by the disablement of the floodlights: *Ong* [2001] 1 Cr App R (S) 117 (CA);

- **users of a public highway,** e.g. all drivers potentially endangered by flying golf balls: *Castle* v *St Augustine's Links* (1922) 38 TLR 615 (DC);

- **small groups of people with common characteristics,** e.g. 13 female recipients of obscene telephone calls within a particular geographic region of the country: *Johnson* [1997] 1 WLR 367 (CA);

- **indirect impact on the community,** e.g. hoax calls to emergency services that diverted public services away from those with genuine need: *Lowrie* [2005] 1 Cr App R (S) 95 (CA).

The House of Lords has doubted whether cases such as *Johnson*, involving nuisance to a number of individuals rather than to the community at large, should fall within public nuisance.

KEY CASE

R v *Rimmington* [2006] 1 AC 459 (HL)

Concerning: class of people

Facts

The defendant sent racially abusive letters to 538 people.

Legal principle

The House of Lords accepted the defendant's argument that public nuisance should not be used for conduct which is also covered by a statutory offence unless there was good reason for doing so (in this case, the conduct would have fallen within section 1 of the Malicious Communications Act 1988). Moreover, public nuisance should not be used as a means to deal with conduct that was directed at several individuals rather than at the community more generally.

 Make your answer stand out

Rimmington is an important case that has immense implications for the operation of public nuisance. A detailed analysis of its implications can be found in Goldberg and Grant's (2005) article, which would make useful reading. Remember that case commentaries can help you to get to grips with the implications of a case, so have a look at Ashworth's (2006) commentary on *Rimmington*.

Special damage

Although public nuisance requires inconvenience to a class of people, an action can only be brought if a particular individual (or individuals) suffers damage over and above the general inconvenience caused to the class (see Figure 7.6).

Figure 7.6

Road safety campaigners take direct action to slow down motorists on a dangerous stretch of road by digging a trench across it in the night. Can motorists Paul and Tom bring an action in public nuisance?

Paul cannot get past the trench and has to take a detour to work, arriving 30 minutes late and getting into trouble with his employer	Tom attempts to edge his small car around the end of the trench but the edge crumbles and his car is damaged
No public nuisance Paul suffers the same harm (delays in his journey) as all other members of the class affected by the nuisance (road users)	**Actionable public nuisance** Tom has suffered additional damage over and above the delays suffered by the other members of the affected class

This requirement limits the multitude of claims that would succeed if public nuisance was actionable on the basis of interference only (just as private nuisance is limited by the requirement of a proprietary interest).

The following kinds of damage fall within the scope of public nuisance:

- personal injury, discomfort or inconvenience;
- damage to property;
- economic loss.

> **□ REVISION NOTE**
>
> Damages that fall within public nuisance must still satisfy the requirement of reasonable foreseeability outlined in *Overseas Tankship (UK) Ltd* v *Morts Dock and Engineering Co Ltd* (*The Wagon Mound*), which is covered in detail in Chapter 3.

■ Defences

In addition to the general defences outlined in Chapter 13, the following defences are applicable to both public and private nuisance except prescription which is applicable to private nuisance only:

- effective defences: prescription, statutory authority;
- ineffective defences: coming to the nuisance, public benefit, acts of others.

Effective defences

These are defences which are available and which allow the defendant to escape liability for the nuisance completely.

Prescription

A defence of prescription is effectively a claim that the defendant has acquired the right to act in a way that constitutes a private nuisance because he has done so for 20 years without interruption.

Sturges v *Bridgman* [1879] LR 11 Ch D 852 (CA)

Concerning: prescriptive right

Facts

The defendant had been carrying on a confectionery business that involved the use of noisy equipment that created strong vibrations for more than 20 years. The doctor who owned the adjacent house was unable to use his newly built consulting room because of the noise and vibration.

Legal principle

This was an actionable nuisance that was not negated by prescription because the nuisance only started once the consulting room was built. The time period commences not from the start of the act in general but from the start of it becoming a nuisance.

✎ EXAM TIP

The distinction in *Sturges* v *Bridgman* is an important one. Remember to consider how long the action has been causing a nuisance rather than how long it has been going on.

Statutory authority

If the defendant's conduct was authorised by statute, it is likely to provide a defence against claims of nuisance. Some statutes specifically state that they preclude the possibility of action for nuisance, e.g. the Civil Aviation Act 1982 provides that a claim cannot lie in nuisance or trespass in relation to aircraft flying over land.

This also covers planning permission (which is granted under delegated powers exercised by local authorities) thus authorised development will not constitute an actionable nuisance unless undertaken in an unreasonable manner: *Wheeler* v *JJ Saunders Ltd* [1996] Ch 19 (CA).

Ineffective defences

These are frequently raised arguments that are ineffectual as defences to nuisance.

Why would we include a section on ineffective defences that can never succeed? The answer is that they are frequently argued as defences to nuisance so it is important to be aware of them in order to reject them as ineffective.

Coming to the nuisance

Unless prescription authorises the nuisance, it is no defence to argue that it has carried on for a long time without attracting complaint. This is often used in situations when the claimant has actually moved into the vicinity of a nuisance that was already well established.

 Make your answer stand out

Do you think that the law has struck the right balance between competing interests here? Consider the following situation: Joe has been running quad-biking events on his land for five years. His previous neighbour did not object but Chris, who moved to the area two months ago, wants an injunction to stop the activity, claiming that the constant noise causes him anxiety. Where do you think that fairness lies? The current law would protect Chris's right to quiet enjoyment of his house without taking into account the well-established nature of Joe's business and the fact that Chris chose to live next door. Why do you think that the law takes this approach? One argument is that it would be unreasonable for Chris not to purchase the house of his choice merely because Joe is already acting unreasonably next door.

Remember that a critical approach to the current law can be a real strength in essays but be sure to present a balanced and objective argument.

Public benefit

The purpose of the defendant's actions is relevant to determination of its reasonableness and certainly action that is for the public good is less likely to be considered unreasonable than an action with a limited range of beneficiaries. This does not mean that a defendant can cite public benefit as a defence to a nuisance claim.

Actions of others

A defendant cannot argue that his action in isolation would not amount to a nuisance if he has knowingly taken part in a collective nuisance, e.g. one performer at an unauthorised music festival that disrupts local residents.

■ Remedies

Damages and injunctions

The principal remedies for nuisance are damages and **injunctions**. Damages are available to compensate a claimant for physical damage to his land and in relation to personal discomfort and inconvenience. Generally, an injunction will not be granted if damages are awarded. Given the need to balance the interests of the claimant and defendant, an injunction may reflect this by limiting the nuisance rather than prohibiting it entirely. For example, in *Kennaway* v *Thompson* [1981] QB 88 (CA), the court granted an injunction limiting the times at which the defendant could hold watersports events.

For damages awarded in lieu of an injunction, see *Watson* v *Croft Promo-Sport Ltd* [2009] 3 All ER 249 (CA).

📖 **REVISION NOTE**

The main remedies for trespass to land, as with so many other torts, are damages and injunctions, covered in Chapter 14. It would be useful to take a moment to refresh your memory and consider the way that these remedies operate in relation to nuisance.

Abatement

Abatement, or self-help, involves the removal of the nuisance by the claimant. In other words, the claimant rectifies the nuisance himself. As this usually involves the entry of the claimant onto the defendant's land, it generally requires prior notification unless there is an emergency situation (or if the situation can be abated without entry onto the defendant's land). If the criteria for the defence are not satisfied, the claimant may be liable for trespass to land if he enters the defendant's property.

■ Putting it all together

Answer guidelines

See the problem question at the start of the chapter. A diagram illustrating how to structure your answer is available on the companion website.

Approaching the question

This is a typical example of a problem question involving nuisance. Make sure that you follow the instructions as it is made clear that negligence should not be discussed. This is quite a usual instruction as there is often a separate question on negligence on the exam paper and examiners want to stop students repeating the same material in a second question. Note also that you are asked only to consider claims that Beth could make, so do not consider whether Rhys may have a claim in tort as there are no marks available for this.

Important points to include

- Take some time to plan your answer before you start writing. Make a list of potential claims so that you can see from the start how much work you have to do to answer the question.

- Beth may claim in private nuisance for the noise caused by the cows that interrupts her sleep and for the building works that interrupt her work during the day. It might be preferable to deal with these issues separately.

- There may be a claim in public nuisance as others in the neighbourhood are affected by the construction work.

- Beth may claim for trespass to land in relation to the debris dropped from the crane.

- Beth may have a claim in either private nuisance or trespass to land in relation to the trees overhanging her driveway.

- Beth's claim in relation to the noise made by the cows requires a methodical assessment of potential liability for private nuisance. Try following the structure suggested in this chapter. (1) Does the claimant have sufficient proprietary interest to bring a claim? Beth is the owner of the house so this is straightforward. (2) Is the defendant's conduct unreasonable? This is tricky. Is keeping cows in a field unreasonable? Consider factors such as the number of cows in relation to the size of the field and the character of the neighbourhood: it will depend on whether this is a residential or rural area. (3) Are any defences available? You could consider whether the cows have been in the field for 20 years but remember that it is only recently since the number of cows has increased that Beth has been disturbed. (4) What remedies are available if Beth is successful? It is likely that she will want an injunction to prevent the continuance of the nuisance.

- Follow the same approach in relation to the building work that disturbs her during the day. The key issue here will be the reasonableness of the defendant's actions, so be sure to take the relevant factors listed in the chapter into account. ▶

- The claim for public nuisance hinges on whether or not 'other people in the neighbourhood' amount to a 'class of people'. Make reference to the definition from *PYA Quarries* and look for similar situations in case law. Remember, however, the implications of the House of Lords' decision in *Rimmington* to the effect that it must be the public that is affected rather than a collection of individuals.

- The key point to remember here is that private nuisance and trespass to land are mutually exclusive, so you will have to conclude that one or the other is relevant here and explain that decision. As this is a one-off incident rather than a continuing problem, the appropriate basis for action in relation to the debris would be trespass to land (see Chapter 9).

- This issue reappears in relation to the overhanging branches. Do not be tempted into concluding that this is a private nuisance because it is ongoing as this tort also requires some harm to be caused and it is questionable whether that is satisfied here unless her car has actually been damaged (the facts are ambiguous on this point: it is hard to park without scratching the car but perhaps she has nonetheless managed to do so). If there is no harm suffered, then an action in trespass to land is actionable *per se* (without need for injury) so will be more appropriate.

 Make your answer stand out

Do not overlook the claim for public nuisance. The question specifies that you should discuss claims that Beth could bring but that does not exclude public nuisance. Remember, though, that it must be established that Beth has suffered some special damage in order to bring a claim.

Do not overlook defences and remedies when answering the question. Too many students concentrate on establishing liability without considering whether the defendant had a defence that would lead to a contrary outcome or what remedies the claimant is likely to want. This point can attract additional credit from the examiners, especially if combined with careful use of the facts to present a balanced argument. For example, Beth may only resort to abatement of the nuisance in relation to the overhanging branches if she gives advance notice or there is an emergency.

READ TO IMPRESS

Ashworth, A. (2006) Public nuisance: elements of offence – requirement of public inquiry. *Criminal Law Review*, p. 153.

Cane, P. (1997) What a nuisance! *Law Quarterly Review*, p. 515.

Goldberg, J. and Grant, G. (2005) Public nuisance, the Orthodox Jew and the racist. 155, *New Law Journal*, p. 1856.

Lee, M. (2003) What is private nuisance? 119, *Law Quarterly Review*, p. 298.

Murphy, J. (2004) The merits of *Rylands v Fletcher*. 24, *Oxford Journal of Legal Studies*, p. 643 (see also Chapter 8; this article covers aspects of nuisance as well).

www.pearsoned.co.uk/lawexpress

 Go online to access more revision support including quizzes to test your knowledge, sample questions with answer guidelines, podcasts you can download, and more!

Rylands v *Fletcher*

8

Revision checklist

Essential points you should know:

- [ ] The elements that must be established for an action under *Rylands* v *Fletcher* to be successful
- [ ] The defences that may be used to avoid liability
- [ ] The relevance of recent case law that explored *Rylands* v *Fletcher*
- [ ] The relationship between *Rylands* v *Fletcher* and other torts

■ Topic map

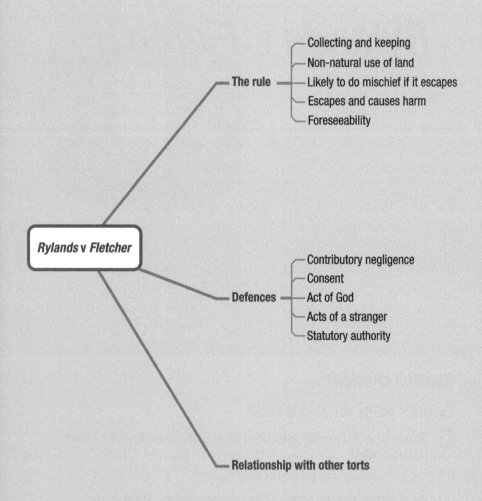

- The rule
  - Collecting and keeping
  - Non-natural use of land
  - Likely to do mischief if it escapes
  - Escapes and causes harm
  - Foreseeability

Rylands v *Fletcher*

- Defences
  - Contributory negligence
  - Consent
  - Act of God
  - Acts of a stranger
  - Statutory authority

- Relationship with other torts

A printable version of this topic map is available from **www.pearsoned.co.uk/lawexpress**

■ Introduction

The position of *Rylands* v *Fletcher* in tort law is somewhat anomalous as it is not often used as a basis for liability and questions have been asked about its role in modern tort law.

This tort stems from a ruling in the case of the same name and has survived for over a hundred years despite the doubts expressed about it. It has survived scrutiny by the House of Lords and so continues to exist as a separate basis of tortious liability (although it was said *obiter* that it was a manifestation of private nuisance). The uncertainty surrounding this tort makes it a topic that necessitates careful consideration but it is a topic that has attracted a great deal of academic comment so there will be no shortage of articles that look at this tort from a number of different perspectives.

ASSESSMENT ADVICE

Essay questions

Essay questions dealing with *Rylands* v *Fletcher* are quite common as it has been the subject of examination by the House of Lords in recent years. Questions tend to focus on the tort's relationship with negligence, nuisance and **trespass to land** and ask whether there is a role for *Rylands* v *Fletcher* in modern tort law.

Problem questions

Problem questions may include an issue relating to *Rylands* v *Fletcher* in order to test your ability to differentiate this from other property-based torts. Look out for a situation in which the defendant has taken something onto land which has escaped and caused harm as that should trigger a consideration of *Rylands* v *Fletcher*. Remember that there is a great deal of overlap with negligence, private nuisance and trespass to land, so it would be useful to treat these as a collective group of revision topics.

■ Sample question

Could you answer this question? Below is a typical essay question that could arise on this topic. Guidelines on answering the question are included at the end of this chapter, whilst a sample problem question and guidance on tackling it can be found on the companion website.

■ The rule in *Rylands* v *Fletcher*

Rylands v *Fletcher* was a case in which damage was caused by the escape of water from a reservoir that flooded a mine. The principle formulated in the case has continued to survive as the basis for tortious liability despite criticisms from the judiciary and academic commentators.

KEY CASE

Rylands v *Fletcher* [1868] LR 3 HL 330 (HL)

Concerning: liability for harm caused by the escape of things brought onto land

Facts

The defendant engaged independent contractors to construct a reservoir to supply water to his mill. This was built over abandoned mine shafts which collapsed due to the weight of the water, causing water to flood into the claimant's colliery. The defendant had not been negligent and there was no basis for a claim in private nuisance as the defendant had taken reasonable care to select a competent and experienced independent contractor.

Legal principle

The defendant's liability was established on the basis that 'the person who for his own purposes brings on his land and collects and keeps there anything likely to do mischief if it escapes, must keep it at his peril, and, if he does not do so, is *prima facie* answerable for all the damage which is the natural consequence of its escape' (*per* Blackburn J at 279 in the Court of Exchequer). This was approved on appeal to the House of Lords with Lord Cairns describing the required use of land as 'non-natural use' (at 339).

This principle can be broken down into its composite elements, each of which will be examined in more detail in the sections that follow:

- collecting and keeping on land;
- non-natural use of land;

- likely to do mischief if it escapes;
- escapes and causes harm to property.

Collecting and keeping

In *Rylands* v *Fletcher*, the defendant collected water on his land and kept it there in a reservoir. The principle requires that something be brought onto the land by the defendant: liability cannot be established if something that occurs naturally on the land escapes and causes harm.

It is important to remember that the thing that is collected and kept on the land might be the thing that escapes (as in *Rylands* v *Fletcher* where it was water brought onto the land and water that escapes) but that this is not a requirement for liability. It may be that the thing that is collected and kept on the land causes something else to escape:

- *Miles* v *Forest Rock Granite Co (Leicestershire) Ltd* (1918) 34 TLR 500 (CA): explosives were collected and kept on the defendant's land in relation to his quarrying business but it was the rocks freed by the explosion that escaped from the land.
- *LMS International* v *Styrene Packaging and Insulation Ltd* [2005] EWHC 2065 (TCC): the defendant's business involved cutting polystyrene blocks with hot wire. The polystyrene was collected and kept on the premises but it was fire caused by the hot wire that escaped.

Non-natural use of land

The non-natural use of land in *Rylands* v *Fletcher* was the construction of a reservoir. The meaning of 'non-natural use' has been explored in case law.

In *Rickards* v *Lothian* [1913] AC 263 (PC) it was held that water escaping from an overflow pipe could not be described as non-natural use of land as this required 'some special use bringing with it increased danger to others . . . not ordinary use of land' (*per* Lord Moulton at 280).

This was confirmed in *Read* v *J Lyons & Co Ltd* [1947] AC 156 (HL) where it was acknowledged that 'what may be regarded as dangerous or non-natural will vary according to the circumstances' taking into account the 'circumstances of the time and the practice of mankind' (*per* Lord Porter at 176).

This change in the way that any particular use of land is categorised as either ordinary or dangerous is illustrated in *Musgrove* v *Pandelis* [1919] 2 KB 43 (CA) where it was held that storage of a car with petrol in its tank in a garage was a danger, and therefore non-natural use of land, thus the defendant was liable under *Rylands* v *Fletcher* when the fuel ignited and fire spread to neighbouring properties. It is inconceivable that keeping a car in a garage would be considered as anything other than ordinary in today's society.

KEY CASE

Transco plc v *Stockport MBC* **[2004] 2 AC 1 (HL)**

Concerning: non-natural use of land, contemporary circumstances

Facts

Escape of water from a pipe owned by the defendant local authority caused an embankment to collapse, which exposed a gas pipe, thus necessitating expensive emergency remedial work by the claimant.

Legal principle

The House of Lords did not accept that this fell within the scope of *Rylands* v *Fletcher* on the basis that the supply of water through pipes was normal and routine and not something that presented a particular hazard. The risk presented by any particular activity had to be considered by contemporary standards. As the pipe carried no more risk of fracture leading to the escape of water than any other pipe, it could not be considered a non-natural use of land. Lord Hoffmann noted that damage to property caused by leaking water was a risk against which insurance was available, which supported the conclusion that this situation did not meet the high threshold of exceptional risk arising from non-natural use that is required if a claim under *Rylands* v *Fletcher* is to succeed.

 Make your answer stand out

Transco is an important case because the House of Lords engaged in a thorough review of the cases in which *Rylands* v *Fletcher* had been applied and gave detailed consideration to the operation of this tort in modern society. All five Law Lords explored these issues and familiarity with their views would be useful for inclusion in an essay question on the topic. In addition to reading the case, you might find it helpful to read commentaries on the case such as Bagshaw's (2004) commentary or articles which consider the impact of the case. For example, Nolan's (2005) article considers how *Rylands* v *Fletcher* sits in relation to negligence and nuisance following the restatement of the rule in *Transco*.

Murphy (2004) seeks to defend the rule in *Rylands* v *Fletcher* arguing that it is quite distinct from private nuisance and futher that it would be wrong to abandon it in favour of a more expansive law of negligence.

! **Don't be tempted to . . .**

Don't oversimplify the meaning of non-natural use of land. This is a concept that has been well developed in case law and it is important that you use the common law precedents to support your position on whether or not a particular use of land is natural or otherwise.

Likely to do mischief if it escapes

This requirement emphasises that the thing collected and kept on land need not be dangerous in itself provided that it is likely to cause harm if it escapes. In *Rylands* v *Fletcher*, the water was not dangerous when it was contained in the reservoir but it was dangerous when it escaped. Other examples of this include:

- *Jones* v *Festiniog Railway* (1867–8) LR 3 QB 733 (DC): a passenger train emitted sparks which set fire to the claimant's haystack.
- *West* v *Bristol Tramways Co* [1908] 2 KB 14 (CA): wood paving used by the defendant was coated in creosote; the fumes from this damaged a neighbour's plants and shrubs.
- *Hillier* v *Air Ministry*, *The Times*, 8 December 1962: the Air Ministry laid electricity cables under the claimant's field; several years later, 19 of the 50 cows in the field were electrocuted simultaneously when electricity escaped from the cables.
- *Crowhurst* v *Amersham Burial Board* (1878–9) LR 4 Ex D 5 (DC): yew trees were planted in the defendant's cemetery but the branches hung into a neighbouring field and were eaten by the claimant's horse which died.

Escapes and causes harm

If the thing that has been brought onto the defendant's land escapes and causes harm, liability under *Rylands* v *Fletcher* will be complete (unless the defendant can rely upon a defence) provided that harm is caused to the claimant's property.

There was case law that suggested that a claimant could recover under *Rylands* v *Fletcher* for personal injury but it is now generally accepted that such claims should be brought under negligence and that *Rylands* v *Fletcher* should only be used in relation to claims for damage to property or damage to interests in property.

Foreseeability

One aspect of the requirement that the escape causes harm that needs to be addressed is whether the potential for harm needs to be foreseeable. In *Rylands* v *Fletcher*, it was clear that the tort was intended to be one of **strict liability**, i.e. if something escaped from land and caused harm, the defendant would be liable even if this was not something that he could have predicted or guarded against. This aspect of the tort was examined by the House of Lords in the *Cambridge Water* case:

KEY CASE

Cambridge Water Co v *Eastern Counties Leather plc* [1994] 2 AC 264 (HL)

Concerning: non-natural use, foreseeability of damage

Facts

The defendant company was a leather manufacturer which used chemical solvents in the tanning process. These chemicals were stored in drums on the defendant's premises. Following new European regulations, tests were carried out on the claimant's water and it was found to be polluted by the chemicals from the tannery as spillages had leaked into the water. At first instance, the claim based on *Rylands* v *Fletcher* was dismissed on the basis that there was not a non-natural use of land due to the amount of time that the tannery had been in operation and the industrial area in which it was located. The Court of Appeal rejected this argument and held that the storage of chemicals was a non-natural use of land and found the defendant liable for the damage caused on a strict liability basis. This issue was reconsidered by the House of Lords.

Legal principle

Lord Goff examined the precise wording of Blackburn J in *Rylands* v *Fletcher*, identifying phrases such as 'anything *likely* to do mischief if it escapes', 'something he *knows* to be mischievous' and 'liability for natural and *anticipated* consequences' (at 302, Lord Goff's emphasis) as evidence that *Rylands* v *Fletcher* required 'at least foreseeability of the risk' as a prerequisite to recovery of damages. He went on to say that the tort was strict liability only in the sense that the defendant would be liable for the consequences of escape even if he had taken steps to prevent it occurring. Lord Goff made reference to *Wagon Mound (No 1)* and concluded that *Rylands* v *Fletcher* required foreseeability by the defendant of the relevant type of damage (at 304).

Applying this principle, as the defendant in the *Cambridge Water* case had not foreseen that chemicals would seep through the floor and contaminate water supplies, there could be no liability under *Rylands* v *Fletcher*.

 Make your answer stand out

In *Cambridge Water*, the House of Lords considered the role and operation of *Rylands* v *Fletcher* and the decision attracted a great deal of academic comment. It would be useful preparation for an essay question to explore some of the different responses to the *Cambridge Water* case: for example, Ghandi (1994) concludes by saying that *Cambridge Water* 'sealed the fate of an already moribund tort' whilst Mullender and Dolding (1995) criticise the case as 'one-sided' for failing to take account of the need to impose liability for environmental pollution.

You might find it helpful to use the diagram in Figure 8.1 to apply the elements of *Rylands* v *Fletcher*.

Figure 8.1

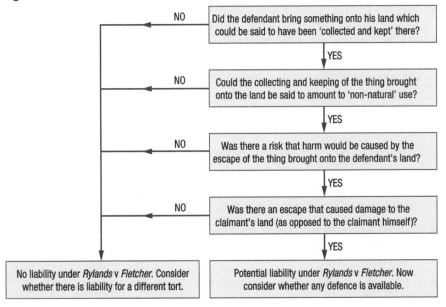

▨ Defences

Once the elements of *Rylands* v *Fletcher* have been established, it is important to consider whether the defendant has a defence which will allow him to avoid or, in the case of contributory negligence, reduce liability:

- **Contributory negligence:** if the claimant was partly to blame for the damage to his property, e.g. by failing to take proper precautions against the sort of harm which occurred, any award of damages may be reduced to reflect this. Contributory negligence is covered in greater detail in Chapter 13.

- **Consent:** if the claimant expressly or impliedly consented to the collecting and keeping of the thing that escaped, he cannot then hold the defendant liable for the consequences of the escape.

- **Act of God:** this relates to unforeseeable natural circumstances that cause the escape. For example, if heavy flooding had caused the water to escape in *Rylands* v *Fletcher*, there would have been scope to argue that the flooding was caused by an act of God.

- **Acts of a stranger:** if an unknown third party takes action which leads to the escape then the defendant will avoid liability. For example, in *Rickards* v *Lothian* [1913] AC 263 (PC), the flood was caused by a third party blocking the outlet and turning on the taps.

- **Statutory authority:** it may be that the defendant's actions are authorised by statute, in which case he will not be liable, provided that he has acted in line with statutory requirements.

▍Relationship with other torts

It is sometimes argued that *Rylands* v *Fletcher* does not play a useful role in modern tort law because it does not cover any situation that is not already covered by other torts:

- In *Burnie Port Authority* v *General Jones Pty* [1994] 68 ALJ 331, the Australian High Court stated that *Rylands* v *Fletcher* should be considered as subsumed within the law of negligence.

- In *Cambridge Water*, Lord Goff commented that *Rylands* v *Fletcher* was a species of private negligence.

- In *RHM Bakeries* v *Strathclyde Regional Council* (1985) SLT 214 (HL), the House of Lords ruled that *Rylands* v *Fletcher* has 'no place in Scots law'.

□ REVISION NOTE

Make sure that you have a grasp of the elements of negligence, private nuisance and trespass to land so that you understand how these torts can be compared to *Rylands* v *Fletcher*.

In light of these views, it is important to consider the extent to which *Rylands* v *Fletcher* does overlap with other torts to determine whether it covers any unique ground so that a claimant could be left unprotected if the tort no longer existed.

	Rylands v *Fletcher*	Negligence	Private nuisance	Trespass to land
Who can claim?	A person whose land or property is harmed by the escape of a dangerous thing	A person who has suffered personal harm or harm to property as a result of a breach of duty of care	A person with a proprietary interest in land who has suffered interference with the quiet enjoyment of land	A person in possession of land who suffers unjustified and direct interference with that land
Who is liable?	The person responsible for the land from which the dangerous thing escaped	The person whose breach of duty of care caused the injury or harm	The person in control of the land from which the nuisance emanates	The person who interferes with the land affected by the trespass
Type of interference?	Direct or indirect harm caused to land or property on the land	Any damage to property or personal injury caused by the breach of duty	Indirect harm in terms of interference with quiet enjoyment of land	Any direct intrusion onto land by a person or property
Harm and/or fault required?	Traditionally seen as strict liability but foreseeability requirement stated in *Cambridge Water*. Requires harm to property	Requires breach of duty and foresight of consequences. Covers harm to person and property	Requires unreasonable use of land which resembles a fault requirement. Harm required	The interference with land must be intentional. It is actionable *per se* (without need for damage)

It is fair to say that *Rylands* v *Fletcher* does cover a narrow band of conduct that is not covered by the other torts but that this has been limited even further by the foreseeability requirement stated by the House of Lords in *Cambridge Water*. In essence, *Rylands* v *Fletcher* imposes liability for harm caused by something emanating from the defendant's land that was brought onto that land by the defendant and which had the potential to cause harm if it escaped. *Cambridge Water* adds the requirement that the risk of escape and damage was foreseeable.

> **!** **Don't be tempted to . . .**
>
> You must pay attention to the relationship between *Rylands* and other torts. This is particularly important if you are required to consider whether or not *Rylands* still has a place as a particular tort itself or whether the situations it specifically covers are already dealt with by other torts. This is a tricky area, so take time to think through the similarities and differences with negligence, private nuisance and trespass to land.

■ Putting it all together

Answer guidelines

See the essay question at the start of the chapter.

Approaching the question

This is a typical essay that asks whether there is still a role for *Rylands* v *Fletcher* in tort. In order to tackle this question, you must be able to explain the scope of the tort, taking into account how this may have changed as a result of recent judicial scrutiny and explain how it relates to other torts that protect property such as negligence, private nuisance and trespass to land.

Important points to include

- Start by outlining the nature of tortious liability under *Rylands* v *Fletcher* and the elements of the tort that must be satisfied in order for liability to be established. Make sure that this does not involve too much descriptive detail as there is more to this question than simply describing *Rylands* v *Fletcher*. Too much description will weaken the focus of your essay. Keep in touch with the question: you were asked about the role of *Rylands* v *Fletcher* so make sure you explain what purpose it serves and give some examples of the sorts of conduct that is covered by this tort.
- Consider how *Rylands* v *Fletcher* overlaps with other torts that also provide protection against damage or harm to property:
  - □ **Negligence:** outline the basis of liability for negligence in a couple of sentences, pointing out that it covers damage caused as a result of a breach of duty of care.

Remember that this is not the place for a lengthy description of negligence: make sure that you capture the essence of the tort in a few lines and then get straight back to the main focus of the essay.

☐ **Private nuisance:** point out that the House of Lords in *Cambridge Water* suggested that *Rylands* v *Fletcher* was subsumed within nuisance and consider whether this is a reasonable statement. For example, private nuisance requires that interference with land is continuous or ongoing whereas liability under *Rylands* v *Fletcher* can be established on the basis of a single incident.

☐ **Trespass to land:** similarly, consider what features distinguish the two torts. For example, trespass to land is actionable *per se* whereas *Rylands* v *Fletcher* requires proof of harm or damage.

■ Make sure that you bring your essay back to the question asked in the conclusion. In the light of what you have discussed, is there a role for *Rylands* v *Fletcher* in tort law in England and Wales? Your answer to this question will depend on the points that you have discussed in the body of your essay.

 Make your answer stand out

When explaining how each tort differs from *Rylands* v *Fletcher*, illustrate your essay by using an example of a situation that would fall within *Rylands* v *Fletcher* but not the other tort.

You could use examples from case law if you can call them to mind or you could make up hypothetical examples to demonstrate your understanding. For example, you might say that if Holly threw snails into her next-door neighbour's garden, this would amount to trespass to land as it is a direct and deliberate interference with the neighbour's property. However, if Holly had a snail farm that she kept in her shed from which 50 snails escaped, there might be a basis for a *Rylands* v *Fletcher* claim if the snails made their way into the neighbour's garden and damaged their vegetables.

READ TO IMPRESS

Bagshaw, R. (2004) Rylands confined. *Law Quarterly Review*, p. 388.

Ghandi, P. (1994) Requiem for *Rylands* v *Fletcher*. *Conveyancer*, p. 309.

Mullender, R. and Dolding, L. (1995) Environmental law: notions of strict liability. *Journal of Business Law*, p. 93.

Murphy, J. (2004) The merits of *Rylands* v *Fletcher*. 24, *Oxford Journal of Legal Studies*, p. 643.

Nolan, D. (2005) The distinctiveness of *Rylands* v *Fletcher*. *Law Quarterly Review*, p. 421.

www.pearsoned.co.uk/lawexpress

Go online to access more revision support including quizzes to test your knowledge, sample questions with answer guidelines, podcasts you can download, and more!

Trespass to land

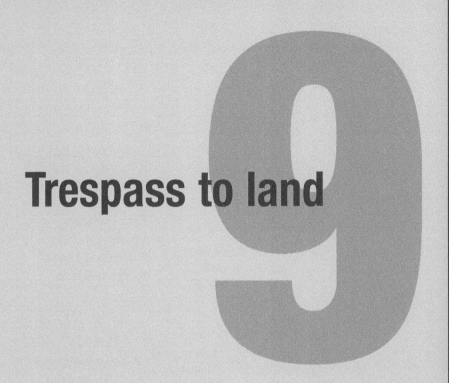

Revision checklist

Essential points you should know:

☐ The nature of trespass to land and its composite elements

☐ Definitions of key concepts such as land, possession and trespass *ab initio*

☐ The relationship between trespass to land and other torts such as nuisance

☐ The availability of defences and remedies

■ Topic map

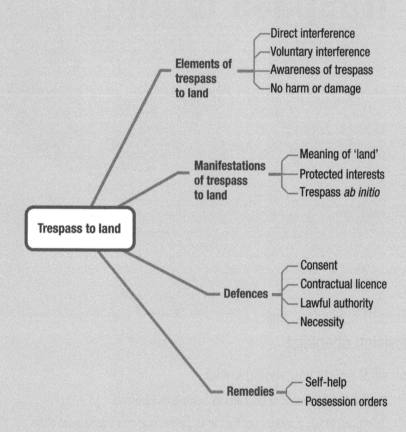

Elements of trespass to land
- Direct interference
- Voluntary interference
- Awareness of trespass
- No harm or damage

Manifestations of trespass to land
- Meaning of 'land'
- Protected interests
- Trespass *ab initio*

Trespass to land

Defences
- Consent
- Contractual licence
- Lawful authority
- Necessity

Remedies
- Self-help
- Possession orders

A printable version of this topic map is available from **www.pearsoned.co.uk/lawexpress**

■ Introduction

Trespass to land is a tort concerned with the prevention of interference with the possession of land.

It tends to be a misunderstood tort, possibly due to the prevalence of misleading notices stating that 'trespassers will be prosecuted' which suggest that it is a criminal offence when this is not (usually) the case. As with any tort that has a commonly understood but legally inaccurate meaning, it is important to approach the revision of this topic with a lawyer's mind to avoid reliance on inaccurate assumptions about the law.

As trespass to land is actionable *per se* (without proof of damage), it can be easy to establish. This means it may be an effective way of establishing tortious liability if other avenues fail, so plays a valuable role in tort law.

ASSESSMENT ADVICE

Essay questions

Essay questions on trespass to land are rare as it is not a complex topic. It is most likely to arise as a more general essay question that looks at how tort protects property rights, in which case you would need to be able to discuss trespass to land in conjunction with other torts, such as private nuisance.

Problem questions

Problem questions are also unlikely to deal exclusively with trespass to land but the topic does crop up frequently as part of a problem question dealing with other torts. Look out for any suggestion that there has been an encroachment onto land by a person or property to trigger a discussion of this topic.

■ Sample question

Could you answer this question? Below is a typical problem question that could arise on this topic. Guidelines on answering the question are included at the end of the chapter, whilst a sample essay question and guidance on tackling it can be found on the companion website.

■ Elements of trespass to land

KEY DEFINITION: Trespass to land

A direct and 'unjustified interference with the possession of land . . . whether or not the entrant knows that he is trespassing'. (Rogers, W.V.H. (2002) *Winfield and Jolowicz on Tort*, 16th edn, London: Sweet & Maxwell, p. 487.)

Trespass to land has four elements which require further exploration:

- There must be direct interference with the land.
- The interference must be voluntary.
- The defendant need not be aware that they are trespassing.
- There is no requirement for harm or damage.

Direct interference

As with all trespass torts, interference with the land must be direct. It is this requirement that is a key means of differentiating between trespass to land and other torts such as nuisance and negligence; see Figure 9.1.

Figure 9.1

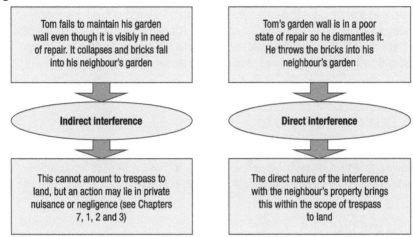

Voluntary interference

It has long been established that a person must enter another's land voluntarily to be liable for trespass: *Stone* v *Smith* (1647) Style 65. A person who is pushed or thrown onto land is not there voluntarily so cannot be liable but the person who pushed him there may be liable. For example, if Adam pushes Ben into Karen's garden, it is Adam who is liable for trespass not Ben.

Awareness of trespass

Although the entry onto the land must be voluntary, there is no requirement that the defendant is aware that he is trespassing by doing so. This gives rise to the possibility of innocent trespass if the defendant is mistaken about the ownership of land or about the availability of permission: *Conway* v *George Wimpey & Co* [1951] 2 KB 266 (CA).

No harm or damage

Trespass to land is actionable *per se* (without any requirement for harm). This is because it is a tort which protects land against interference by allowing the owner to exclude other people and property rather than compensating for damage caused to property.

✎ **EXAM TIP**

Remember that trespass to land is a continuing tort. This means that fresh liability arises as long as the tortious conduct continues. For example, if Mark places a ladder on Dawn's land, he is liable for trespass at that point in time and will incur further liability if he subsequently refuses to remove the ladder upon Dawn's request.

! Don't be tempted to . . .

Don't automatically look for harm or damage to land in order to establish liability for trespass to land. It is actionable *per se* (of itself), so there is no need for there to be damage or injury as there would be, for example, in nuisance.

Manifestations of trespass to land

Trespass to land can be satisfied in four distinct ways (Figure 9.2). It is important to note these as they create far broader scope for the tort than you might expect.

Figure 9.2

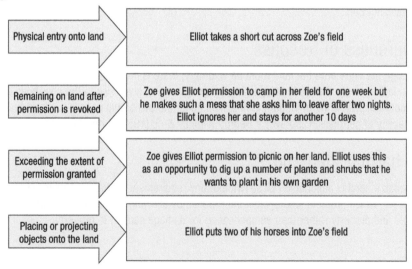

Physical entry onto land	Elliot takes a short cut across Zoe's field
Remaining on land after permission is revoked	Zoe gives Elliot permission to camp in her field for one week but he makes such a mess that she asks him to leave after two nights. Elliot ignores her and stays for another 10 days
Exceeding the extent of permission granted	Zoe gives Elliot permission to picnic on her land. Elliot uses this as an opportunity to dig up a number of plants and shrubs that he wants to plant in his own garden
Placing or projecting objects onto the land	Elliot puts two of his horses into Zoe's field

There are also three concepts that must be understood in order to appreciate the scope of trespass to land and to ensure that you recognise it when it arises:

- the meaning of 'land';
- the interest in land which is protected;
- trespass *ab initio*.

Meaning of 'land'

'Soil' and 'property' are commonly used synonyms for 'land' but the definition adopted in relation to trespass is far broader. It includes not only the soil itself and any property built upon it as well as temporary structures and plants but also, with limits, the airspace above the land and the subsoil below the ground.

KEY CASE

Bernstein v *Skyviews and General Ltd* [1978] QB 479 (DC)

Concerning: airspace; land

Facts

The defendant took aerial photographs of houses and offered them for sale to the owners. The claimant objected to this and claimed that the defendant had trespassed on his airspace in order to take the photograph.

Legal principle

It was held that the defendant had flown over the claimant's land without permission but that the right to ownership of airspace was limited to a 'height as is necessary for the ordinary use and enjoyment of land'. This did not extend to the height at which the aircraft had flown, hence, the action failed.

Protected interests

It is common to refer to the owner of the land in relation to trespass but the tort actually protects against interference with the possession of land, rather than ownership (although the two may frequently coincide). If there is a division in ownership and possession, i.e. landlord and tenant, the interest that is protected is the party who is entitled to exclusive possession. This was emphasised in *AG Securities* v *Vaughan* [1990] 1 AC 417 (HL) where it was also highlighted that those with licences such as guests, visitors and lodgers lack exclusive possession so cannot bring an action in trespass to land.

Trespass *ab initio*

A person who has permission to enter land is not a trespasser. However, an initially lawful entry becomes an actionable trespass if the defendant abuses their permission to enter the land. This is trespass *ab initio* (from the beginning) as the abuse of permission negates it from the point of entry onto the land.

✎ EXAM TIP

Trespass *ab initio* is based upon abusive behaviour by someone with permission to be on the land. Determine whether behaviour is abusive by considering whether it was consistent with express or implied permission to enter: what was it reasonable to expect that the defendant would do on the land? For example, customers have implied permission to enter to browse and make purchases but will become trespassers if they steal whilst in a shop.

■ Defences

There are four main defences to trespass to land:

- **Consent:** a person who has permission to enter is not a trespasser. Ensure that the defendant has not exceeded the limits of his permission if you are using this defence.
- **Contractual licence:** such as payment of an entry fee or purchase of tickets for a sporting event.
- **Lawful authority:** particular people may have permission to enter particular premises in particular circumstances such as court bailiffs and the police (Police and Criminal Evidence Act 1984).
- **Necessity:** this justifies trespass in emergency situations to deal with a perceived threat. It does not matter if the threat is real provided the defendant believes that it is real.

■ Remedies

In addition to damages and injunction, there are two remedies of particular importance to trespass to land:

- **Self-help:** a landowner may use reasonable force to repel or expel trespassers provided that the trespasser has not obtained full possession of the land, i.e. force cannot be used to evict squatters. Self-help can also be used to remove objects placed on land, e.g. a landowner can cut branches from trees that are encroaching onto his land, although he must ensure that the property (the cut branches) is returned to the possession of its owner.
- **Possession orders:** if a trespasser has full possession of land, an order for possession must be obtained to restore the land to its rightful owner.

The main remedies for trespass to land, as with so many other torts, are damages and injunction, covered in Chapter 14. It would be useful to take a moment to refresh your memory and consider the way that these remedies operate in relation to trespass to land.

■ Putting it all together

Answer guidelines

See the problem question at the start of the chapter.

Approaching the question

This is not a typical example of a problem question in this area as it raises several different manifestations of trespass to land whereas problem questions usually include one or two instances in combination with other torts such as private nuisance. This question has been formulated to demonstrate how a range of different issues relating to trespass to land could arise.

Important points to include

Start by introducing the topic effectively by identifying trespass to land as the relevant tort arising on the facts and explaining the nature of this tort, e.g. it is a tort that protects against unjustified interference with land and so is appropriate because visitors to the gallery are behaving in a way that is contrary to the conditions of entry.

Deal with each party in turn to determine his/her liability:

■ **Desmond.** Desmond entered the gallery so his physical presence may amount to trespass. The gallery has invited visitors in but requires that they pay a fee, thus placing conditions on entry. Desmond has entered through a window to avoid paying the fee, so he is a trespasser as he has not complied with the condition of entry.

■ **Emma.** Although Emma paid to enter the gallery and was initially a lawful visitor, she has stayed after the gallery has closed. It may seem as if she has exceeded the permission to enter that was granted by the gallery but her presence on the land is not voluntary as she fell asleep, thus it is likely that she is not liable for trespass to land. ▶

- **Nelson.** It is presumed the Nelson paid to enter the gallery and so is initially a lawful visitor, but he has exceeded the extent of this permission by his breach of the rules prohibiting smoking. The gallery is entitled to place conditions on entry and his failure to comply with those conditions renders Nelson a trespasser.

- **Julie.** Julie is also a lawful visitor who has exceeded the permission to enter granted by the gallery by taking photographs, thus, like Nelson, her entry becomes unlawful.

- **Terry.** As with Nelson and Emma, Terry has broken the rules of the gallery, and thus is a trespasser. It is irrelevant that none of the parties has caused harm to the premises as all that is required to render them liable for trespass is that they have exceeded the permission given to them to enter the land.

 Make your answer stand out

You should deal with each party and issue separately even though they are all potentially liable for the same tort. Students often get their answers into a terrible muddle by trying to deal with all the parties collectively to save time but the confusion that this creates will limit the success of your answer. A methodical approach will impress your examiner and ensure that you do not miss any important issues, so give some thought to the structure and organisation of your answer.

There is a clear focus on trespass *ab initio* in the question, so make sure that you deal with that issue thoroughly. By linking this to the fact that trespass to land is actionable *per se*, you could make a clever point about the purpose of the tort to protect against unwanted intrusion to land rather than to guard against damage caused to land, thus drawing a comparison with other torts.

READ TO IMPRESS

Murdoch, J. (2000) Trespass against us. *Estates Gazette*, p. 140.

Murdoch, S. and Murdoch, J. (1996) Forgive us our trespasses. *Estates Gazette*, p. 107.

Pawlowski, M. (2008) Trespass revisited. 151, *Solicitors Journal*, p. 1548.

www.pearsoned.co.uk/lawexpress

 Go online to access more revision support including quizzes to test your knowledge, sample questions with answer guidelines, podcasts you can download, and more!

10

Trespass to the person

Topic map

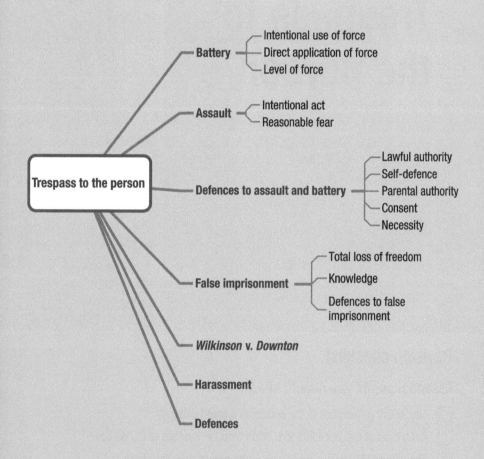

Trespass to the person
- Battery
  - Intentional use of force
  - Direct application of force
  - Level of force
- Assault
  - Intentional act
  - Reasonable fear
- Defences to assault and battery
  - Lawful authority
  - Self-defence
  - Parental authority
  - Consent
  - Necessity
- False imprisonment
  - Total loss of freedom
  - Knowledge
  - Defences to false imprisonment
- *Wilkinson* v. *Downton*
- Harassment
- Defences

A printable version of this topic map is available from **www.pearsoned.co.uk/lawexpress**

■ Introduction

Trespass to the person covers a collection of torts that protect the inviolability of the individual.

These torts cover a selection of ways in which an individual may suffer interference from others: physical and psychological harm, curtailment of freedom and harassment.

The ever-increasing reliance on negligence has led to trespass to the person seeming of less importance. This is unfortunate as trespass to the person, unlike negligence, is actionable *per se*, meaning that liability arises if the defendant commits the relevant act without any requirement that the claimant suffers harm. The new tort of harassment tends to be viewed as a form of trespass to the person. Although introduced to combat stalking, harassment is a broad and flexible tort that has been used in a variety of situations: domestic violence, neighbour disputes and protest situations.

These easily established torts therefore have a useful role to play in protecting individuals against interference from others and should not be overlooked in the revision process.

ASSESSMENT ADVICE

Essay questions

Essay questions could cover trespass to the person as a broad category, e.g. how effectively does tort protect an individual from unwanted interference, or any of the individual torts, e.g. discuss the extent to which the tort of harassment plays a useful role in today's society. The potential for a question on a particular tort, such as harassment, will depend on the prominence it has been given in your syllabus.

Problem questions

Problem questions usually combine trespass to the person with other torts to test your ability to identify and deal with a selection of torts. It is also possible that questions will require the ability to distinguish trespass to the person – which involves direct interference to another but requires no harm to be caused – from other torts with different requirements.

■ Sample question

Could you answer this question? Below is a typical essay question that could arise on this topic. Guidelines on answering the question are included at the end of the chapter, whilst a sample problem question and guidance on tackling it can be found on the companion website.

■ Battery

KEY DEFINITION: Battery

'Battery is the intentional and direct application of force to another person.' (Rogers, W.V.H. (2002) *Winfield and Jolowicz on Tort*, 16th edn, London: Sweet & Maxwell, p. 71.)

Battery is a straightforward tort that has the characteristics described in the sections that follow.

Intentional use of force

Battery requires that the defendant intentionally makes contact with the body or clothing of the claimant.

KEY CASE

Letang v *Cooper* [1965] 1 QB 232 (CA)

Concerning: intentional force

Facts

The defendant accidentally drove over the claimant's legs whilst she was sunbathing in a car park. She sought damages on the basis of trespass to the person as a claim in negligence was time-barred.

Legal principle

The claimant could not recover damages on the basis of trespass to the person as the defendant's actions were accidental and not intentional.

Lord Denning reiterated the mutually exclusive operation of negligence and trespass to the person:

> If [the action] is intentional, it is a tort of assault and battery. If negligent and causing damage, it is the tort of negligence . . . [The claimant's] only cause of action here . . . (where the damage was unintentional) was negligence and not trespass to the person.

> **!** **Don't be tempted to . . .**
>
> Some students confuse liability for battery and liability in negligence. The distinction made by Lord Denning in *Letang* v *Cooper* is an important one: a defendant cannot be liable for battery and negligence on the basis of the same facts. These torts are mutually exclusive which means that liability must be for one or the other. This is an area where mistakes are made with students often concluding that there is liability for both negligence and battery. Be sure to avoid this common mistake by ensuring that you remember:
>
> - intentional action: battery;
> - unintentional action: negligence.

Direct application of force

Battery requires that force is applied directly to the body of the claimant as a result of the defendant's intentional act. This requirement of directness has been interpreted broadly by the courts:

- **Contact by a third party.** *Scott* v *Shepherd* (1773) 96 ER 525: the defendant threw a lighted squib into a crowded market. It was thrown again by a third party to prevent damage to his stall, hitting the victim in the eye. The defendant was liable despite third-party intervention.
- **Contact made indirectly.** *Pursell* v *Horn* (1838) 112 ER 966: the defendant threw water over the claimant and was liable despite the indirect nature of the contact.
- **Direct contact with the wrong person.** *Livingstone* v *MoD* [1984] NI 356 (CA): a soldier fired at a rioter but missed and struck the claimant. The doctrine of transferred malice (D intends to hit A but misses and hits B) was used to establish liability for battery.

Level of force

Reference to 'force' to describe the contact required between defendant and claimant is misleading. There is no requirement that battery causes harm, indicating that the level of force may be extremely low. In *Cole* v *Turner* (1704) 6 Mod Rep 149, it was held that 'the least touching in anger is a battery'.

The reference to anger has been interpreted to mean that the contact must be 'hostile' (*Collins* v *Wilcock* [1984] 1 WLR 1172 (DC)) which has in turn been interpreted to mean that the actions were 'unlawful' (*F* v *West Berkshire HA* [1990] 2 AC 1 (HL)) in the sense of being non-consensual.

> **! Don't be tempted to . . .**
>
> Don't automatically conclude that there is no battery because the claimant has not suffered an injury. Remember that there is no requirement of harm caused for a battery, unlike the tort of negligence which requires that harm be caused to the claimant.

■ Assault

> **KEY DEFINITION: Assault**
>
> An assault is an act which causes another person to apprehend the infliction of immediate, unlawful force on his person: *Collins* v *Wilcock* [1984] 1 WLR 1172 (DC) *per* Lord Goff.

> **✎ EXAM TIP**
>
> The most common error occurs when students apply the everyday meaning of 'assault' (for example, meaning 'attack') and thus confuse assault (which involves no physical contact) with battery (which does require contact).
>
> Focus on the legal meaning of the words and concentrate on establishing the elements of the torts to avoid this problem. It can help to remember that assault usually precedes a battery.

See Figure 10.1 which illustrates the distinction between assault and battery.

Intentional act

Assault requires a deliberate act by the defendant. Although historically, 'no words or singing can amount to an assault' (*R* v *Meade and Belt* (1823) 1 Lew CC 184), it is now clear that assault can be committed by words as well as conduct.

Figure 10.1

Assault	Battery
Definition	
The defendant causes the victim to apprehend immediate unlawful violence	The defendant applies non-consensual physical contact to the victim's body
In other words	
The victim sees that an attack is imminent	The attack on the victim takes place
For example	
Vincent sees Derek running towards him with an axe	Derek hits Vincent over the head with the axe

---

KEY CASE

R v *Ireland* [1998] AC 147 (HL)

Concerning: words as assault

Facts

The defendant made silent telephone calls to the victims. In dealing with the issue of silence as an assault, the House of Lords tackled the issue of words as an assault.

Legal principle

The proposition that 'words can never suffice [for the basis of assault] is unrealistic and indefensible. There is no reason why something said should be incapable of causing an apprehension of immediate personal violence' (*per* Lord Steyn).

Reasonable fear

The conduct must cause the claimant *reasonable fear* that attack is imminent. The reasonableness is judged according to the claimant's perceptions of the defendant's actions: *R* v *St George* (1840) 9 C&P 483. The claimant must believe that the threatened attack is possible and will be carried out: *Thomas* v *National Union of Mineworkers* [1986] Ch 20 (DC). See Figure 10.2.

Figure 10.2

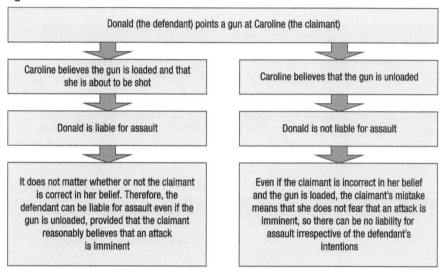

■ Defences to assault and battery

In addition to the general defences discussed in Chapter 13, there are a range of defences specific to assault and battery.

Lawful authority

Certain interferences with the person are authorised by statute such as the Police and Criminal Evidence Act 1984 which entitles the police to use reasonable force in furtherance of an arrest and the Mental Health Act 1983 which authorises the compulsory detention and treatment of those suffering from specified mental disorders.

Self-defence

A person may use such force as is reasonable to protect against an actual or perceived threat of harm against themselves or another person. The force used must be proportionate to the threat, i.e. it must be no more than is necessary to repel the threat. Force which is disproportionate will not fall within self-defence.

📖 **REVISION NOTE**

Have a look at the key case of *Revill* v *Newberry* that you will find in Chapter 13. Self-defence was not available to this householder as his actions in shooting the burglar were disproportionate to the threat posed to his property.

In *Ashley* v *Chief Constable of Sussex Police* [2008] 1 AC 962 (HL) the House of Lords held that in cases where the assailant had acted in a mistaken belief that he was being attacked, this mistaken belief must be honestly *and reasonably* held in order for self-defence to be available against a civil claim in assault or battery.

Parental authority

The right of a parent to use physical force to chastise a child is a hugely debated topic and one which is increasingly cited as involving human rights issues due to the possibility of contravention of Article 3 of the European Convention on Human Rights (freedom from inhumane and degrading treatment).

The use of force in punishing a child may amount to battery if the level of force is disproportionate to the child's behaviour or if the child does not understand the purpose of the punishment (*A* v *UK* [1998] 2 FLR 959 (ECHR)).

Consent

If, for example, a person has consented to the application of force to their body a claim for battery will be defeated. Although consent is covered as a general defence later (in Chapter 13), it has a particular application in relation to trespass to the person. Consent may be express or implied. Consent must be given freely by a person who has the mental capacity to exercise choice and to give or withhold consent.

 Make your answer stand out

Consent in relation to trespass to the person has been particularly problematic as regards medical treatment. Many medical and surgical procedures involve bodily contact that would amount to an actionable tort of battery if the patient did not consent to the contact. This raises questions of the extent to which patients are entitled to withhold consent to necessary and often life-saving medical treatment. The issue can be complicated by questions of mental competency. The full extent of this area and the ethical issues that it raises are beyond the scope of this book but Wicks's (2001) article provides a clear analysis of the topic that takes into account questions of human rights and would make useful reading in preparation for an essay question.

Necessity

The essence of this defence is that interference with another person may sometimes be necessary to protect them from a greater evil, e.g. grabbing someone to stop them falling over the edge of a cliff. As with consent, necessity has been used as a means of authorising medical treatment of those who are regarded as lacking the capacity to give consent, e.g. the sterilisation of a female mental patient who was involved in a sexual relationship with another patient: *F* v *West Berkshire HA* [1990] 2 AC 1 (HL).

■ False imprisonment

KEY DEFINITION: False imprisonment

'The infliction of bodily restraint which is not expressly or impliedly authorised by the law.' (Rogers, W.V.H. (2002) *Winfield and Jolowicz on Tort*, 16th edn, London: Sweet & Maxwell, p. 81.)

False imprisonment focuses on situations in which the claimant's liberty or movement is constrained, whether this is by arrest, detention or other confinement.

□ REVISION NOTE

Many cases involve the arrest or detention of suspected offenders. A stronger understanding of this area can be gained by ensuring that you are familiar with the common law and statutory powers of arrest (Police and Criminal Evidence Act 1984, as amended by section 110 of the Serious Organised Crime and Police Act 2005).

Total loss of freedom

False imprisonment requires total restraint of the claimant's movements:

- It is not enough that the defendant cannot go where he wants provided that he can go somewhere.
- If there is reasonable means of escape, there is no false imprisonment.
- Restraint need not be physical. A person who is told not to leave and complies with this instruction suffers a total loss of freedom.

> **KEY CASE**
>
> *Bird* v *Jones* (1845) 7 QB 742
> *Concerning: partial constraint*
>
> **Facts**
>
> The claimant partially crossed Hammersmith Bridge when it was closed during a regatta. He was prevented from continuing to the end of the bridge and claimed that this limitation on his freedom to proceed amounted to false imprisonment.
>
> **Legal principle**
>
> The claim failed because there was only partial restraint on the claimant's movement. He was not permitted to proceed but was free to retrace his steps. False imprisonment requires total, not partial, constraint on the claimant's free movement.

Knowledge

An action for false imprisonment may arise if the claimant was not aware that he was being detained at the time of the detention.

> **KEY CASE**
>
> *Murray* v *Ministry of Defence* [1988] 1 WLR 692 (HL)
> *Concerning: knowledge of constraint*
>
> **Facts**
>
> The claimant's house was searched in her presence and she was arrested 30 minutes later. It was unclear whether she was aware that she was not free to leave during the period prior to her arrest.
>
> **Legal principle**
>
> The House of Lords held that there was no requirement 'that the victim should be aware of the fact of denial of liberty . . . [however] if a person is unaware that he has been falsely imprisoned and has suffered no harm, he can normally expect to recover no more than nominal damages' (*per* Lord Griffiths).

Defences to false imprisonment

In addition to the general defences covered in Chapter 13, the following will provide a defence to false imprisonment:

- **Reasonable condition for release:** if the defendant's detention of the claimant is contingent upon the performance of a reasonable condition, i.e. payment of a toll or delay based on the need to wait for appropriate transport, but the claimant refuses to comply, his continued detention will be considered voluntary.

- **Lawful arrest:** an arrest that is made properly according to the requirements of the Police and Criminal Evidence Act 1984 (as amended) will not amount to false imprisonment nor will a detention made in furtherance of the common law right to effect a citizen's arrest.

- **Medical detention:** there are circumstances when a person requires protection from their own behaviour and thus detention may be authorised by the provisions of the Mental Health Act 1983. Individuals suffering from particular contagious diseases may be detained against their will according to the Public Health (Control of Disease) Act 1984.

■ *Wilkinson* v *Downton*

This case gave rise to a separate category of tortious liability based upon the infliction of indirect harm to another.

KEY CASE

Wilkinson v *Downton* **[1897] 2 QB 57 (DC)**

Concerning: indirect harm

Facts

The defendant told the claimant that her husband had been seriously injured in an accident. This was untrue and had been meant as a practical joke. The claimant suffered a serious shock which led her to suffer adverse physical symptoms for a period of time.

Legal principle

It was held that a person who has 'wilfully done an act calculated to cause physical harm to the plaintiff – that is to say, to infringe her legal right to safety, and has in fact thereby caused physical harm to her' has provided a good cause of action (*per* Wright J).

Despite its obvious potential, particularly as it pre-dated the development of cases concerning nervous shock (see Chapter 1), this case was rarely used in this jurisdiction. The requirements for liability were clarified in *Wong* v *Parkside NHS Trust* [2003] 3 All ER 932:

- There must be actual harm (physical harm or recognised psychiatric illness). This differentiates this tort from other forms of trespass as they are actionable *per se*.

- The defendant must have acted intentionally.

- The conduct must be of such a degree that it is calculated to cause harm so that the defendant cannot say he did not mean to cause it.

 Make your answer stand out

It is sometimes questioned whether the rule in *Wilkinson* v *Downton* should fall within trespass to the person. It involves the indirect infliction of harm to an individual so satisfies the general requirement of interference with personal integrity that characterises these torts, but it does require that actual harm be suffered, which is inconsistent with the rule that trespass is actionable *per se* (without the need for harm or damage). There is an excellent discussion of the rule of *Wilkinson* v *Downton* in modern tort law in *Wainwright* v *Home Office* [2004] 2 AC 406 in which the House of Lords considered whether an action could be based upon the distress caused to visitors to a prison being strip-searched in a way that contravened prison rules. This was later held by the European Court of Human Rights (*Wainwright* v *United Kingdom* (2006) (application no 12350/04) (ECtHR)) to be a violation of their rights under Article 8 (privacy) and the failure to provide a remedy in tort was also a violation of their Article 13 rights (effective remedy). It would also be useful to read Lunney's (2002) assessment of *Wilkinson* v *Downton*.

■ Harassment

Prior to the enactment of the Protection from Harassment Act 1997 (PFHA), *Wilkinson* v *Downton* was one of a variety of means used to impose tortious liability on those who caused distress and anxiety to others. The introduction of a statutory tort of harassment under section 3 PFHA obviated the need for creative use of other torts.

KEY STATUTE

Protection from Harassment Act 1997, section 1

Harassment is defined as the pursuit of a course of conduct that the defendant knows or ought to know amounts to harassment of another.

This breaks down into three elements, illustrated in Figure 10.3, all of which must be established for a claim of harassment to succeed.

Figure 10.3

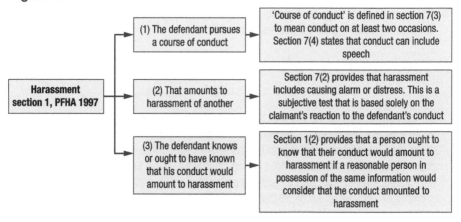

There is no requirement that the claimant suffers physical or psychological harm as a result of the harassment. The tort is satisfied if the claimant experiences alarm or distress as a consequence of the defendant's actions, something which will vary according to the character of the victim (some people are more readily distressed than others). Once harassment is established, the claimant may obtain an injunction to prevent further harassment.

■ Defences

If the claimant establishes the elements of one of the trespass torts, the defendant may still avoid liability by reliance on a defence. The general defences that are applicable to most torts are covered in Chapter 13, whilst defences that are specific to particular torts involving trespass to the person have been discussed throughout this chapter.

📖 REVISION NOTE

Make sure you are clear on which defences apply to which torts. Many students get confused on this point and lose marks as a consequence. Try making a list of each tort that details which defences are available and noting how they are likely to apply to that particular tort, i.e. consent is a general defence but the answer to the question 'consent to what?' will vary according to which tort is under consideration.

■ Putting it all together

Answer guidelines

See the essay question at the start of the chapter.

Approaching the question

This is an essay question dealing with one facet of trespass to the person. The role of the rule in *Wilkinson* v *Downton* in modern tort law has been questioned by academics and the judiciary, so there is plenty of scope for debate about its value. Make sure you know enough about the topic before you select this question: it would not be enough merely to be able to state the rule, you must also be able to assess how it relates to other torts so that you can assess whether there is a role for this tort.

Important points to include

■ Start by explaining the rule in *Wilkinson* v *Downton*. Make sure that you can state the legal principle from the case as well as the facts. You should be able to explain what conduct is covered by this tort: an intentional act that causes harm to the victim. An ability to list the characteristics of the tort as outlined by the Court of Appeal in *Wong* would be useful.

■ Think about other torts and consider whether there is any overlap with *Wilkinson* v *Downton*. Try approaching this by considering whether any of the other torts could cover the same conduct as *Wilkinson* v *Downton*.

■ **Battery:** requires physical contact so does not cover the same sort of wrongful conduct as *Wilkinson* v *Downton* as this tends to involve words that cause injury to the claimant.

■ **Assault:** like *Wilkinson* v *Downton*, assault can be founded on words but the consequences of the words differ as assault requires that the words cause the victim to apprehend immediate personal violence, whilst *Wilkinson* v *Downton* requires that the words cause physical or psychological harm to the victim.

■ **Negligence:** at the time that *Wilkinson* v *Downton* was decided, the tort of negligence was not formulated with precision and it was not possible to recover for psychiatric injury based on shock. This position changed since *Dulieu* v *White* [1901] 2 KB 669, so the sort of injury covered by *Wilkinson* v *Downton* is also recoverable under negligence. The difference lies in the way that such injury is caused as *Wilkinson* v *Downton* requires that the defendant's conduct be 'calculated to cause injury', i.e. that it be intentional rather than negligently caused.

▶

- **Harassment:** the tort of harassment was introduced by section 3 of the Protection from Harassment Act 1997 and requires that there be a course of conduct, i.e. conduct on at least two occasions. Liability under the rule in *Wilkinson* v *Downton* can be established on the basis of a single occasion.

- Having situated *Wilkinson* v *Downton* within the context of other torts, you will now be in a position to comment on whether this tort has a rule to play. Reference to cases such as *Wong* and *Wainwright* v *Home Office* would be valuable here as the Court of Appeal and House of Lords discussed the role of *Wilkinson* v *Downton* in detail.

 Make your answer stand out

Avoid the common pitfall of providing excessive amounts of descriptive detail about the torts in your essay. This will distract attention (yours and that of the examiner) away from the central focus of the question.

You should always strive to include examples from case law in your answer but *Wilkinson* v *Downton* has not been applied in many cases, so you might find it useful to incorporate hypothetical examples into your essay to demonstrate your points. For example, it would be valuable if you could think of a situation that is covered by *Wilkinson* v *Downton* but not by any of the other torts.

READ TO IMPRESS

Finch, E. (2002) Stalking the perfect stalking law: an evaluation of the efficacy of the Protection from Harassment Act 1997. *Criminal Law Review*, p. 703.

Lunney, M. (2002) Practical joking and its penalty: *Wilkinson* v *Downton* in context. *Tort Law Review*, p. 168.

Wicks, E. (2001) The right to refuse medical treatment under the European Convention on Human Rights. *Medical Law Review*, p. 17.

www.pearsoned.co.uk/lawexpress

 Go online to access more revision support including quizzes to test your knowledge, sample questions with answer guidelines, podcasts you can download, and more!

11

Liability for defective products

Revision checklist

Essential points you should know:

- [ ] The elements of common law liability for defective products
- [ ] The provisions of the Consumer Protection Act 1987 as they relate to strict liability for defective products
- [ ] The statutory defences available to a potential defendant under the Act

■ Topic map

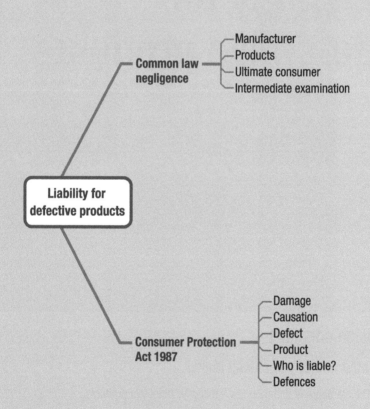

◼ Introduction

Defective products which cause damage can give rise to liability in tort.

This liability traditionally arose under the common law. However, the common law position places the burden on the claimant to establish causation, which is not always straightforward, particularly where the damage arose as a result of a design defect on the part of the manufacturer. This potential failure in the common law position led to growing pressure for a strict liability approach to product liability which was implemented at the European level by Directive 85/374/EEC and transposed into domestic law by the Consumer Protection Act 1987. This chapter will consider both the position at common law (which still applies) as well as the statutory position under the Act.

ASSESSMENT ADVICE

The area of product liability could be tested by either an essay or a problem question, although in general problem questions are more commonly used.

Essay questions

Essay questions on product liability could ask you to compare and contrast the position at common law and the statutory position under the Consumer Protection Act 1987. This will require a good level of knowledge of the composite elements of each basis for liability and the analytical skills to differentiate between them. Having explored the differences, you would need to be able to weigh up the advantages and disadvantages of each position (with reasons).

Problem questions

Problem questions on product liability are more common and would generally involve the application of the common law and statute law to a scenario in which someone has suffered loss or damage arising from a defective product. You must cover both areas of law separately and ensure that you cover all the necessary points before reaching your conclusions. Remember that the outcome under the Act may well be different to that at common law.

■ Sample question

Could you answer this question? Below is a typical problem question that could arise on this topic. Guidelines on answering the question are included at the end of this chapter, whilst a sample essay question and guidance on tackling it can be found on the companion website.

PROBLEM QUESTION

Sophie is out shopping in Tatmart Ltd, her local department store, when she notices an assistant demonstrating the Steamo-2000 steam cleaner. The assistant explains that the cleaner allows all sorts of surfaces to be cleaned using just tap water. It is particularly effective at cleaning soap film from tiles. He also says that the Steamo-2000 comes with a 12-month guarantee from the manufacturer Steamo Enterprises Ltd, and that there is £150 off the normal price of £379 as an introductory offer. Sophie decides to buy one, and pays £229 in cash.

Sophie decides to use her cleaner straight away to do some cleaning in her bathroom shower cubicle. Carefully following the instructions, she fills the tank with water, and leaves the cleaner to heat up for the recommended 10 minutes. After about five minutes, she hears a strange noise coming from the bathroom and, as she goes to check, the cleaner explodes. Flying debris shatters the mirrored bathroom cabinet and hits Sophie, causing painful but fortunately minor cuts.

That evening, Sophie's husband, who is an electrical engineer, takes a look at the remains of the cleaner; he is certain that a defective thermostat caused it to overheat.

Sophie goes back to Tatmart to complain, but the assistant tells her that she must pursue any complaint with the manufacturer.

What claims in tort can Sophie make against the manufacturer?

■ Liability for defective products

Defective products can give rise to liability in a variety of ways. Claims may arise in contract law or consumer law involving various statutes including the Sale of Goods Act 1979, the Sale and Supply of Goods Act 1994, the Supply of Goods and Services Act 1982, the Unfair Contract Terms Act 1977 and the Unfair Terms in Consumer Contract Regulations 1999. A detailed discussion of these areas is naturally beyond the scope of a tort revision guide. However, it is worth being aware that there is a distinction between causes of action in contract and tort in relation to defective products. In relation to tort, liability can arise:

- under the common law in negligence; and/or
- under the Consumer Protection Act 1987.

Common law negligence

The basis of the common law position can be found in the 'narrow rule' from *Donoghue* v *Stevenson* [1932] AC 562 (HL). You first encountered the 'neighbour principle' from this case in Chapter 1. This is sometimes called the 'wide rule' from *Donoghue* v *Stevenson*. However, there is also part of the judgment which deals specifically with the relationship between the manufacturer and the ultimate consumer of those products:

KEY CASE

Donoghue v *Stevenson* [1932] AC 562 (HL)

Concerning: duty of care between manufacturer and ultimate consumer

Facts

Mrs Donoghue and a friend visited a café. Mrs Donoghue's friend bought her a bottle of ginger beer. The bottle was made of opaque glass. When filling Mrs Donoghue's glass, the remains of a decomposed snail – which had somehow found its way into the bottle at the factory – floated out. Mrs Donoghue developed gastroenteritis as a result.

Legal principle

Lord Atkin explained the narrow rule as follows:

> . . . a manufacturer of products, which he sells in such a form as to show that he intends them to reach the ultimate consumer in the form in which they left him with no reasonable possibility of intermediate examination, and with the knowledge that the absence of reasonable care in the preparation or putting up of the products will result in an injury to the consumer's life or property, owes a duty to the consumer to take that reasonable care.

There are a number of elements to this rule:

- manufacturer;
- products;
- ultimate consumer;
- intermediate examination.

Manufacturer

As well as the ordinary sense of the word, for the purposes of the narrow rule, a 'manufacturer' has been held to include any party who creates the danger inherent in the goods such as:

- assemblers;
- installers;
- service engineers/repairers (*Haseldine* v *Daw & Son Ltd* [1941] 2 KB 343 (CA));
- retailers;
- suppliers (*Andrews* v *Hopkinson* [1957] 1 QB 229 (QBD)).

Products

Although *Donoghue* v *Stevenson* concerned drinks, a 'product' is considered to be anything manufactured which is capable of causing damage including such diverse articles as underpants (*Grant* v *Australian Knitting Mills* [1936] AC 85 (PC)), lifts (*Haseldine* v *Daw & Son Ltd* [1941] 2 KB 343 (CA)) and hair dye. It extends to the packaging, labelling and safety instructions (*Vacwell Engineering Co Ltd* v *BDH Chemicals Ltd* [1971] 1 QB 111 (CA)).

Ultimate consumer

The 'ultimate consumer' of a product is construed very widely. It includes anyone who may foreseeably be affected by the defective product (*Stennett* v *Hancock and Peters* [1939] 2 All ER 578 (KBD)).

Intermediate examination

This area is linked to causation in negligence (see Chapter 3). In essence, if an intermediary is reasonably expected to make an examination of the product which would (or should) have revealed the defect and then fails to do so, then this may be sufficient to break the chain of causation. However, if the intermediate examination of the product is only foreseeable (rather than likely), this will not be sufficient to absolve the manufacturer from liability:

KEY CASE

Griffiths v *Arch Engineering Co* **[1968] 3 All ER 217 (Newport Assizes)**

Concerning: common law product liability; intermediate examination

Facts

The claimant, a workman, was injured by a portable grinding tool which he borrowed from the first defendants. The tool was owned by the second defendants. There was no intermediate examination of the tool before its use by the injured workman.

> **Legal principle**
>
> The first defendants were liable since they had an opportunity to examine the tool and did not do so. The second defendants were *also* liable since they had no reason to believe that an intermediate examination would be carried out.

However, if intermediate inspection reveals a defect, the manufacturer will probably avoid liability (*Taylor* v *Rover Car Co Ltd* [1966] 1 WLR 1491 (Birmingham Assizes)). This will also be the case if the intermediary ignores a clear warning to examine the product before use (*Kubach* v *Hollands* [1937] 3 All ER 907 (KBD)).

A manufacturer who had no reason to believe that an intermediate examination will take place (either by the consumer or by a third party) will be potentially liable. However, if the defect arose after manufacture then the manufacturer will not be liable (*Evans* v *Triplex Safety Glass Co Ltd* [1936] 1 All ER 283 (KBD)).

■ Consumer Protection Act 1987

The Consumer Protection Act 1987 came into force on 15 May 1987 and gave effect to EC Directive 85/374/EEC on the approximation of the laws, regulations and administrative provisions of the member states concerning liability for defective products.

KEY STATUTE

> **Consumer Protection Act 1987, section 2(1)**
>
> 2. Liability for defective products
> (1) Subject to the following provisions of this Part, where any damage is caused wholly or partly by a defect in a product, every person to whom subsection (2) below applies shall be liable for the damage.

In essence, any supplier of defective products within the EU (even products which are imported from *outside* the EU) is strictly liable in tort if the defect causes damage.

Therefore, the claimant is not required to show that the defendant is at fault or has been careless. All the claimant needs to do is prove that a defect in the product resulted in injury.

Damage

Damage includes loss of or damage to personal property provided that it exceeds £275 in value (section 5(4)). However, this £275 minimum only applies to property damage not to personal injury (section 5(1); section 5(4)). It does *not* include the cost of repairing or replacing the product itself (section 5(2)). Damage caused to *business* property is *outside* the scope of the Act (section 5(2)).

Causation

In relation to causation, the claimant carries the burden of proof; the usual 'but for' test applies (see Chapter 3).

Defect

The meaning of 'defect' is defined in section 3.

KEY STATUTE

Consumer Protection Act 1987, section 3

3. Meaning of "defect"

(1) Subject to the following provisions of this section, there is a defect in a product for the purposes of this Part if the safety of the product is not such as persons generally are entitled to expect; and for those purposes 'safety', in relation to a product, shall include safety with respect to products comprised in that product and safety in the context of risks of damage to property, as well as in the context of risks of death or personal injury.

(2) In determining for the purposes of subsection (1) above what persons generally are entitled to expect in relation to a product all the circumstances shall be taken into account, including –

   (a) the manner in which, and purposes for which, the product has been marketed, its get-up, the use of any mark in relation to the product and any instructions for, or warnings with respect to, doing or refraining from doing anything with or in relation to the product;

   (b) what might reasonably be expected to be done with or in relation to the product; and

   (c) the time when the product was supplied by its producer to another; and nothing in this section shall require a defect to be inferred from the fact alone that the safety of a product which is supplied after that time is greater than the safety of the product in question.

In essence, defective products are 'unsafe': the Act applies to dangerous products as opposed to products which are simply defective. Section 3(2) sets out the 'consumer expectations' test providing the factors which the court will take into account in determining whether the product is in fact defective.

Product

'Product' is widely defined in section 1(2) as including:

- any goods;
- electricity;
- a product which is comprised in another product, whether by virtue of being a component part or raw material or otherwise.

'Goods' are further defined in section 45(1) as including:

- substances;
- growing crops;
- things comprised in land by virtue of being attached to it;
- any ship, aircraft or vehicle.

Information is not covered by the Act.

Who is liable?

The range of potential defendants is identified in section 2(2) of the Act:

KEY STATUTE

Consumer Protection Act 1987, section 2(2)

This subsection applies to –

(a) the producer of the product;

(b) any person who, by putting his name on the product or using a trade mark or other distinguishing mark in relation to the product, has held himself out to be the producer of the product;

(c) any person who has imported the product into a Member State from a place outside the Member States in order, in the course of any business of his, to supply it to another.

The *producer* of the product is usually its manufacturer. However, 'producer' also includes the manufacturers of the component parts of the product. Therefore, if a component is faulty, both the manufacturer of the part and of the whole product are liable.

Section 2(2)(b) refers to *own-branders*. These are suppliers who put their own name to a product which they have not actually made themselves (a familiar example of this can be found in supermarkets who often display goods made for them by other producers as their own-brand). *Importers of goods* into the EU also fall within the Act. Section 2(3) of the Act includes 'forgetful suppliers' as potential defendants – that is any supplier who is unable to meet a victim's request to identify any of the entities involved in the supply chain (e.g. wholesalers or manufacturers). Suppliers are otherwise not liable under the Act.

Liability is joint and several: that is, any or all defendants could be sued (section 2(5)).

Liability may not be excluded (section 7).

Defences

Section 4 of the Act provides some defences:

Section	Defence
Section 4(1)(a)	The defect was attributable to compliance with legal requirements.
Section 4(1)(b)	The defendant did not supply the product to another (applies to stolen or counterfeit goods).
Section 4(1)(c)	The defendant did not supply the product in the course of a business.
Section 4(1)(d)	The defect did not exist in the product at the time it was supplied (covers wear and tear, misuse and 'best before' dates on perishable foodstuffs or medical supplies).
Section 4(1)(e)	This is the 'development risks' (or 'state of the art') defence – the defendant must prove that the state of scientific or technical knowledge was such that the defect was unknown and unforeseeable when the product was circulated (see *A and Others* v *National Blood Authority and Others* [2001] 3 All ER 289 (QBD)).
Section 4(1)(f)	The manufacturer of component parts is not liable for a defect in the finished product which is wholly attributable to the design of the finished product or to compliance with the instructions given by the manufacturer of the finished product.

There is also a **limitation** period of 10 years from when the product was circulated by the defendant. Within those 10 years, the defendant must claim within three years from injury or damage. These restrictions do not apply to common law liability.

> **!** Don't be tempted to . . .
>
> Don't just concentrate on one basis of claim for defective products at the expense of the other. It is also important that you remember the key differences between claims under common law negligence and under the Consumer Protection Act 1987. Common law negligence requires proof of negligence whereas the statutory claim is founded in strict liability. However, a successful claim in negligence allows recovery for the cost of the defective item, whereas the statutory claim does not allow recovery of the cost of the defective product and damage to other property is only recoverable over £275.

■ Putting it all together

Answer guidelines

See the problem question at the start of the chapter. A diagram illustrating how to structure your answer is available on the companion website.

Approaching the question

This question requires you to examine the common law and statutory position for Sophie in relation to the damage caused by her faulty steam cleaner. You should attack each basis for a claim separately. Do not be tempted to try and amalgamate the two; it will inevitably lead to an answer that is harder to follow.

Important points to include

In order to claim in negligence, Sophie must show that:

- Steamo Enterprises Ltd owed her a duty of care. This is well established between manufacturer and ultimate consumer (*Donoghue* v *Stevenson*).
- Steamo Enterprises Ltd was in breach of that duty. The cleaner was made with a defective thermostat and it would have been reasonable to expect that Steamo would realise that the absence of reasonable care in the manufacture of the cleaner (which involved boiling water and steam) will result in an injury to the consumer or his/her property.
- Causation and remoteness are unproblematic here but you should still cover them. The damages which resulted would not have done so but for the cleaner exploding and it is reasonably foreseeable that both physical and property damage would result from an exploding overheated electrical appliance.

For a claim under the Consumer Protection Act 1987, Sophie must show that:

- she suffered damage (cuts and a shattered cabinet);
- the damage was caused by a defect (the thermostat);
- the problem was in the product (which is widely defined to include the cleaner);
- there appeared to be no statutory defences available to the manufacturer.

She could also potentially claim against Tatmart Ltd as the supplier, but Tatmart could quickly exonerate itself from liability by naming Steamo Enterprises Ltd as its own supplier.

However, it is not possible to recover the cost of the defective product itself and damage to other property (in this case, the bathroom cabinet) is only recoverable over £275. ▶

✓ Make your answer stand out

Keep the claims separate, otherwise your answer will lack clarity.

Ensure that you cover all the elements of both claims fully, even where they seem to be obvious (such as the definition of product). It is important to demonstrate that you understand all the required elements of a potential claim and can show how the law applies to the facts of the problem.

The cost limitations on recovery under the Consumer Protection Act 1987 are often overlooked.

READ TO IMPRESS

Mildred, M. (2007) Pitfalls in product liability. *Journal of Personal Injury Law*, p. 141.

Shears, P. (2007) The EU Product Liability Directive – twenty years on. *Journal of Business Law*, p. 884.

www.pearsoned.co.uk/lawexpress

 Go online to access more revision support including quizzes to test your knowledge, sample questions with answer guidelines, podcasts you can download, and more!

12

Defamation and privacy

Revision checklist

Essential points you should know:

☐ The definitions of libel and slander and the distinction between them

☐ The elements of defamation

☐ The availability and operation of the defences

☐ The underlying tension between an individual's right to privacy and another's right to freedom of expression

☐ The key provisions of the Defamation Act 2013 and their effect on the pre-existing law

☐ The tort of misuse of private information

■ Topic map

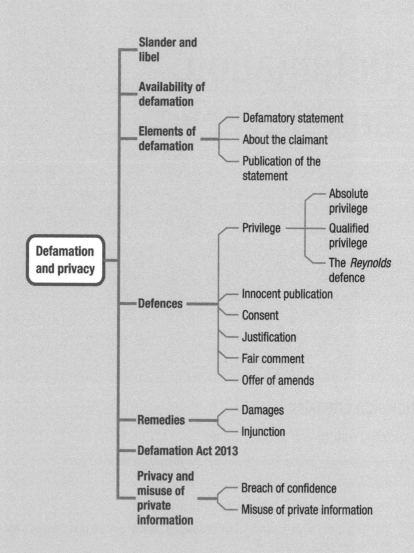

■ Introduction

Defamation is a tort which protects a person from loss of reputation by prohibiting the publication of information likely to attract negative attention from others. Misuse of private information is a relatively new related tort.

Although defamation and misuse of private information are torts which can be relied upon by any individual, many cases involve high-profile public figures in conflict with the media. This encapsulates the struggle of the law to balance between two competing rights: an individual's right to privacy (Article 8 of the European Convention on Human Rights) and the media's right to freedom of expression (Article 10). The involvement of these conflicting rights has led defamation to become more prominent as a topic for consideration since the enactment of the Human Rights Act 1998 and this establishes it as an important revision topic. The Defamation Act 2013 came into force on 1 January 2013. This chapter sets out both the law as it was prior to the Defamation Act 2013 and then provides a summary of the main changes. You should keep a close watch on developments in this area since you will see from the Act that there are considerable amendments to the law.

ASSESSMENT ADVICE

Essay questions

Essay questions dealing with defamation are popular with students as the topic does not really overlap with other areas of tort, so it can be revised as a stand-alone topic. It is also a relatively straightforward tort, which further increases its popularity. The tension between freedom of expression and the right to privacy is one of the key complexities of the topic, so be sure to pay that particular attention as part of revision.

Problem questions

Problem questions that raise issues of defamation will either deal exclusively with this tort or be combined with other topics. It is quite common to have a problem question dealing largely with other torts and have a defamatory statement in them that often goes unnoticed, so be sure to look out for any evidence of defamation. The elements of defamation are relatively easy to apply but remember to consider whether any defences are available.

◼ Sample question

Could you answer this question? Below is a typical problem question that could arise on this topic. Guidelines on answering the question are included at the end of the chapter, whilst a sample essay question and guidance on tackling it can be found on the companion website.

PROBLEM QUESTION

The *World of News* publishes a story about a prominent actor, Jasper Hardy, on its front page under the headline 'Pulling Power of Mr Ugly'. The story alleges that Jasper has had affairs with several married women and also a homosexual relationship. The newspaper names the first of these married women as a well-known celebrity, Gertrude Tobias, who co-presents a television show on relationship problems with her husband, Toby. The second person is described as 'drug-taking legal eagle, Delores Dennis, from Manchester'. This refers to a law student named Delores Dennis but many people assume it is the high-profile barrister of the same name who is based in Manchester. The final person named is Kelvin Costa, who died last year from AIDS.

Consider the strengths and weaknesses of each party's claim for defamation:

(i) before the Defamation Act 2013 came into force and

(ii) after the Defamation Act 2013 came into force.

◼ Slander and libel

KEY DEFINITION: Defamation

'Defamation is the publication of a[n untrue] statement which reflects on a person's reputation and tends to lower him in the estimation of right-thinking members of society generally or tends to make them shun or avoid him.' (Rogers, W.V.H. (2002) *Winfield and Jolowicz on Tort*, 16th edn, London: Sweet & Maxwell, p. 405.)

Slander and **libel** are both forms of **defamation** that differ in two ways:

- ◼ the manner in which the statement is publicised;
- ◼ the consequences that are required before damages are paid.

See Figure 12.1 which illustrates these two differences.

Figure 12.1

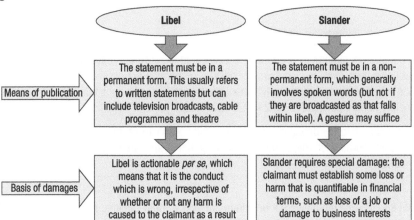

In relation to slander, there are four exceptions to the requirement for special damage to be shown. Slander is actionable *per se* if the imputation is that the claimant:

- has committed a serious criminal offence;
- is unchaste or has committed adultery (female claimants only);
- has a contagious or infectious disease that prevents others from associating with him; or
- is unfit, dishonest or incompetent in relation to his trade, profession or business.

■ Availability of defamation

The following points should be noted:

- The dead cannot bring or defend an action for defamation; both parties must be alive.
- There was a right to trial by jury if the case was not too complex: section 69, Senior Courts Act 1981. This position changed when the Defamation Act 2013 came into force.
- Claims must be brought within 12 months: section 4A, Limitation Act 1980.
- There is no public funding for defamation, hence, the tort favours those who can afford to protect their reputations.
- Defamation involves an unusual two-stage process. The judge determines whether the facts are capable of amounting to defamation whilst the jury decides whether the facts actually do defame the claimant. Note that the presumption in favour of jury trial was removed when the Defamation Act 2013 came into force.

■ Elements of defamation

A defamatory statement is one that is 'calculated to injure the reputation of another, by exposing them to hatred, contempt or ridicule' (*Parmiter* v *Coupland* (1840) 6 M & W 105) and which tends to 'lower the [claimant] in the estimation of right-thinking members of society': *Sim* v *Stretch* [1936] 2 All ER 1237 (HL).

There is a statutory definition of 'statement' in section 15 of the Defamation Act 2013 as 'words, pictures, visual images, gestures or any other method of signifying meaning'.

What sort of allegation lowers a person in the eyes of right-thinking members of society? The elements are set out in Figure 12.2.

Figure 12.2

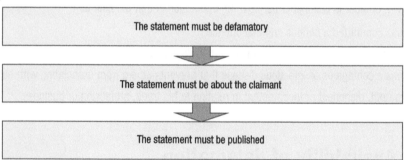

- The statement must be defamatory
- The statement must be about the claimant
- The statement must be published

Byrne v *Deane* [1937] 1 KB 818 (CA)

Concerning: reputation; right-thinking persons

Facts

The claimant was a member of a golf club who was vilified in verse for reporting the presence of a popular but illegal gaming machine in the clubhouse.

Legal principle

Anyone who would think less of a person for reporting illegal activity to the police was not a right-thinking member of society so the words could not be defamatory on that basis. (The case succeeded as the verse also implied disloyalty to his club, something that would erode his standing in the eyes of right-thinking members of society.)

The following have amounted to **defamatory statements**:

- An actor was described as hideously ugly: *Berkoff* v *Burchill* [1996] 4 All ER 1008 (CA).

- An actor was said to be homosexual and deliberately suppressing this to preserve an image of heterosexuality: *Donovan* v *The Face* (1992, unreported).

- A married woman was depicted as unmarried thus suggesting she was 'living in sin' (a serious social problem at the time): *Cassidy* v *Daily Mirror Newspapers Ltd* [1929] 2 KB 331 (CA).

- An amateur golfer was portrayed as endorsing a well-known chocolate manufacturer (which would have removed his amateur status): *Tolley* v *Fry & Sons Ltd* [1931] AC 333 (HL).

✎ EXAM TIP

Remember that a statement can be impliedly defamatory. In the last two examples above, there were no explicit statements that the claimant was unmarried or sponsored by a chocolate manufacturer. Liability arose from pictures and their accompanying captions: in the first case describing the wife as a fiancée, whilst the second was an advertisement that implied that the claimant endorsed the product.

If a statement is not explicitly defamatory, take note of the meaning that the right-thinking person would take from the publication as a whole.

About the claimant

The claimant must establish that the defamation refers to him. This is usually obvious if he is named or otherwise identified in the statement.

A claimant may also have an action if a statement does not refer to him but there are grounds upon which others might think that it did:

KEY CASE

Newstead v *London Express Newpaper Ltd* [1940] 1 KB 377 (CA)
Concerning: misidentification of claimant

Facts

The defendant newspaper reported that Harold Newstead, aged 30 of Camberwell, was convicted of bigamy. Although this was true, another Harold Newstead from Camberwell of that age brought an action for libel on the basis that it was untrue (and defamatory) in relation to him.

Legal principle

It was held that the statement was defamatory as the reasonable person would think that the statement referred to the claimant.

- The claimant need not be named provided there is sufficient information from which he can be identified, even wrongly, with the statement: *Morgan* v *Odhams Press* [1971] 1 WLR 1239 (HL). It is irrelevant that the publisher intended to refer to someone else other than the claimant and did not know that the claimant existed or that others would think that the statement referred to him.

- A statement which is defamatory to a broad class of persons, e.g. university lecturers, cannot be relied upon by individuals within that class unless they are specifically identified. Only if the class is defined sufficiently narrowly, e.g. lecturers in a particular subject at a specific university, so that it could be seen as referring to them as individuals, can it form the basis of defamation: *Knuppfer* v *London Express Newspapers* [1944] AC 116 (HL).

Publication of the statement

It is usual to think of publication of defamatory statements to the world in general via the media but defamation only requires that one other person must hear or read the statement. The publication requirement reinforces the purpose of defamation, which is to protect the reputation of the individual, not his feelings; a statement made exclusively to the claimant cannot damage his reputation in the eyes of others so cannot be defamatory. A claimant cannot, however, presume that material on an internet website has been published: this must be proved either directly or by inference. It is for the jury to decide as a question of fact whether or not there had been substantial publication within the jurisdiction (*Al Amoudi* v *Brisard* [2007] 1 WLR 113 (QB)).

> **!** **Don't be tempted to . . .**
>
> It is a mistake to think that defamation requires some sort of mass publication. As long as only one other person hears or reads the statement, that is enough.

■ Defences

There is a range of defences that may defeat a claim for defamation even if the claimant has established the elements of the tort.

Privilege

This refers to circumstances in which it is regarded as imperative that people are able to express their views without fear of legal action. As such, it represents the primacy of the interests of freedom of expression over the rights of the individual in protecting his reputation.

- **Absolute privilege** covers statements made during judicial and Parliamentary proceedings where there is an interest in ensuring that parties are able to speak freely without fear of legal proceedings. Any statements covered by absolute privilege cannot be relied upon in legal proceedings and so cannot be used as the basis for a defamation claim. In *Buckley* v *Dalziel* [2007] 1 WLR 2933 (QB), the court held that absolute privilege was available to a person who provided information to the police even though the claimant alleged that the statement made to the police was defamatory.

- **Qualified privilege** covers situations in which there is a moral or legal duty to disclose information even if it is unfavourable to the claimant, such as an employment reference. Disclosures covered by qualified privilege can only be the basis of a defamation claim if the defendant acted with malice in making the defamatory statement.

Sections 6 and 7 of the Defamation Act 2013 deal with the protection under privilege.

The *Reynolds* defence

In *Reynolds* v *Times Newspapers* [2001] 2 AC 127 (HL), the House of Lords considered qualified privilege for publication of defamatory statements in the public interest.

KEY CASE

Reynolds v *Times Newspapers* [2001] 2 AC 127 (HL)

Concerning: defamation; qualified privilege

Facts

The Times had published an article in Ireland stating that Reynolds, the former Irish Prime Minister, had misled the Irish Parliament. This article was subsequently published in the UK but did not include the explanation that Reynolds had given for the events, which had been printed in the original article. Reynolds brought an action for defamation. The defences of justification (see below) and fair comment were unavailable, given the factual nature of the article. The question for the House of Lords was whether the defence of qualified privilege should be extended to cover the mass media.

Legal principle

In his judgment, Lord Nicholls provided a list of 10 criteria against which attempts to use the *Reynolds* defence should be judged:

> The elasticity of the common law principle enables interference with freedom of speech to be confined to what is necessary in the circumstances of the case. This elasticity enables the court to give appropriate weight, in today's conditions, to the importance of freedom of expression by the media on all matters of public ▶

concern. Depending on the circumstances, the matters to be taken into account include the following. The comments are illustrative only.

(1) The seriousness of the allegation. The more serious the charge, the more the public is misinformed and the individual harmed, if the allegation is not true.

(2) The nature of the information, and the extent to which the subject-matter is a matter of public concern.

(3) The source of the information. Some informants have no direct knowledge of the events. Some have their own axes to grind, or are being paid for their stories.

(4) The steps taken to verify the information.

(5) The status of the information. The allegation may have already been the subject of an investigation which commands respect.

(6) The urgency of the matter. News is often a perishable commodity.

(7) Whether comment was sought from the plaintiff. He may have information others do not possess or have not disclosed. An approach to the plaintiff will not always be necessary.

(8) Whether the article contained the gist of the plaintiff's side of the story.

(9) The tone of the article. A newspaper can raise queries or call for an investigation. It need not adopt allegations as statements of fact.

(10) The circumstances of the publication, including the timing.

This list is not exhaustive. The weight to be given to these and any other relevant factors will vary from case to case. Any disputes of primary fact will be a matter for the jury, if there is one. The decision on whether, having regard to the admitted or proved facts, the publication was subject to qualified privilege is a matter for the judge. This is the established practice and seems sound. A balancing operation is better carried out by a judge in a reasoned judgment than by a jury. Over time, a valuable corpus of case law will be built up.

The *Reynolds* defence was upheld by the House of Lords in *Jameel (Mohammed)* v *Wall Street Journal Europe Sprl (No. 3)* [2007] 1 AC 359 (HL) in which Lord Hoffmann stated that Lord Nicholls's *Reynolds* criteria were not to be seen as obstacles or hurdles that any journalist had to overcome in order to avail him or herself of the privilege. See also *Charman* v *Orion Publishing Group Ltd* [2008] 1 All ER 750 (CA) and *Roberts* v *Gable* [2008] QB 502 (CA) for further considerations of the *Reynolds* defence and the distinction between the defendant reporting that A had said something defamatory about B and the defendant using A's words as their own.

The Privy Council had held that the *Reynolds* defence has a wider ambit than the press and broadcast media and extends to publication of material in the public interest in any medium so long as the *Reynolds* criteria were satisfied (*Seaga* v *Harper* [2009] 1 AC 1 (PC)).

The *Reynolds* defence was abolished when the Defamation Act 2013 came into force.

Innocent publication

It is not defamation for a person, who is not the author, editor or publisher of the material, to reproduce material that they did not believe contained defamatory comment provided that they took reasonable care in publishing the statement: section 1, Defamation Act 1996.

In *Bunt* v *Tilley* [2007] 1 WLR 1243 (QB) it was held that an Internet service provider which performed no more than a passive role in facilitating postings on the Internet could not be deemed to be a publisher at common law.

Consent

A person who consents to publication cannot subsequently bring an action for defamation.

Justification

A statement which is true in relation to the claimant cannot be defamatory so the defendant may rely on the defence of justification if he is able to establish the accuracy of the statement. The law requires only that he establishes that the central defamatory thrust of the statement is true; justification will still provide a defence if there are peripheral inaccuracies in the statement: section 5, Defamation Act 1952. This defence was abolished when the Defamation Act 2013 came into force.

Fair comment

This defence applied to critical comment based upon true facts. It generally involved media comments about matters of public interest and the defence regarded that the person making the comment must have believed it to be based in truth and must not have been acting maliciously. It was, in effect, opinion based upon true statements.

In relation to whether the comment was fair, it had been said that 'the true test is whether the opinion, however exaggerated, obstinate or prejudiced, was honestly held by the person expressing it': *Reynolds* v *Times Newspapers* [2001] 2 AC 127 (HL). This approach to the fairness of the comment was regarded as important in protection of freedom of expression: *Silkin* v *Beaverbrook Newspapers* [1958] 1 WLR 743 (DC).

In *Lowe* v *Associated Newspapers Ltd* [2007] QB 580 (DC), the court set out the relationship between fact and comment:

- in order for a defendant to be permitted to rely upon the defence of fair comment, readers of the words complained of must be able to distinguish facts from comment, either because the facts had been set out or referred to in the words complained of, or because the facts were sufficiently widely known for readers to recognise the comment as comment; and

- the ultimate test of a defence of fair comment was the objective one of whether someone could have expressed the commentator's defamatory opinion upon the facts known to the commentator, at least in general terms, and upon which he was purporting to comment.

The scope of the defence was also covered by the Court of Appeal in *Associated Newspapers Ltd* v *Burstein* [2007] 4 All ER 319 (CA).

This defence was abolished when the Defamation Act 2013 came into force.

Offer of amends

This is not a defence, strictly speaking, as it allows a defendant to pre-empt legal proceedings.

KEY STATUTE

Defamation Act 1996, section 2

This provides that the publisher of a defamatory statement may make amends and thus avoid liability if he:

- makes a suitable correction and apology;
- publishes these in a reasonable manner;
- pays compensation to the claimant.

▇ Remedies

Remedies in tort are discussed in more detail in Chapter 14. The following outlines the points that are particularly pertinent to defamation.

Damages

The primary remedy for a successful claimant is damages which, unusually, are determined by the jury following the issue of guidelines by the judge about the likely impact of their decision: *Sutcliffe* v *Pressdram* [1991] 1 QB 153 (CA). The Courts and Legal Services Act 1990 provides that the quantum of damages can be reassessed by the Court of Appeal if the award by the jury is inappropriate, such as the reduction from £250,000 to £110,000 in *Rantzen* v *Mirror Group Newspapers* [1994] QB 670 (CA).

Whilst the general aim of an award of damages is to compensate the claimant for loss suffered as a result of the defendant's tortious behaviour, the law acknowledges the difficulties of quantification of the loss involved in defamation by allowing the award of exemplary damages to take account of both the loss of reputation and the 'distress, hurt and humiliation' caused by the publication: *John* v *Mirror Group Newspapers* [1997] QB 586 (CA).

Injunction

There are two roles for injunction in defamation cases (*Bonnard* v *Perryman* [1891] 2 Ch 269 (CA)):

- An interlocutory injunction can be obtained to prevent publication of defamatory material if the claimant is aware that this is likely.

- An injunction can be sought after a successful defamation claim if the claimant can establish that there is a real risk of repetition of the publication.

In *Greene* v *Associated Newspapers* [2005] QB 972 (CA), it was held that the rule from *Bonnard* v *Perryman* did not constitute an infringement of Article 8 of the European Convention on Human Rights (privacy). The Human Rights Act 1998 had not affected the rule that a court would not grant an interlocutory injunction to restrain the publication of an allegedly defamatory statement unless it was clear that the alleged libel was untrue.

Defamation Act 2013

The Defamation Act 2013 received Royal Assent on 25 April 2013. It was brought into force by Statutory Instrument on 1 January 2014. The following table gives a summary of the changes that were introduced by the key provisions of the Act when it came into force.

Section	Effect
1	Requirements for serious harm: a statement is not defamatory unless its publication has caused or is likely to cause serious harm to the reputation of the claimant. Where the claimant is a profit-making body, harm is not serious unless it has caused, or is likely to cause, serious financial loss.
2	**Defence of truth** It is a defence to show that the imputation conveyed by a statement is substantially true. The common law defence of justification is abolished. Section 5 of the Defamation Act 1952 is repealed.

Section	Effect
3	**Defence of honest opinion** It is a defence to show that: - the statement complained of was a statement of opinion; - the statement complained of indicated the basis of the opinion; - an honest person could have held the opinion based on any fact which existed at the time that the statement was published (or anything asserted as fact in a privileged statement published before the statement complained of). If the defendant did not hold the opinion, the defence is defeated. The common law defence of fair comment is abolished. Section 6 of the Defamation Act 1952 is repealed.
4	**Public interest defence** It is a defence to show that the statement complained of was on a matter of public interest and that the defendant reasonably believed that publishing that statement was in the public interest. The *Reynolds* defence is abolished.
5	**Websites** This section deals with 'notice and takedown' procedures for statements published online: - If the poster can be identified and served with legal proceedings, there is a complete defence for the website operator and the claimant must pursue the poster. - If the poster is anonymous, and the website operator has received a complaint, the operator must respond to the complaint. - In all other circumstances, unless the website operator decides that it wants to defend the content on one of the other available grounds of defence, it will need to remove the content complained of.
6	Provides protection for academics and scientists publishing in peer-reviewed journals, the content of which is privileged under certain conditions.
7	Updates and extends the circumstances in which the defences of absolute and qualified privilege are available.
8	**Single publication rule** Claimants are prevented from bringing an action in relation to publication of the same material by the same publisher after the expiry of a one-year limitation period from the date of the first publication of that material to the public, or a section of the public.

Section	Effect
9	**'Libel tourism'**
	Provides that a court does not have jurisdiction to hear and determine an action in defamation unless it is satisfied that, of all the places in which the statement complained of has been published, England and Wales is clearly the most appropriate place in which to bring an action in respect of the statement.
10	**Secondary publishers**
	Prohibits actions for defamation brought against secondary publishers (such as booksellers) except where it is not reasonably practicable for the claimant to bring the action against the author, editor or publisher.
11	**Jury trials**
	Removes the presumption of trial by jury.

▓ Privacy and misuse of private information

The Human Rights Act 1998 incorporates Article 8 of the European Convention on Human Rights which sets out the basic right of respect for privacy:

KEY STATUTE

Human Rights Act 1998, schedule 1, Article 8

(1) Everyone has the right to respect for his private and family life, his home and his correspondence.

(2) There shall be no interference by a public authority with the exercise of this right except such as is in accordance with the law and is necessary in a democratic society in the interests of national security, public safety or the economic well-being of the country, for the prevention of disorder or crime, for the protection of health or morals, or for the protection of the rights and freedoms of others.

Section 6 of the Act requires that public authorities (expressly including the courts) must not act in a way that is incompatible with Convention rights. It follows that the courts must interpret existing causes of action with regard to those rights. As Baroness Hale said in *Campbell* v *Mirror Group Newspapers* [2004] UKHL 22; [2004] 2 AC 457:

> The [Human Rights Act 1998] does not create any new cause of action between private persons. But if there is a cause of action applicable, the court as a public authority must act compatibly with both parties' Convention rights.

Breach of confidence

Before the Human Rights Act 1998, however, the notion of breach of conscience existed in equity (not as a tort): disclosing information given in confidence would be unconscionable (*Douglas* v *Hello!* [2001] QB 267 (CA)). The three requirements necessary to prove breach of confidence were:

- The information must have the necessary quality of confidentiality (see e.g. *Stephens* v *Avery* [1988] Ch 449 (DC); *Attorney-General* v *Guardian* [1987] 1 WLR 1248 (HL)).
- There must be an obligation on the recipient to keep the information confidential (*Attorney-General* v *Guardian (No. 2)* [1990] 1 AC 109 (HL)).
- The interest in confidentiality must outweigh the public interest in disclosure (see e.g. *W* v *Egdell* [1990] Ch 359 (CA)).

There are three main exemptions (*Attorney-General* v *Guardian*) in which confidence will not apply:

- if the information is in the public domain;
- if the information is useless or trivial; or
- if there is some overriding public interest in publishing or disclosing the information.

Misuse of private information

After the Human Rights Act 1998 came into force in October 2000, a body of case law developed which provides some protection against the misuse of private information. It combines elements of breach of confidence with Article 8 rights. It was defined in *Campbell* v *Mirror Group Newspapers* [2004] UKHL 22; [2004] 2 AC 457:

KEY CASE

Campbell v *Mirror Group Newspapers* **[2004] UKHL 22; [2004] 2 AC 457**

Concerning: privacy; misuse of private information

Facts

The claimant, the model Naomi Campbell, volunteered information to the media including the assertion that she did not take drugs. The defendant newspaper published articles disclosing her drug addiction and that she was attending Narcotics Anonymous including photographs of her in a street as she was leaving a group meeting. The claimant sued the newspaper for breach of confidentiality.

Legal principle

The requirement for an initially confidential relationship was no longer necessary and that the law of breach of confidence had developed such that there was a tort that was better encapsulated as misuse of private information.

There are two requirements as part of this tort:

- The claimant must have a 'reasonable expectation of privacy' in the information (or images) in question.

- The court must balance the interest in keeping the information private against the interest in revealing the information.

Whether there is a 'reasonable expectation of privacy' depends on all the circumstances of the case, including:

- the particular attributes of the claimant, such as whether they are celebrities or children (celebrities have less expectation of privacy, whereas children have a greater expectation);

- the nature of the activity in which the claimant was engaged;

- the place at which it was happening;

- the nature and purpose of the intrusion;

- the absence of consent and whether it was known or could be inferred;

- the effect of the publication on the claimant;

- the circumstances in which and the purposes for which the information came into the hands of the publisher.

If there is a reasonable expectation of privacy, the court must then consider whether or not to interfere with the right to privacy, protected by Article 8. Any interference with that right by the court must be done according to law, be necessary and proportionate, and must be in furtherance of one of the legitimate aims listed in Article 8(2) of the Convention. Most commonly this involves the right of freedom of expression in Article 10.

This balance between the competing rights must be done on a case-by-case basis:

KEY CASE

A v B plc [2003] QB 195 (CA)

Concerning: privacy; freedom of expression

Facts

A professional footballer sought to prevent publication of 'kiss and tell' revelations on the basis that they interfered with his right to a private life.

Legal principle

It was held that scurrilous stories of casual sexual encounters deserved little protection so the right of the other party involved and the newspaper to freedom of expression should prevail. The Court of Appeal was clear that the newspapers should be free to publish without constraint provided they were within the Press Complaints Commission Code.

The story in this case was true so the claimant could not rely on defamation to prevent publication either.

 Make your answer stand out

Defamation cannot protect individuals who wish to suppress the publication of unfavourable or sensitive information if it is true. This makes defamation of only limited value in protecting an individual's reputation as it is limited in scope to untrue statements. The role of defamation in modern society and its role in the balance between rights to privacy and freedom of expression are outlined with clarity in Squires's (1999) article, which would be valuable reading in preparation for an essay question.

If there is an infringement of Article 8 rights which outweighs the competing right to freedom of expression, publication of the private information will amount to misuse of that information, allowing the court to order an injunction to prohibit publication, or award damages in respect of the breach of privacy. However, the European Court of Human Rights commented in *Mosley* v *United Kingdom* [2011] ECHR 774 that, in that particular case, 'it is clear that no sum of money awarded after disclosure of the impugned material could afford a remedy'.

■ Putting it all together

Answer guidelines

See the problem question at the start of the chapter.

Approaching the question

This is a typical example of a problem question focusing on defamation. The question requires an evaluation of the claims of each of the parties, so make sure that everyone with a potential claim is identified and discussed, even if it seems inevitable that their claim will fail.

Important points to include

Discuss each party in turn, dealing with each of the elements of defamation but be sure to avoid excessive repetition by referring back to earlier discussion rather than writing out the same points over and over again.

Jasper is an actor and a story has been published in the newspaper that calls him 'Mr Ugly' (see *Berkoff* v *Burchill*), alleges that he has had affairs with married women and that he has had a homosexual encounter. Consider whether there is a basis for a defamation claim following the structure outlined in this chapter:

■ Is this a defamatory statement? This depends upon whether the statement is true and the question does not provide this information, so you will need to consider it from both perspectives, i.e. on the basis (a) that the statement is true and (b) that it is false. If the statement is false, is it likely to lower him in the minds of right-thinking people?

■ Does the statement refer to Jasper? This seems straightforward here as the article refers to him by name and to his occupation as an actor.

■ Has the statement been published? It is in a national newspaper so this element of defamation is not difficult to establish.

■ Does the newspaper have any defences?

Gertrude is identified in the paper as one of the people with whom Jasper has had an affair. Be sure that you do not confuse slander and libel here: the statement is published in a newspaper, so it falls under libel not slander. If the statement had fallen under slander, it would have been relevant that it concerned allegations of adultery. As it falls under libel, this is not relevant and the ordinary steps of establishing defamation should be followed.

Toby is married to Gertrude so it is possible that he may have an action on the basis of the allegation about her infidelity if this would affect his reputation. You should take into account what Gertrude and Toby do for a living not in relation to whether he has suffered (that would only be required in relation to slander) but in terms of whether he would be exposed to ridicule.

Delores is a barrister and is not the person referred to in the newspaper. The question is whether anyone would think that the article referred to her (*Newstead*). Given that both women share a name, city of residence and legal occupation, it is likely that a reasonable person would think that the statement referred to Delores the barrister.

Kelvin cannot bring a claim irrespective of whether the statement made about him is defamatory as he is dead.

▶

Under the new law

There has to be a requirement of serious harm (section 1). Did the statement cause (or was it likely) to cause harm to Gertrude, Jasper, Toby or Delores?

Consider whether there was a defence of truth (section 2) or honest opinion (section 3). Was publication in the public interest (section 4)?

 Make your answer stand out

Remember to make effective use of the facts. Kelvin cannot bring a claim in defamation because he is dead, so there is no merit in considering whether the statement that he died of AIDS is defamatory. However, it might be useful to consider the relevance of this statement in relation to the claims brought by other parties, given the communicable nature of the disease.

Remember to discuss defences as well as liability. If you conclude that a particular party has a good claim in defamation without considering whether the newspaper has a defence, then there is a danger that you have reached an inaccurate conclusion.

READ TO IMPRESS

Decam, P. (2006) Defamation on the internet: getting caught in a world-wide web. *Practical Law Companies*, p. 33.

Lewis, D. (2005) Whistleblowers and the law of defamation: time for statutory privilege? 3, *Web Journal of Current Legal Issues*.

Squires, D.B. (1999) Striking a balance between kissers and tellers: the law of breach of confidence. *Entertainment Law Review*, p. 240.

www.pearsoned.co.uk/lawexpress

 Go online to access more revision support including quizzes to test your knowledge, sample questions with answer guidelines, podcasts you can download, and more!

13

Defences

■ Topic map

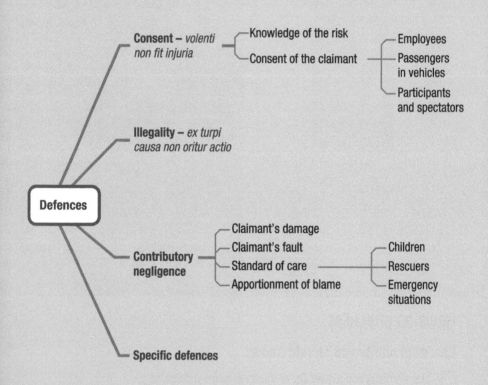

■ Introduction

Once all the elements of any of the torts outlined in this guide have been established, the only way in which a defendant may escape liability is to rely upon a defence.

Defences may be general, i.e. they apply to all torts (such as consent), or specific, i.e. they are applicable only to particular torts (such as self-defence which is a defence to trespass against the person). This chapter outlines the three main general defences: consent, contributory negligence and illegality and provides a table of the specific defences (as these are covered in more detail in the chapters dealing with the torts to which they apply).

Awareness of the defences is crucial to understanding of tort law so they should not be overlooked as part of the revision process. Every defendant who faces liability will want to know whether they have a defence and, conceptually, the availability of defences is part of the way in which the boundaries of actionable tort are established. In practical terms, as any problem question could raise any of the general defences, it is not a topic that should be omitted from your revision.

ASSESSMENT ADVICE

Essay questions

Essay questions addressing the role of remedies in tort are relatively common as are questions focusing on a particular defence such as consent. The more specific the question, the greater the depth of knowledge that is needed to answer the question so make sure that you know enough about the topic before tackling an essay about it.

Problem questions

Problem questions involving defences are common but will always arise in combination with some other tort: a defendant does not need a defence unless the elements of one of the torts have first been established. A question may tell you to discuss liability for tort including any defences that are available or it may remain silent but this failure to instruct you to address any defences that are raised does not mean they should be omitted from your answer. You should always consider whether a defendant has a defence as part and parcel of establishing whether or not he has incurred tortious liability.

■ Sample question

Could you answer this question? Below is a typical problem question that could arise on this topic. Guidelines on answering the question are included at the end of the chapter, whilst a sample essay question and guidance on tackling it can be found on the companion website.

PROBLEM QUESTION

Alison is driving very slowly as she is towing a horsebox containing two horses. Basil, driving behind in a stolen car, gets impatient at the slow speed and overtakes Alison on a bend, crashing into Caroline who was driving in the opposite direction. Caroline was not wearing a seatbelt because she did not want to crease her new dress. She sustains serious head injuries as a result of the accident. Her passenger, Derek, who knew that the car had just failed its MOT due to faulty brakes, was also badly injured. Basil's passenger, Eric (who helped Basil steal the car) suffered a broken leg. Freddie (aged eight) heard the sound of the collision and ran into the road to see what was happening and was struck by Alison's car. Freddie suffered a broken pelvis. Alison was paying insufficient attention to the road at the time that Freddie ran out in front of her as she was sending a text to her husband to tell him about the accident.

Identify the potential defendants; consider their liability and advise them as to what defences they could use to avoid or limit their liability.

■ Consent – *volenti non fit injuria*

KEY DEFINITION: Consent, *volenti non fit injuria*

The defence of consent is frequently referred to by the Latin term *volenti non fit injuria*. The literal translation of this is 'there can be no injury to one who consents' although it is often said to mean 'voluntary assumption of risk'.

The basis of this defence is that a person who consents to harm or consents to an activity which carries a risk of harm should not be able to hold the person who caused that harm liable in tort. Consent is a complete defence; if it is argued successfully, the defendant will not be liable for the claimant's loss.

Before the defence can be considered, it must be shown that the defendant has in fact committed a tort. Once this has been established, the defendant must then prove:

- that the claimant had knowledge of the risk involved (the nature and extent of the risk); and

- that the claimant willingly consented to accept that risk (a voluntary acceptance of that risk as the claimant's own free choice).

Knowledge of the risk

The first requirement of the defence is that the claimant must have had knowledge of the nature of the risk involved. This requires more than a vague awareness of danger but of a more specific knowledge of the type of risk involved in a particular activity. This is a subjective test.

KEY CASE

***Morris* v *Murray* [1991] 2 QB 6 (CA)**

Concerning: consent; knowledge of the risk

Facts

The claimant went drinking with a friend for some hours. The claimant's friend then suggested that they go on a joyride in his light aircraft. The aircraft, piloted by the claimant's friend, took off down wind and uphill, in conditions of poor visibility, low cloud and drizzle when other flying at the aerodrome had been suspended. The aircraft crashed. The pilot was killed and the claimant was seriously injured in the crash. An autopsy on the pilot showed that he was more than three times the legal alcohol limit for driving. The claimant brought an action against the deceased's estate claiming damages for personal injury. The judge awarded him £130,900 damages. The estate appealed against the award.

Legal principle

The court applied a subjective test and held that the claimant was aware of the risk he was taking and therefore his claim against the deceased's estate was barred by the defence of consent.

EXAM TIP

As with any subjective test, you will have to find evidence of what the claimant knew or was thinking. This means that you should analyse the facts of a problem question carefully, looking for clues as to the claimant's awareness of the risk. Remember that any reference to 'obvious' risks will suggest to the examiner that you are applying an objective (reasonable person) test so avoid this and concentrate on the claimant's knowledge of the risk.

Consent of the claimant

The defendant must prove that the claimant freely consented to run the risk of injury. Knowledge of the risk is not the same as consent to running it.

Free consent implies that the claimant must have had a choice as to whether or not to accept the particular risk. The defence will therefore not succeed where the claimant had no choice but to accept the risk (*Smith* v *Charles Baker & Sons* [1891] AC 325 (HL)) or where they lack the mental competence to agree: *Gillick* v *West Norfolk and Wisbech AHA* [1986] AC 112 (HL).

There are certain categories of claimants who have received particular attention from the courts in terms of their consent to harm. Three of these, in particular, will be considered:

- employees;
- passengers in vehicles;
- participants and spectators at sporting events.

Employees

Employees are in a difficult position. Their job may involve the risk of harm but the financial reality of life probably means that most people cannot consider the option of leaving their employment to avoid the risk of harm. It was held in *Smith* v *Charles Baker & Sons* [1891] AC 325 (HL) that continuing to work in a job that is known to carry risks cannot be taken as consent to the risk. For this reason, consent is rarely successful in relation to tortious claims by injured employees.

Passengers in vehicles

The courts have been reluctant to find that a person who is injured by poor driving, even by an obviously intoxicated driver, has consented to the injury (although there may be an issue of contributory negligence). Section 149(3) of the Road Traffic Act 1988 makes it clear that the willing acceptance of the risk of negligence by a passenger does not absolve the driver of liability.

Participants and spectators

By voluntarily taking part in a sporting activity, individuals are deemed to have consented to the risks inherent in that sport. This will vary according to the nature of the activity: rugby carries more risk of injury than darts, for example. The general principle is that participation implies consent to injuries sustained during the course of normal play but not to unsporting behaviour that is in breach of the rules of the game: *Smoldon* v *Whitworth and Nolan* [1997] PIQR 133 (CA).

Some sports, such as motor racing, carry risks to spectators. The general rule seems to be that spectators are deemed to have consented to the risk of harm arising from 'error of judgement or lapse of skill' by a participant but not to injuries caused by negligence: *Wooldridge* v *Sumner* [1963] 2 QB 43 (CA).

Make your answer stand out

The judicial approach to consent in relation to participants and spectators at sporting events demonstrates its flexible nature. In other words, the courts will assess the situation and determine what level of risk of harm it is reasonable to deem an individual to have consented to by dint of their presence or participation.

For further insight into the complexities of the boundaries of consent, see Fafinski's (2005) article which considers the relationship between civil and criminal liability for sporting injuries.

■ Illegality – *ex turpi causa non oritur actio*

KEY DEFINITION: Illegality, *ex turpi causa non oritur actio*

The defence of illegality is frequently referred to by the Latin term *ex turpi causa non oritur actio* which means 'no action arises from a disgraceful claim'. In other words, if the claimant was knowingly engaged in an unlawful enterprise at the time he was injured, it would be contrary to public policy to allow his claim to succeed.

There must be a close connection between the injury sustained by the claimant and the criminal enterprise in which he is involved. For example, if two thieves were on their way to commit a burglary and one punched the other, there would be no defence of **illegality** to prevent a claim in tort for trespass to the person because the attack was unconnected with the planned criminal enterprise.

There is a fair degree of dissent amongst the case law as to the application of illegality. Some cases have taken a strong line and held that the claimant's participation in unlawful activity deprives him of any claim for injury sustained during the criminal enterprise:

- A burglar bitten by a guard dog had no claim due to illegality: *Cummings* v *Granger* [1977] QB 397 (CA).

- A claim for negligence against the police for injuries sustained by a prisoner, whom they failed to prevent from jumping out of a window, was rejected on the basis of illegality: *Vellino* v *Chief Constable of Greater Manchester Police* [2002] 1 WLR 218 (CA).

- A claimant who started a fight but was severely injured by his opponent was prevented from claiming for the injuries sustained due to illegality: *Murphy* v *Culhane* [1977] QB 74 (CA).

- A claimant suffering post-traumatic stress disorder following the negligent act of the defendant was unable to recover damages for loss of earnings after being found guilty of manslaughter due to diminished responsibility and detained in a secure mental hospital: *Gray* v *Thames Trains Ltd* [2009] 1 AC 1339 (HL).

Although there is a fair amount of case law that shows that claimants have been unsuccessful because of illegality, there have been cases in which the courts have been reluctant to allow illegality to defeat the claim for damages:

KEY CASE

***Revill* v *Newberry* [1996] QB 567 (CA)**

Concerning: illegality

Facts

The claimant went to steal property from a shed but the owner was in wait with a shotgun. The owner fired the gun in panic when the claimant started to enter the shed and he sustained serious injuries.

Legal principle

The court held that the claimant should not be deprived of a claim on the basis of illegality, saying that it was too 'far-reaching to deprive [the claimant] even of compensation for injury which he suffers and which otherwise he is entitled to recover at law'.

 Make your answer stand out

Although the defence of illegality was rejected in *Revill*, a defence of contributory negligence succeeded in reducing the damages he was awarded by two-thirds. Part of the reluctance of the courts to admit defences of consent and illegality arises from the fact that they entirely defeat a claim that has otherwise satisfied the requirements of the tort in question. By contrast, contributory negligence allows the claim to succeed but adjusts the level of damages awarded to reflect the claimant's responsibility for his own injury.

Awareness of the relationship between the defences and the policy considerations that have influenced the development of case law is necessary in order to write an essay on this topic. Further insight into these issues can be gained by reading Glofcheski's (1999) article which engages with the policy issues in this area.

■ Contributory negligence

> **KEY STATUTE**
>
> **Law Reform (Contributory Negligence) Act 1945, section 1(1)**
>
> Where any person suffers damage as the result partly of his own fault and partly of the fault of any other person . . . a claim in respect of that damage shall not be defeated . . . but the damages recoverable in respect thereof shall be reduced to such an extent as the court thinks just and equitable having regard to the claimant's share in the responsibility for the damage.

Unlike consent and illegality, contributory negligence is not a complete defence but a partial defence that reduces the level of damages payable to the claimant. It applies when the claimant's carelessness has in some way caused, or contributed to, his own injuries.

> **!　Don't be tempted to . . .**
>
> It is a mistake to think that contributory negligence is only a defence (as its name might lead you to think) to the tort of negligence. The reference to negligence relates to the claimant's fault in contributing to his own injury, not the means by which the defendant caused him injury so it is applicable to most torts. The Law Reform (Contributory Negligence) Act 1945, section 4, specifies, in addition to negligence, breach of statutory duty or other act or omission which gives rise to a liability in tort. This gives contributory negligence a very broad applicability as a partial defence to a whole range of torts.

Claimant's damage

The requirement that the claimant has suffered damage includes, but is not limited to, death and personal injury (section 4). As such, it would include any other loss for which damages could be awarded in tort such as damage to property and economic loss.

Claimant's fault

In order for a defence of contributory negligence to succeed, it must be established that the claimant failed to take care of his own safety in a way that at least partially caused the damage that he suffered.

KEY CASE

Jones v *Livox Quarries* [1952] 2 QB 608 (CA)

Concerning: foreseeability of harm

Facts

The claimant was injured at work when two quarrying vehicles collided. The claimant was sat on the back of one of the vehicles at the time of the collision, without the driver's knowledge and in contravention of the explicit prohibition on doing so.

Legal principle

It was held that this did amount to contributory negligence as the claimant 'ought to have foreseen that, if he did not act as a reasonable, prudent man, he might be hurt himself'.

Therefore, the injury which the claimant suffered must have been a foreseeable consequence of his own behaviour even though the injury was caused by the defendant:

- In *Badger* v *Ministry of Defence* [2006] 3 All ER 173 (QB), the damages recoverable by the widow of a man who had contracted lung cancer as a result of exposure to asbestos by the defendant were reduced by 20% since her late husband had continued to smoke when he knew or should have known that his doing so was liable to damage his health and he had been told to stop: a prudent man would have known of the risks.

- However, in *St George* v *Home Office* [2009] 1 WLR 1670 (CA) the claimant was not held to be contributorily negligent in respect of injuries he sustained due to the negligence of prison staff. The claimant was addicted to drugs and alcohol and informed prison staff that he suffered seizures when in withdrawal. He was allocated a top bunk from which he fell during such a seizure which left him permanently and very severely disabled. Although the claimant would not have suffered a withdrawal seizure and fallen but for his addiction, the claimant's fault in becoming addicted was too remote in time, place and circumstance and was not sufficiently connected with the negligence of the prison staff to be properly regarded as a potent cause of the injury.

✎ EXAM TIP

The essence of contributory negligence is that it takes into account the conduct of both the claimant and the defendant so remember to examine the behaviour of both parties. In particular, ask 'did the claimant do anything to put himself at risk of suffering this injury or to increase the seriousness of his injuries?', as, if so, this is a good indication that contributory negligence will be established.

Standard of care

The standard of care is that of the reasonably prudent person. In other words, a defence of contributory negligence will succeed if it can be established that the claimant failed to recognise that he was jeopardising his own safety if this would have been obvious to the ordinary person.

Children

There is an exception to this in relation to children as the courts have acknowledged that children are less likely to recognise the risks inherent in their conduct than adults.

KEY CASE

Gough v *Thorne* [1966] 1 WLR 1387 (CA)

Concerning: age of the claimant

Facts

The 13-year-old claimant was struck by a car as she was crossing the road. Her view had been obscured by a lorry but the driver had indicated that it was clear to cross the road. Unfortunately, a car swerved past the lorry and struck the claimant and the issue was whether her damages should be reduced on the basis of contributory negligence.

Legal principle

The court held that there was no contributory negligence as the claimant had done all that could be expected of a child of her age:

> A very young child cannot be guilty of contributory negligence. An older child may be; but it depends on the circumstances. A judge should only find a child guilty of contributory negligence if he or she is of such an age as reasonably to be expected to take precautions for his or her own safety; and then he or she is only to be found guilty if blame is to be attached to him or her (*per* Lord Denning).

The key question in relation to child claimants is whether their behaviour showed a level of care for their own safety that was appropriate for their age:

- An 11-year-old claimant was injured after being struck by a car whilst playing with a football in the middle of a busy road. A 75% reduction in damages was made for contributory negligence because this risk would be obvious to an ordinary 11-year-old: *Morales* v *Eccleston* [1991] RTR 151 (CA).

- A nine-year-old claimant suffered serious burns after setting fire to some petrol supplied by the defendants. This was not contributory negligence as he was not of an age where he would appreciate the danger of playing with petrol: *Yachuk* v *Oliver Blais Co Ltd* [1949] AC 386 (PC).

Further evidence of differential standards being applied to children can be seen in relation to occupiers' liability. You might find it useful to refresh your memory about this approach (see Chapter 6) and consider how it compares to contributory negligence. This would be particularly useful to ensure that you were prepared for a question involving child claimants.

Rescuers

The objective standard of care is also modified in relation to rescue situations where it becomes the standard of the reasonable rescuer: only if a rescuer has shown 'wholly unreasonable disregard for his or her own safety' will there be a finding of contributory negligence: *Baker* v *TE Hopkins & Son Ltd* [1959] 1 WLR 966 (CA).

Emergency situations

It is also recognised that a person faced with sudden peril may respond in a way that does not seem to be the best course of action when viewed with the benefit of hindsight. A person acting 'in the agony of the moment' is not expected to take time to weigh up the risk of his action and this is taken into account in relation to contributory negligence. In *Jones* v *Boyce* (1816) 1 Stark 492 (CCP), it was held that the question is whether the claimant's actions were reasonable in the context of the dangerous situation in which he was placed.

Apportionment of blame

If a defendant establishes contributory negligence, the court will look at the contribution of both parties to the harm suffered by the claimant and apportion a percentage of responsibility to each party. The claimant's damages will then be reduced by that percentage. In *Stapley* v *Gypsum Mines Ltd* [1953] AC 663 (HL), it was held that there are two factors to be taken into account when deciding how to apportion blame:

- **Causation:** the extent to which the claimant's own behaviour caused or contributed to his injuries;
- **Culpability:** the relative blameworthiness of the claimant and defendant for the injuries sustained by the claimant.

Notice that the focus is on the claimant's contribution to his injuries. This is different from a requirement that he contributed to the accident that caused the injuries. The claimant may be entirely blameless in terms of causing the accident in which he was injured but may have his damages reduced for contributory negligence if he has contributed to his own injuries.

> **KEY CASE**
>
> *Froom* v *Butcher* [1976] QB 286 (CA)
>
> *Concerning: reduction for contribution to injury*
>
> **Facts**
>
> The claimant was injured when the car in which she was a passenger was struck by an oncoming vehicle, driven dangerously by the defendant. The claimant was not wearing a seatbelt and the issue was whether this could amount to contributory negligence.
>
> **Legal principle**
>
> It was held that contributory negligence was concerned with the cause of the claimant's injuries, not the cause of the accident in which the injuries were sustained. The injury was caused in part by the defendant's bad driving and in part by the claimant's failure to wear a seatbelt and, as such, she had contributed to her own injuries and a reduction in the quantum of damages was appropriate.

The Court of Appeal went on to establish a scale of reductions based upon failure to wear a seatbelt:

- Injuries would have been avoided altogether if a seatbelt had been worn: 25% reduction.
- Injuries would have been less severe if a seatbelt had been worn: 15% reduction.
- Injuries would have been the same even if a seatbelt had been worn: no reduction.

As *Froom* v *Butcher* makes clear, the focus of attention must not be on the claimant's behaviour in isolation but in how the claimant's behaviour has contributed to his injuries. If the claimant has behaved badly but would have been just as seriously injured if he had been behaving in an impeccable fashion, there will be no contributory negligence; see Figure 13.1.

Figure 13.1

Iestyn is cycling home from work through busy traffic. He is not wearing his cycle helmet because he has a headache. A car, driving erratically, clips the wheel of his bicycle and Iestyn falls, hitting his head on the kerb and suffering a broken arm	**Contribution to the injuries** →	Iestyn makes no contribution to the accident. His failure to wear his cycle helmet has contributed to his injuries as his head would have been less badly injured had he been wearing it. A reduction in damages on the basis of contributory negligence is likely
Iestyn is coming home from the pub after drinking heavily. He finds it hard to steer and is weaving about. A car rounds the bend at a high speed on the wrong side of the road. It knocks Iestyn off his bicycle and he sustains serious injuries in the accident	**No contribution to the injuries** →	Although Iestyn is being careless in the way that he is riding his bicycle, this makes no contribution to his injuries. It is likely that the accident would have occurred in th e same way and resulted in the same injuries irrespective of his drunkenness and inability to steer his bicycle

▉ Specific defences

Unlike the general defences outlined in this chapter, those in the following table are limited in application to a particular tort. They are listed here for the sake of completeness but you will find a more detailed account in the chapter dealing with the relevant tort.

Tort	Defences
Occupiers' liability (Chapter 6)	Warning notices
Nuisance (Chapter 7)	Prescription
	Statutory authority
Trespass to land (Chapter 9)	Contractual licence
	Lawful authority
	Necessity
False imprisonment: trespass to the person (Chapter 10)	Reasonable condition for release
	Lawful arrest
	Medical detention
Assault and battery: trespass to the person (Chapter 10)	Lawful authority
	Self-defence
	Parental authority
	Consent
	Necessity
Defamation (Chapter 12)	Privilege
	Innocent publication
	Consent
	Justification
	Fair comment
	Offer of amends

◼ Putting it all together

Answer guidelines

See the problem question at the start of the chapter.

Approaching the question

This is a typical example of a problem question that focuses on defences. There is a need to establish liability as there is no need for a defence unless *prima facie* liability is established but the bulk of your answer should be focused on defences. Problems often arise with such a question as students are tempted to answer it on the basis that the negligence issues are extremely straightforward so it seems like an easy question. Bear in mind that the negligence issues are so easy so that attention can be devoted to the issues concerning defences. It would be a mistake to tackle this question if you were only able to deal with the negligence aspects of it.

Important points to include

- One of the difficulties of tackling a question such as this comes in identifying the appropriate defendant in relation to each claimant. This is particularly complex here as Alison would not initially attract liability but is likely to do so at a later stage in relation to Freddie. Take time before you start writing your answer to make a plan that allows you to be absolutely clear about who the defendant is in relation to each claimant.
- **Basil** overtakes on a bend and crashes into Caroline who is driving in the opposite direction. Establish his liability before considering whether there is a defence available to any of the potential claimants.
- **Caroline** suffered head injuries as a result of the collision. She was not wearing a seatbelt so her award of damages might be reduced on the basis of contributory negligence (*Froom* v *Butcher*).
- **Derek** was badly injured in the collision but is his claim against Basil (who crashed into the car in which Derek was a passenger whilst overtaking on a bend) or Caroline (who was driving a car with faulty brakes)? As there is no suggestion that Caroline's failure to brake contributed to the accident, it would be more appropriate to concentrate on Basil's liability here. Derek's knowledge of the faulty brakes does not seem to raise any defence for Basil here.
- **Eric** was a passenger in the car which Basil was driving so establishing negligence is not a problem here. Does Eric's contribution to the theft of the car provide a defence for Basil?

▶

■ **Alison** is potentially liable for negligence as she was sending a text message whilst driving and hit Freddie (aged eight) when he ran into the road. Whether she has a defence of contributory negligence will depend on whether it was reasonable for Freddie to appreciate the risks attached to his actions. Consideration of *Gough* v *Thorne* and other cases discussed in this chapter would be relevant here.

 Make your answer stand out

There should be two stages to dealing with each issue here: (1) establish negligence and (2) explore possible defences. Take care not to confuse the facts relevant to these two stages. For example, by overtaking on a bend, Basil's conduct would be negligent even if he were driving his own car so it is not relevant to the first stage of establishing negligence that the car is stolen. This point is relevant in considering whether Basil may argue a defence of illegality in relation to Eric's injuries.

Do not get drawn into a discussion of Alison's liability for the accident as to do so would suggest misunderstanding of the operation of the tort of negligence. Alison is driving slowly which is why Basil overtook her on a bend but we are not concerned with establishing the cause of the accident but with whether any of those involved have been negligent. What basis is there to argue that Alison is negligent in relation to the collision between Basil and Caroline? She was not driving carelessly: in fact, she was taking extra care by driving slowly as she was towing a horsebox.

READ TO IMPRESS

Fafinski, S. (2005) Consent and the rules of the game: the interplay of civil and criminal liability for sporting injuries. *Journal of Criminal Law*, p. 414.

Glofcheski, R.A. (1999) Plaintiff's illegality as a bar to recovery for personal injury. *Legal Studies*, p. 6.

Ryan, R. and Ryan, D. (2006) Pleading contributory negligence: recent developments. *Quarterly Review of Tort Law*, p. 7.

www.pearsoned.co.uk/lawexpress

 Go online to access more revision support including quizzes to test your knowledge, sample questions with answer guidelines, podcasts you can download, and more!

14

Remedies

Revision checklist

Essential points you should know:

- [ ] The circumstances in which damages are awarded
- [ ] The distinction between the different categories of damages
- [ ] The different types of injunction and their application
- [ ] The relationship between damages and injunctions

■ Topic map

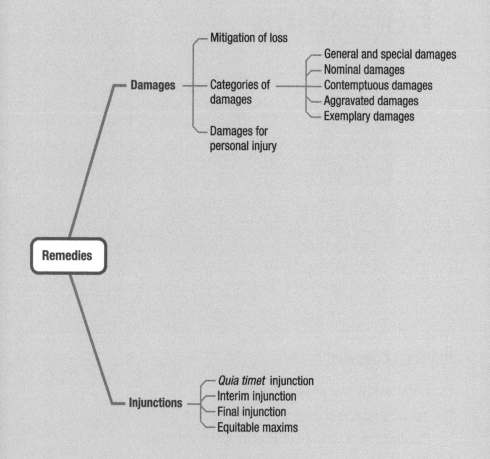

■ Introduction

This chapter focuses on the two main remedies available in tort: damages and injunctions.

These remedies are of general application and are supplemented by some specific remedies that are available only to particular torts, such as abatement in relation to the tort of nuisance. Most claimants who have suffered a tortious wrong are concerned either to prevent the continuation or repetition of the problem (injunction) or to obtain financial recompense for the harm they have suffered (damages). Damages are a legal remedy that are available 'as of right' to a successful claimant, i.e. he is entitled to an award of damages, whereas injunctions are equitable remedies so are available at the court's discretion; a successful claimant will not automatically be granted an injunction.

Remedies are frequently omitted from tort revision. This is unfortunate as it is one of the two key issues for a client who is a claimant or defendant in a tort case: (1) will I be successful or liable? and (2) what will I get (if I win) or have to pay (if I lose)? Moreover, an understanding of the heads of damage will help you to identify potential causes of action so this will enhance your ability to deal with liability in relation to the substantive torts that you have studied.

ASSESSMENT ADVICE

Essay questions

Essay questions dealing with remedies would require not only a detailed knowledge of the types of damages and injunctions and their application but also of the policy underlying their use. The issues are not complex but do require careful attention to detail: for example, students often confuse the different types of damages.

Problem questions

Problem questions that require a strong focus on remedies usually make this clear from their instructions, e.g. consider the remedies available to the claimant, or from the wording of the facts, e.g. a detailed account of the losses suffered by the claimant, particularly in relation to future losses.

■ Sample question

Could you answer this question? Below is a typical essay question that could arise on this topic. Guidelines on answering the question are included at the end of this chapter. Another sample question and guidance on tackling it can be found on the companion website.

ESSAY QUESTION

Assess the extent to which each of the following remedies strikes an appropriate balance between the interests of the claimant and the defendant:

(a) mandatory injunction

(b) interim injunction

(c) nominal damages

(d) aggravated damages.

■ Damages

Damages are the primary remedy available in tort. The principle is that the award of damages should return the claimant to the position that they would have been in had the tort not occurred. This is not always straightforward as some tortious harms are less amenable to quantification than others; for example, if the defendant's trespass to land damages the claimant's wall, the cost of repairing or replacing the wall can be calculated but other sorts of harm are less easy to represent in financial terms. There are three basic situations:

- harm, loss or injury that is amenable to quantification, such as damage to property;

- harm, loss or injury that is harder to quantify typically involving personal injury;

- torts which are actionable *per se*, i.e. there is no requirement of harm where the damages represent the wrong arising from interference with the claimant's legal interest (e.g. damages for trespass to the person reflect the interference with the claimant's right to bodily integrity and freedom from interference).

In addition to the difficulties of calculating the value of certain kinds of damage, there are also other factors to take into account such as the claimant's duty to mitigate their loss and situations in which the courts award damages that go beyond mere recompense for loss.

Mitigation of loss

A claimant who suffers loss as a result of the defendant's tort is entitled to an award of damages to ensure that they are not 'out of pocket'. However, a claimant must take reasonable steps to ensure that the losses that they are claiming are kept to a minimum. For example, a claimant who is not able to continue in his usual employment due to the defendant's conduct must seek reasonable alternative employment in order to mitigate his loss.

Categories of damages

General and special damages

These are illustrated in the following table:

Special damages	General damages
Those which are capable of being calculated at the time of the trial and which are presented to the court in a form of calculation	Those which are not capable of being calculated at the time of trial so are left to the court to quantify
Loss of earnings before trial	Loss of future earnings
Medical expenses prior to trial	Cost of future medical expenses
Damage to property, e.g. loss of a vehicle in an accident	Pain and suffering

Nominal damages

These damages are awarded when the claimant's rights have been infringed but little harm has been caused. This type of damages is frequently awarded in relation to torts which are actionable *per se* and cases in which the primary aim of the claimant was to obtain an injunction:

- The defendant abandoned a broken-down car on the claimant's land. There is liability for trespass to land but little actual damage.

- The defendant persistently parks his car on the claimant's land. The claimant is concerned to obtain an injunction to prevent him from doing so rather than obtaining damages.

Contemptuous damages

These damages are also awarded when the level of harm caused is low. They differ from **nominal damages** in that the court feels that the action should not have been brought (even though the claimant has been successful in establishing the elements of a tort). To reflect the court's view that the claimant was wrong to bring a claim, an award of contemptuous damages is extremely low, often the lowest value currency available: 1p damages.

Aggravated damages

These damages are awarded over and above the damages that are necessary to return the claimant to the position that he would have been in had the tort not occurred. They are additional sums of money to reflect that the initial harm was made worse by some aggravating factor, often injury to feelings or anxiety and distress caused by the defendant. As such, they are often awarded in cases involving defamation and trespass to the person.

KEY CASE

Thompson v *Metropolitan Police Commissioner* **[1998] QB 498 (CA)**
Concerning: aggravated damages

Facts

The claimant was lawfully arrested for a driving offence but the police used excessive force to place her in a cell.

Legal principle

It was held that additional damages should be awarded when there are aggravating features about the case that mean that the claimant would not otherwise receive sufficient compensation. The court held that aggravating features 'can include humiliating circumstances . . . or any conduct of those responsible . . . which shows that they had behaved in a high-handed, insulting, malicious or oppressive manner'.

Exemplary damages

There is often some confusion about the distinction between aggravated damages (above) and exemplary damages as the latter is also an additional award that reflects the court's disapproval of the defendant's conduct. There is, however, a crucial distinction between the two types of damages as Figure 14.1 illustrates.

KEY CASE

Rookes v *Barnard* **[1964] AC 1129 (HL)**
Concerning: distinction between aggravated and exemplary damages

Facts

After a disagreement, the claimant left his union. The defendant, an unpaid union official, told the claimant's employer that there would be a strike unless the claimant was dismissed. Following his dismissal, the claimant brought a civil action founded in conspiracy against the defendant and others.

Legal principle

The House of Lords considered the distinction between aggravated and exemplary damages. It was held that the purpose of aggravated damages was to compensate the claimant for loss or harm suffered whilst the purpose of exemplary damages was to punish the defendant for unacceptable behaviour and deter others from similar behaviour. It was held that there are three situations that justify the imposition of exemplary damages:

(1) Oppressive, arbitrary or unconstitutional action by the servants of the government.

(2) Cases where the defendant is calculated to make a profit that will exceed the compensation otherwise payable to the claimant.

(3) In situations where exemplary damages are explicitly authorised by statute.

Figure 14.1

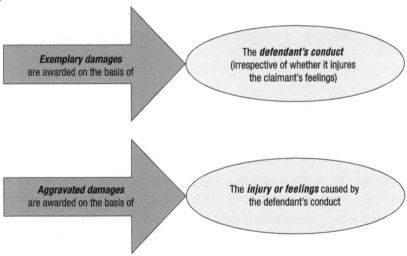

Damages for personal injury

The quantification of damages in personal injury cases is particularly complex due to the wide range of heads of damage that may arise. For example, a person who is seriously injured in an accident may wish to recover for some or all of the following:

- the cost of replacing personal property damaged in the accident;
- loss of earnings (1) between the accident and trial and (2) after the trial;
- loss of earning capacity if he is unable to perform the same level of work after the accident;

- damages for pain and suffering (before and after the trial);

- damages for loss of amenity if he is no longer able to engage in social and leisure pursuits that he enjoyed prior to the accident;

- the costs of any private medical care (a claimant is entitled to private treatment even if NHS treatment is available) incurred before and after the trial;

- the expenses involved in obtaining care assistance in the home if his injuries leave him unable to care for himself;

- the costs of having his home adapted to his needs, i.e. ramps, lowered surfaces.

 Make your answer stand out

This list of potential heads of damage gives an indication of the complexity of a personal injury claim, particularly as some of the losses are clearly not amenable to mathematical calculation (non-pecuniary losses). The intricacies of the calculation of personal injury claims is beyond the scope of this revision guide so if this is covered in detail on your syllabus you will need to consult a specialist text that deals with the issue.

■ Injunctions

An **injunction** is a discretionary remedy which takes the form of a court order that requires that the defendant behave in a particular way. This can take two forms:

- **Prohibitory:** the most common form of injunction which requires the defendant to refrain from doing something; in other words, to stop committing the tort that he is committing.

- **Mandatory:** these compel the defendant to take a particular action to rectify the situation that has arisen due to his tortious behaviour. As they require positive action, they are considered to be an onerous burden to impose upon the defendant and are relatively uncommon and in strictly limited circumstances:

KEY CASE

Redland Bricks Ltd v *Morris* **[1970] AC 652 (HL)**

Concerning: conditions for granting a mandatory injunction

Facts

The claimants (respondents) and defendants (appellants) owned adjoining land. The appellants (Redland Bricks) used their land to quarry clay and their activities caused the land belonging to the respondents (Morris), who were market gardeners, to subside.

Further slips were predicted that would make the respondents' land unworkable as a market garden. The estimated cost of remedying the slippage was £30,000, which greatly exceeded the value of the respondents' land (£12,000). Notwithstanding this, the trial judge granted a mandatory injunction requiring that the damage be remedied.

Legal principle

The House of Lords overturned the injunction. As the cost of remedial action would exceed the value of the land, it was not appropriate to impose a mandatory injunction. Four criteria were:

(1) a strong possibility of substantial damage in the future;

(2) pecuniary remedies, i.e. damages, would be inadequate;

(3) the defendants have behaved 'wantonly or unreasonably';

(4) the injunction must be capable of reflecting exactly what the defendant was compelled to do.

Although injunctions can be used in relation to any tort, they are most common in relation to problems that are likely to continue so are used most frequently in relation to nuisance, trespass to land, harassment and defamation. Failure to comply with an injunction amounts to a contempt of court and may be punishable by a fine or imprisonment.

There are three kinds of injunction that vary according to the time at which they are obtained in relation to the commission of the tort, see Figure 14.2.

Figure 14.2

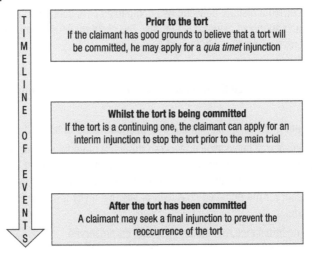

TIMELINE OF EVENTS

Prior to the tort
If the claimant has good grounds to believe that a tort will be committed, he may apply for a *quia timet* injunction

Whilst the tort is being committed
If the tort is a continuing one, the claimant can apply for an interim injunction to stop the tort prior to the main trial

After the tort has been committed
A claimant may seek a final injunction to prevent the reoccurrence of the tort

Quia timet injunction

This is an injunction which is obtained prior to the commission of a tort in order to prevent its occurrence. For example, a person who knows that a neighbour plans to hold a noisy event may wish to apply for a *quia timet* injunction to prevent its occurrence. Such injunctions are only granted if:

- there is a high likelihood that a tortious event will occur;
- this event would cause significant damage or disruption to the claimant; and
- the defendant will not desist unless an injunction is granted.

Interim injunction

This is also known as an interlocutory injunction and may be granted once an action has been commenced pending the full hearing of the issue. In other words, if a claimant initiates an action in nuisance, there will be a lapse of time before the claim is heard so the claimant may seek an **interim injunction** to prevent the continuation of the nuisance until the matter is resolved. The guidelines for granting an interim injunction have been outlined by the House of Lords:

KEY CASE

American Cyanamid v *Ethicon* [1975] AC 396 (HL)

Concerning: conditions for granting an interim injunction

Facts

The case concerned a dispute between two companies both concerned with the manufacture and supply of disposable sutures. The claimant sought an interim injunction to prevent an alleged breach of patent law.

Legal principle

The House of Lords outlined the conditions that must exist for an interim injunction to be granted:

(1) The claimant must establish that there is a serious issue to be tried.

(2) That the balance of convenience favoured the grant of an injunction, i.e. whether damages would be an adequate remedy at the end of the trial must be balanced against the consideration of whether damages would be sufficient to compensate the defendant for the enforced cessation of lawful activity if the claim was unsuccessful.

(3) If there is no imbalance, the status quo must be preserved.

Figure 14.3

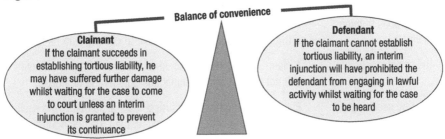

The reference to the balance of convenience (Figure 14.3) between the parties gets to the heart of the difficulty associated with the grant of interim injunctions. As the case has not been heard, the court is not sure whether or not a tort is actually being committed.

It is for this reason that a claimant must undertake to pay damages to the defendant if an interim injunction is granted but there is eventually found to be no liability in tort.

Final injunctions

The usual remedy in tort is damages and a claimant will not be granted an injunction unless he is able to establish that damages would not be an adequate remedy.

 Make your answer stand out

In situations where there is a risk of ongoing tortious behaviour, damages will not be adequate. For example, a financial award would do little for a claimant whose sleep is repeatedly disturbed by noise emanating from a neighbouring building (private nuisance, see Chapter 7) or a claimant whose everyday life was blighted by persistent harassment from the defendant (harassment, see Chapter 10). To award damages in such a case would be the equivalent of allowing the defendant to purchase the right to commit a tort.

Equitable maxims

As injunctions are **equitable remedies**, their availability is limited by general equitable principles. Therefore, claimants must ensure that the circumstances of their case do not offend against key equitable maxims, as the following table illustrates:

Equitable maxim	Meaning in relation to injunctions
Equity does nothing in vain	An injunction will not be granted if it would be ineffective, e.g. if the defendant would not be able to comply with its terms
Delay defeats equity	A claimant who has not acted promptly in bringing an action will not be awarded an injunction against the defendant
He who seeks equity must do equity	Equity is concerned with fairness thus a claimant who seeks an injunction must not have encouraged the defendant in his tortious behaviour or acquiesced to its existence

! Don't be tempted to . . .

Be careful you don't state that injunctions are *always* available in situations where the claimant really wants the defendant to do (or stop doing) something. Injunctions are equitable remedies which are discretionary, so whether or not they are available will depend on whether they are appropriate taking into account all the circumstances of the case and particularly in the light of the key equitable maxims.

■ Putting it all together

Answer guidelines

See the essay question at the start of the chapter.

Approaching the question

This is an example of an essay question involving damages. Although it may not look like a typical essay question, it has been worded like this to make it easier for students to appreciate what issues they need to address. A more typical manifestation of this question would be 'using examples to illustrate your answer, assess the extent to which remedies in tort take into account the interests of the claimant and the interests of the defendant'. Whatever its format, this is a very common question.

Important points to include

■ The different categories of damages and injunctions does lead to a fair amount of confusion amongst students so this is not a question that should be attempted by anyone who is not absolutely clear about the precise meaning of each of the remedies listed. It is common, for example, for students to confuse aggravated and exemplary damages and this is a question that would expose that confusion, whereas other less specific questions on remedies would allow it to remain hidden. For example, if the question reads 'assess the extent to which different types of remedies strike an appropriate balance between the interests of the claimant and the defendant' then the student could be selective with which remedies were included and omit altogether ones where there was misunderstanding or confusion. However, the precision added to the question by listing particular types of remedies offers no such hiding place.

■ Make sure that you know enough about each of the remedies to tackle this question. This should include:

  □ an explanation of the nature of the remedy and its application;

  □ any case law that demonstrates its operation;

  □ a factual example of how it applies to demonstrate understanding.

■ For example, a mandatory injunction is a court order which compels the defendant to behave in a particular way thus is regarded as more onerous and a far greater burden than a prohibitory injunction which merely prevents the defendant from doing that which he would be otherwise able to do. It is an equitable remedy that may be awarded to a successful claimant if the criteria outlined in *Redland Bricks Ltd* v *Morris* [1970] AC 652 are satisfied: (1) there must be a strong possibility of damage in the future; (2) pecuniary remedies (damages) would be inadequate; (3) the defendants have behaved unreasonably; and (4) the injunction must be able to provide a clear and precise indication of what the defendant is required to do.

✓ Make your answer stand out

Make sure that your answer goes beyond a straightforward descriptive account of each of the remedies. This should be the foundation of your answer but build upon this by tackling the issue raised by the question to improve your essay. Think about what you have said about each remedy and consider whether it favours the claimant or the defendant. For example, the stringent conditions attached to the grant of a mandatory injunction favour the defendant because they ensure that it is only in the rarest of occasions that the court will grant an injunction that imposes a positive burden on the defendant. Then think about why the courts take this approach. ▶

In relation to a mandatory injunction, it is because the imposition of a positive burden may necessitate the expenditure of money or effort thus can only be justified in extreme circumstances. (Note the requirement for unreasonable behaviour outlined in *Redland Bricks* that suggests that this type of injunction may be used to reflect the court's disapproval of the defendant's unreasonable behaviour.)

Always strive to incorporate academic opinion into an essay. Locate suitable articles and include as part of your revision, and ensure that you are familiar with the views expressed by the writer. It can help to summarise the main arguments in the article as a series of bullet points that will be easier to remember and introduce into your essay.

READ TO IMPRESS

Murphy, J. (2007) Rethinking injunctions in tort law. 27, *Oxford Journal of Legal Studies*, p. 509.

Smith, S. (1997) Rights, remedies and normal expectations in tort and contract. 113, *Law Quarterly Review*, p. 426.

www.pearsoned.co.uk/lawexpress

 Go online to access more revision support including quizzes to test your knowledge, sample questions with answer guidelines, podcasts you can download, and more!

And finally, before the exam . . .

By using this revision guide to direct your work, you should now have a good knowledge and understanding of the way in which the various torts work in isolation and the ways in which they are interrelated. What is more, you should have acquired the necessary skills and techniques to demonstrate that knowledge and understanding in the exam, regardless of whether the questions are presented to you in essay or problem format.

Test yourself

☐ Look at the **revision checklists** at the start of each chapter. Are you happy that you can now tick them all? If not, go back to the particular chapter and work through the material again. If you are still struggling, seek help from your tutor.

☐ Attempt the **sample questions** in each chapter and check your answers against the guidelines provided.

☐ Go online to **www.pearsoned.co.uk/lawexpress** for more hands-on revision help and try out these resources:

    ☐ Try the **test your knowledge** quizzes and see if you can score full marks for each chapter.

    ☐ Attempt to answer the **sample questions** for each chapter within the time limit and check your answers against the guidelines provided.

    ☐ Listen to the **podcast** and then attempt the question it discusses.

    ☐ **'You be the marker'** and see if you can spot the strengths and weaknesses of the sample answers.

    ☐ Use the **flashcards** to test your recall of the legal principles of the key cases and statutes you've revised and definitions of important terms. ▶

☐ Make sure that you take into account the different levels of knowledge required for essays and problem questions in tort. Problem questions require that you state and apply the current law whilst essays require far greater depth of knowledge.

☐ Follow up some of the suggested reading to ensure that you have the necessary level of understanding to tackle an essay question and impress your examiner.

Linking it all up

This text provided a series of questions on specific areas of tort but you should remember that these topics can be combined to create questions that require knowledge of a whole range of different areas of tort. In essence, a problem question could combine any number of tortious acts and defences not to mention involving multiple parties so it is important that you cover as much of the syllabus as possible in your revision so that you are equipped to tackle any question that you encounter. Selective revision can leave you in the difficult position of being able to tackle only part of a problem question.

Check where there are overlaps between subject areas. (You may want to review the 'revision note' boxes throughout this book.) Make a careful note of these as knowing how one topic may lead into another can increase your marks significantly. Here are some examples:

✔ Almost any tort can be combined with vicarious liability where there is an employer involved.

✔ All torts could open up a discussion of defences or remedies.

✔ There are many special situations which affect the basic operation of the tort of negligence.

Knowing your cases

Make sure you know how to use relevant case law in your answers. Use the table below to focus your revision of the key cases in each topic. To review the details of these cases, refer back to the particular chapter.

Key case	How to use	Related topics
Chapter 1 – Negligence: the duty of care		
Donoghue v *Stevenson*	To show the origin of the neighbour principle	Manufacturer liability for defective products
Caparo Industries v *Dickman*	To explain the elements of the duty of care	Negligent misstatement
Smith v *Littlewoods*	To show when a duty of care is owed in relation to acts of third parties	
Mitchell v *Glasgow City Council*	To show when there is liability in negligence for the criminal acts of another	
Hedley Byrne v *Heller*	To establish that a person could be liable in tort for negligent misstatement	
Caparo Industries v *Dickman*	To show what is required for negligent misstatement	General duty of care
Spartan Steel and Alloys v *Martin*	To distinguish between consequential economic loss and pure economic loss	
Anns v *Merton LBC*	To provide an example of economic loss being recoverable	*Murphy* v *Brentwood DC*
Junior Books v *Veitchi*	To provide an example of economic loss being recoverable	
Murphy v *Brentwood DC*	To show the current position regarding pure economic loss. Overrules *Anns*.	*Anns* v *Merton LBC*
Alcock v *Chief Constable of South Yorkshire*	To define shock; to set out the factors to be considered for a duty of care in psychiatric injury	
Page v *Smith*	To demonstrate primary and secondary victims in psychiatric injury	
McLoughlin v *O'Brian*	To set out the requirements of proximity in psychiatric injury	

▶

Key case	How to use	Related topics
Van Colle v *Chief Constable of Hertfordshire Police; Smith* v *Chief Constable of Sussex Police*	To show the duty of care owed by public authorities	
Chapter 2 – Negligence: breach of duty		
Blyth v *Birmingham Waterworks*	To show the basic standard of care is that of the reasonable man	Duty of care
Bolam v *Friern Hospital*	To establish the standard of care in medical negligence cases	
Bolitho v *City and Hackney HA*	To show that doctors can be liable in negligence even if there is a body of medical opinion in favour	*Bolam*
Nettleship v *Weston*	To establish the standard of care in negligence cases which involve unskilled defendants	
Mullin v *Richards*	To establish the standard of care in negligence cases which involve children	
Wooldridge v *Sumner*	To establish the standard of care in sporting negligence cases involving spectators	
Bolton v *Stone; Miller* v *Jackson*	To illustrate contrasting cases which involve the likelihood of injury affecting the standard of care	
Paris v *Stepney BC*	To show how the standard of care varies for claimants who are at risk of suffering greater injury than normal	
Latimer v *AEC*	To demonstrate the cost and practicability of precautions against risk	Employers' liability
Scott v *London & St Katherine Docks*	To show when *res ipsa loquitur* is available	

Key case	How to use	Related topics
Chapter 3 – Negligence: causation and remoteness of damage		
Cork v *Kirby MacLean Ltd*	To set out the 'but for' test	
Barnett v *Chelsea and Kensington Hospital*	To illustrate the operation of the 'but for' test	
Bonnington Castings v *Wardlaw*	To show the position where there are multiple causes of damage	
Wilsher v *Essex Area HA*	To illustrate multiple causes of damage	
McGhee v *National Coal Board*	To show that a material increase in risk can give rise to liability	
Hotson v *East Berkshire AHA*	To show that 'lost chances' are not recoverable	Lost chances
Gregg v *Scott*	To illustrate various reasons for and against recover of a lost chance	Lost chances
Performance Cars v *Abraham*	To show the position regarding multiple consecutive causes of damage	
Baker v *Willoughby; Jobling* v *Associated Dairies*	To show contrasting circumstances in which the courts will consider the act of a third party to have broken the chain of causation	*Novus actus interveniens*
McKew v *Holland & Hannen & Cubitts*	To show how acts of the claimant can affect liability	*Novus actus interveniens*
Carslogie Steamship Co v *Norwegian Government*	To show how acts of nature can affect liability	*Novus actus interveniens*
Re Polemis	To show unlimited liability for the direct consequences of a negligent act	Remoteness
The Wagon Mound (No 1)	To show liability for the reasonably foreseeable consequences of a negligent act	Remoteness

▶

Key case	How to use	Related topics
Smith v *Leech Brain*	To illustrate the 'egg-shell skull' rule	Remoteness
Lagden v *O'Connor*	To show liability for the damages of an impecunious claimant	

Chapter 4 – Vicarious liability

Key case	How to use	Related topics
Ready Mixed Concrete v *Minister of Pensions*	To show whether a worker is an employee	
Century Insurance v *NI Road Transport Board*	To show that doing an authorised act in an unauthorised manner can still be in the course of employment	
Beard v *London Omnibus Co*	To show that acts beyond the scope of employment do not give rise to vicarious liability	
Lister v *Hesley Hall*	To set out the test concerning whether employers can be liable for intentional wrongful acts of employees	

Chapter 5 – Employers' liability

Key case	How to use	Related topics
Latimer v *AEC*	To show that an employer must take reasonable steps to safeguard employees from defective premises	Cost and practicability of precautions
Knowles v *Liverpool County Council*	To show when an employer is liable for existing defects	
Speed v *Thomas Swift & Co*	To show the features of a safe system of work	
Lonrho v *Shell Petroleum*	To show whether breach of a statute gives rise to civil liability	Breach of statutory duty
Hartley v *Mayoh*	To show that there must be a statutory duty for the tort of breach of statutory duty to arise	Breach of statutory duty. Duty of care
John Summers & Sons v *Frost*	To show that failure to meet a strict statutory duty will be a breach (even in the absence of fault)	Breach of statutory duty. Duty of care

Key case	How to use	Related topics
Gorris v *Scott*	To establish that the damage suffered by the claimant must be of the type protected by the statute	Breach of statutory duty. Remoteness of damage

Chapter 6 – Occupiers' liability

Lowery v *Walker*	To show that failure to stop or limit known trespasser can give rise to implied permission to enter land	
Phipps v *Rochester Corporation*	To show that defendants cannot be expected to protect children from unforeseeable risks	
Glasgow Corporation v *Taylor*	To show that a duty can exist if there are concealed dangers or allurements that tempt children into danger	
Keown v *Coventry NHS Trust*	To distinguish between dangers caused by the state of a building and dangerous use of well-maintained premises	

Chapter 7 – Nuisance

Hunter v *Canary Wharf*	To show the requirement for a proprietary interest in land for nuisance	
Robinson v *Kilvert*	To show that unusually sensitive claimants cannot rely on nuisance that would not have disturbed a reasonable person	
Hollywood Silver Fox Farm v *Emmett*	To show that malicious actions may be nuisance even if they are not an unreasonable use of land	
Attorney-General v *PYA Quarries*	To establish that public nuisance requires disturbance of a class of people	
R v *Rimmington*	To show that public nuisance should not be used for conduct that is also a statutory offence without good reason	

▶

Key case	How to use	Related topics
Sturges v *Bridgman*	To show that the time period for actionable nuisance commences from the start of the nuisance not the act causing it	
Chapter 8 – *Rylands* v *Fletcher*		
Rylands v *Fletcher*	To establish liability for the harm caused by the escape of things brought onto land	
Transco v *Stockport MBC*	To distinguish natural and non-natural use of land and to show that risks must be judged by contemporary standards	
Cambridge Water v *Eastern Counties Leather*	To show that *Rylands* v *Fletcher* requires at least foreseeability of risk as a prerequisite to recovery of damages	Foreseeability
Chapter 9 – Trespass to land		
Bernstein v *Skyviews*	To show that right to ownership of airspace is not unlimited	
Chapter 10 – Trespass to the person		
Letang v *Cooper*	To show that trespass to the person requires intentional force	
R v *Ireland*	To show that words can amount to an assault	
Bird v *Jones*	To demonstrate that false imprisonment requires total constraint on movement	
Murray v *Ministry of Defence*	To show that the victims need not know that they are being falsely imprisoned	
Wilkinson v *Downton*	To show that a claim in tort can arise from the infliction of indirect harm	
Chapter 11 – Liability for defective products		
Donoghue v *Stevenson*	To show that manufacturers have a duty of care to the ultimate consumer	Duty of care

Key case	How to use	Related topics
Griffiths v *Arch Engineering*	To show that a reasonable expectation of intermediate inspection may break the chain of causation	Causation

Chapter 12 – Defamation and privacy

Key case	How to use	Related topics
Byrne v *Deane*	To demonstrate the requirement for a right-thinking member of society in defamation cases	
Newstead v *London Express*	To show that defamation can be available even if the claimant is misidentified	
Campbell v *Mirror Group Newspapers*	To exemplify the tort of misuse of private information	
A v *B plc*	To demonstrate how rights to privacy and freedom of expression are balanced on a case-by-case basis	

Chapter 13 – Defences

Key case	How to use	Related topics
Morris v *Murray*	To show the requirement for the claimant to have had knowledge of the nature of the risk for the defence of consent to be available	
Revill v *Newberry*	To show that illegality is not always a bar to a successful claim	
Jones v *Livox Quarries*	To show that the claimant must have failed to take care of their own safety for contributory negligence to succeed	Foreseeability. Contributory negligence
Gough v *Thorne*	To show that the age of the claimant is relevant to contributory negligence	Foreseeability. Standard of care
Froom v *Butcher*	To demonstrate the distinction between the cause of the claimant's injuries and the cause of the accident in which they were sustained	Contributory negligence

▶

Key case	How to use	Related topics
Chapter 14 – Remedies		
Thompson v *Metropolitan Police Commissioner*	To set out the criteria for the award of aggravated damages	
Rookes v *Barnard*	To distinguish between aggravated and exemplary damages	
Redland Bricks v *Morris*	To establish the conditions for granting a mandatory injunction	
American Cyanamid v *Ethicon*	To establish the conditions for granting an interim injunction	

■ Sample question

Below is a problem question that incorporates overlapping areas of the law. See if you can answer this question drawing upon your knowledge of the whole subject area. Guidelines on answering this question are included at the end of this section.

PROBLEM QUESTION

Each year, the local authority grants permission to a travelling fair to stay on a park for two weeks. On the day of its arrival, the fair was subject to a rigorous safety inspection that tested all of the rides and investigated the procedures used by staff to set up and run the rides. The result of the inspection was that all aspects of the fair were exemplary. That evening, a bolt securing one of the carriages on the Twizzler ride snapped and the carriage flew through the air. Fortunately, nobody was in the carriage at the time. The bulk of the carriage smashed into a house adjoining the park which was owned by Dafydd. He was out at the time but his lodger, Dewi, was injured when the roof and wall of the house collapsed following the impact of the carriage. A chunk of metal from the flying carriage fell into Tomas's garden and is still there some three months after the accident.

Discuss the tortious liability arising from this situation.

Answer guidelines

Approaching the question

The most sensible approach to tackling this question is to take each issue and consider which tort(s) are relevant and to consider whether liability is established. This problem could potentially bring up issues of private nuisance, trespass to land, negligence, *Rylands* v *Fletcher* and trespass to the person.

Important points to include

- **Damage to Dafydd's house:** this is damage to his property so consider which of the torts that cover this sort of damage could be relevant.

- **Private nuisance:** this is a single incident rather than an ongoing or continuous problem so private nuisance is not the most appropriate basis for liability.

- **Trespass to land:** this tort requires that the interference is intentional and direct. It is clear that the owner of the fair did not intend to send a carriage into Dafydd's house.

- **Negligence:** this may seem like the most obvious basis of liability but there does not seem to have been a breach of the duty of care. The fair was inspected and considered to be exemplary so how would you establish breach of duty?

- ***Rylands* v *Fletcher***: this little-used tort might have a role here as the fair could be seen as non-natural use of land that carried a risk that harm would be caused if (parts of) it 'escaped' so it seems like an arguable basis for liability. Remember to include reference to the foresight requirement introduced by the House of Lords in *Cambridge Water*.

- **Dewi's injuries:** would not be covered by *Rylands* v *Fletcher* because this tort does not cover personal injury only damage to property. The same problem arises in relation to negligence as was outlined in relation to the damage to the house. Dewi cannot bring a claim in private nuisance as he does not have a proprietary interest in the land: *Hunter* v *Canary Wharf*. There is no basis for a claim under trespass to land so the only arguable basis for liability would be battery.

- **Metal in Tomas's garden:** the only basis for liability here would be trespass to land because no harm has been caused. ▶

Make your answer stand out

Ensure that you consider the less obvious torts – for instance, the possible application of *Rylands* v *Fletcher.*

Similarly, you should discuss why certain torts do not apply – such as *Rylands* and private nuisance in respect of Dewi's injuries.

Be thorough in your analysis – look at where loss or damage has occurred and think about which torts might be relevant.

Consider whether any defences might be applicable and what sort of damages could potentially be recoverable.

Glossary of terms

The glossary is divided into two parts: key definitions and other useful terms. The key definitions can be found within the chapter in which they occur, as well as in the glossary below. These definitions are the essential terms that you must know and understand in order to prepare for an exam. The additional list of terms provides further definitions of useful terms and phrases which will also help you answer examination and coursework questions effectively. These terms are highlighted in the text as they occur but the definition can only be found here.

■ Key definitions

Assault	An act which causes another person to apprehend the infliction of immediate, unlawful force on his person: *Collins* v *Wilcock*.
Battery	The intentional and direct application of force to another person.
Consent	A defence which is often referred to by the Latin phrase *volenti non fit injuria*. The literal translation of this is 'there can be no injury to one who consents' although it is generally said to mean 'voluntary assumption of risk'.
Control test	This distinguishes an employee from an independent contractor on the basis of whether the employer had the right to control the work done and, most importantly, how it is done: *Yewen* v *Noakes*.
Defamation	The publication of an untrue statement which reflects on a person's reputation and lowers him in the estimation of right-thinking members of society.
Defamatory statement	One that is 'calculated to injure the reputation of another by exposing them to hatred, contempt or ridicule': *Parmiter* v *Coupland*.

Economic loss	Financial loss which is not attributable to physical harm caused to the claimant or his property. It includes loss of profits, loss of trade and loss of investment revenue.
False imprisonment	'The infliction of bodily restraint which is not expressly or impliedly authorised by the law'.
Frolic of one's own	A phrase used to describe conduct that falls outside the course of employment, being something that the employee has done within working time that is unrelated to his work and undertaken on his own account: *Joel* v *Morison*.
Illegality	A defence which is frequently referred to by the Latin phrase *ex turpi causa non oritur actio* which means 'no action arises from a disgraceful claim'. In other words, if the claimant was knowingly engaged in unlawful activity at the time he was injured, it would be contrary to public policy to allow the claim to succeed.
Joint liability	This arises if two or more people cause harm/damage to the same claimant and they are (1) engaged in a joint enterprise; (2) one party authorises the tort of the other; and (3) one party is vicariously liable for the torts of the other.
Negligence	Breach of a legal duty to take care that results in damage to the claimant.
Novus actus interveniens	A new act intervenes.
Occupier	A person who exercises an element of control over premises: *Wheat* v *Lacon*.
Organisation test	This distinguishes between a contract of service whereby 'a man is employed as part of the business and his work is done as an integral part of the business' and a contract for services whereby 'work, although done for the business, is not integrated into it but is only accessory to it': *Stevenson, Jordan and Harrison*.
Private nuisance	A tort that protects interests in property against 'the unreasonable use of man of his land to the detriment of his neighbour': *Miller* v *Jackson*.
Public nuisance	'Materially affects the reasonable comfort and convenience of life of a class of Her Majesty's subjects': *A-G* v *PYA Quarries*.
Res ipsa loquitur	A Latin phrase meaning 'the thing speaks for itself'.
Several liability	Occurs in all cases that do not fall within joint liability but where more than one defendant has caused harm to the same claimant.

Trespass to land	A direct and unjustified interference with the possession of land whether or not the entrant knows he is trespassing.
Trespasser	A person who goes onto land without invitation and whose presence is either unknown to the proprietor or if known is practically objected to: *Addie* v *Dumbreck*.

■ Other useful terms

Equitable remedy	Remedies that originated in the Court of Exchequer. These were discretionary and less rigid than common law remedies.
Ex turpi causa (ex turpi causa non oritur actio)	The law will not allow a claim if it is based on something illegal.
Injunction	Court order to do or refrain from doing something.
Interim injunction	A temporary injunction in force until the issue can be determined at a full hearing. Previously known as an interlocutory injunction.
Libel	Defamatory statement in permanent form.
Limitation	Time period within which a tort claim may be brought.
Mitigation	Process in which a claimant takes steps to minimise his or her losses.
Nominal damages	A token sum of damages awarded when a legal right has been infringed but where the claimant has suffered no substantial loss.
Slander	Defamatory statement in temporary form.
Statutory duty	Duty imposed by legislation.
Strict liability	Imposition of liability without proof of fault.
Tortious	Tort-like.
Vicarious liability	Liability of one legal person for the tort of another.
Volenti (volenti non fit injuria)	A general defence available when a claimant gives his consent with prior knowledge of the risk involved. A voluntary assumption of risk.

Index